Early 20th-Century German Plays

The German Library: Volume 58

Volkmar Sander, General Editor

EARLY
20TH-CENTURY
GERMAN PLAYS

Edited by
Margaret Herzfeld-Sander

CONTINUUM · NEW YORK

2002
The Continuum Publishing Company
370 Lexington Avenue, New York, NY 10017

The German Library
is published in cooperation with Deutsches Haus,
New York University.
This volume has been supported by Inter Nationes.

Printed in the United States of America

Library of Congress Cataloging-in-Publication Data

Early 20th-century German plays / edited by Margaret Herzfeld-Sander.
p. cm. — (The German library ; v. 58)
Contents: Spring awakening. The marquis of Keith / Frank Wedekind
—Tales from the Vienna Woods / Ödön von Horváth — Purgatory in
Ingolstadt / Marieluise Fleisser.
ISBN 0-8264-0960-1. — ISBN 0-8264-0961-X (pbk.)
1. German drama—20th century—Translations into English.
I. Wedekind, Frank, 1864–1918. II. Horváth, Ödön von, 1901–1938.
III. Fleisser, Marieluise, 1901–1974. IV. Herzfeld-Sander,
Margaret. V. Series.
PT1258.E27 1998
432'.91208—dc21   97-32743
                                                            CIP

For performance rights *The Marquis of Keith* and
Tales from the Vienna Woods, contact
Carl R. Mueller, UCLA, Department of Theater,
102 East Melnitz, Box 951622,
Los Angeles, California 90095-1622

Acknowledgments will be found on page 255,
which constitutes an extension of the copyright page.

Contents

Introduction

Classic dramatic form and theatrical convention were still evident in Germany in the nineteenth century. However, the appearance of what was to develop into post–World War I modern drama concerned with the circumstances, conflicts, and problems of unheroic people, a flexible structure, and an alienating dialogic discourse, occurred already before the turn of the century. The importance of reality influencing and weighing down individual aspirations and the more open plot structures had manifested themselves already in the drama of the Sturm and Drang (The German Library, vol. 14) during the late eighteenth century, and then even more so in the plays of Georg Büchner, Christian Dietrich Grabbe, and Johann Nepomuk Nestroy during the nineteenth century.

From Bismarck and the rule of Kaiser Wilhelm to World War I and postwar Weimar, the essential features of modern German drama became more visible. Although there was still some form of censorship of sociopolitically suspicious plays until the beginning of the Weimar, Republic (1918–33), the theater as the forum of public events and human passions saw ever more plays that exposed the social milieu encroaching on the development of the individual, threatening its degradation and dissolution. The experience of World War I further enhanced the precarious position of the individual. In his essay on "The Sociology of Modern Drama" (cf. The German Library, vol. 83 *Essays on Theater*) Georg Lukács elaborates on the idea that the new drama is the drama of the hero confronted by external forces. The hopes and convictions of human beings are constrained by the pressures of the outside world. "The realization and maintenance of personality had become on the one hand a conscious problem of living; the longing to make the personality prevail grows increasingly pressing and urgent. On the other hand, external circumstances, which rule out this possibility from the first, gain even greater weight" (op. cit. p. 148). Thus the dramatic construct shows the interdependence of the social environment opposed to the views and desires of individual characters and their struggle for survival. To unfold this frequently hostile relationship, playwrights use a plethora of aesthetic means to enlighten the audience about the change in human conditions in a rapidly changing world. Even before the turn of the century, playwrights had tried to capture the transformations of social conditions by experimenting with dramatic discourse and theatrical representation. Various innovative formal devices became popular, such as fast scene changes, expressionist, fragmented dialogue and monologue, explosive eruptions, extended silences, and the replacement of a final closure by the open-ended text. The most lasting influence, eventually, was to be exerted by Bertolt Brecht with his radical conception of epic theater informing the public about the contradictory nature of the social order and of men and women through the process of alienation on the stage in order to demonstrate the new subject matter and to destroy the illusionary identification of the audience with the plot. The theater of the new drama tried to find a symbiosis between modern sensibilities and innovative technical means. Many playwrights pondering the social and spiritual convulsions of their time engaged in theoretical reflections on the task and possibilities of the drama and the theater as a civic forum. Particularly since Lessing and Schiller, German theater had been conceived as a moral and emancipatory institution. This tradition has lasted to this day: constant essayistic attempts to reconsider the dramatic genre and the stage as important cultural contributions abound throughout the nineteenth century, during the Weimar Republic, and again after World War II.

Both in theory and practice, the three playwrights included in this volume to varying degrees show many of the tendencies that were to become fully integrated into modern and postmodern drama. Frank Wedekind, Ödön von Horváth, and Marieluise Fleisser do not any longer adhere to classic structures, dramatic techniques, and autonomous characters. The pluralistic nature of the new drama had established itself.

Frank Wedekind (1864–1918)

Frank Wedekind challenged established views and exploded classic forms of dramatic theater. He inspired quite a few playwrights, notably Bertolt Brecht, Ödön von Horváth, and Friedrich Dürrenmatt. Wedekind's demand for recognizing human instincts, sexual freedom, the emancipation of women and a more humane social order still hold the interest of contemporary audiences. At the beginning Wedekind's objectives and dramatic output were subject to misunderstandings and vicious attacks. Gradually, however, Wedekind was recognized as a novel force in the theatrical world and considered as remarkable a predecessor of antinaturalistic drama as August Strindberg, Carl Sternheim, Ernst Toller, and Georg Kaiser; and more lastingly revolutionary in his concepts and dramatic devices than many of his contemporary playwrights, such as Gerhart Hauptmann, Max Halbe, Arno Holz, and Johannes Schlaf. The affinity between his works and the modern theater is striking. The use of humor and satire, of the bizarre and the grotesque, leads directly to expressionistic drama and points to Brecht, Dürrenmatt, Ionesco, and Beckett. With many writers, he shared an uneasiness about modern civilization that led him, in his own way, to protest emphatically against its very structure and moral fiber.

The necessity of freedom from social and political pressures was instilled in him early. Both his parents had lived abroad for a considerable length of time. Having sided with and openly supported the Liberals in 1848, his father, a doctor, left Germany after the failure of the Revolution, emigrated to America, and settled as a general practitioner in San Francisco. He married an actress who had come to America to make a living—the daughter of a German political refugee who had settled in Switzerland. The Wedekinds, who had become naturalized American citizens, returned to Germany in 1864; on July 24 Frank (Benjamin Franklin) Wedekind was born in Hanover. Eight years later his parents went to Switzerland, where they bought an estate; here he grew up in very comfortable circumstances. After school he went on to study German and French literature at Lausanne, but under parental persuasion he changed to law, only to discontinue his studies altogether in order to become a writer. A brief interlude as a press agent was followed by years of restless wanderings. He lived in Berlin, Munich, Paris, London, before finally settling in Munich, the lively and intellectually stimulating atmosphere of which he preferred.

Wedekind was not only interested in the theater but also fascinated by the outer fringes of the entertainment world: the circus, variety shows, music halls, and cabarets. He temporarily held engagements as a circus clown, pantomime actor, singer, journalist, actor, and director. In addition, he was a member of the *Simplizissimus* circle, the leading satirical magazine of his day, to which he also contributed. At the turn of the century, from June 1899 to March 1900, he was imprisoned for publishing poetry against the German Kaiser. He returned to Munich after his release and joined "The Eleven Executioners," a political cabaret, where he recited his satirical ballads while playing the lute. This was where Brecht got to know him in 1917–18. Brecht was captivated not only by Wedekind's ironic, provocative songs, but above all by the man himself, whose dissent and aggressive vitality irritated and challenged the proper bourgeoisie. We have a description of Wedekind and his friends at the time by Heinrich Mann, who recollects their singularly shocking impression on an audience both affronted and tickled. Their wild aggressiveness revealed their defiant posture and their contempt. The young Brecht was fascinated by them and it was under their impact that he began to write *Baal.*

In 1906 Max Reinhardt, one of the most progressive stage directors at the time, produced *Spring Awakening,* which Wedekind had completed in 1891. Performed in Berlin, the play created a scandal and achieved a sensational success. But for Wedekind there was to be no lasting recognition. He finally took acting lessons in order to appear in his own plays, for censorship and misinterpretation abounded. In 1906, Wedekind married the actress Mathilde Newes, and she began to perform with him in his plays. She was particularly successful as Lulu in his *Earth Spirit* and *Pandora's Box.* Wedekind, for his part, while not the most talented of actors, was always exciting; and although the censor continued to plague him, he finally lived to see his works accepted by notable critics and liberal segments of the public. At the outbreak of World War I, Wedekind initially rendered half-hearted support to the national cause but soon recognized his mistake and, like Heinrich Mann, declared himself a pacifist and above national loyalties. He died unexpectedly after an operation on March 9, 1918.

In all of Wedekind's writings we detect an unfaltering interest in the afflictions of modern man, the problems of the artist as an exile, and the plight of the outsider, as well as an urge to expose what he considered the destructive powers and obsolete values of a disoriented, hypocritical society. Today his fame rests primarily on his dramatic writings. His early plays are among his best and are still being performed. They were written just before and after 1900: *Frühlings Erwachen* (1890–91), *Fritz Schwigerling—Der Liebestrank* (1891–92), *Erdgeist* and *Die Büchse der Pandora* (1893–94), *Der Kammersänger* (1897), *Der Marquis von Keith* (1900), *König Nicolo oder So ist das Leben* (1901), *Hidalla oder Karl Hetmann, der Zwergriese* (1903–4), *Tod und Teufel* (1905), and *Musik* (1906). He deemed it necessary to shock and antagonize the bourgeoisie, but the thematic preoccupation with the problems of sexual freedom and the neglect of the artist by society limited his artistic scope. His later plays: *Schloß Wetterstein* (1910), *Franziska* (1911), *Simson* (1913), *Bismarck* (1915), and *Herakles* (1916–17), are more rigid in outlook and merely tend to vary his original themes or to acquire the tone of autobiographical confessions.

Wedekind's attempts to find the reasons for the discord and dissatisfaction in modern life were generally ignored or wrongly interpreted by the greater part of the artistic world throughout his most productive years. During the rise and later fame of German naturalistic drama in the eighteen-nineties, Wedekind remained a literary outsider because of his opposition to the philosophical theories of Hippolyte Taine and the doctrines of Emile Zola, which were then spreading from France all over Europe. These theories emphasized the molding and subjugation of man by his socioeconomic environment and summoned the writer to depict the material circumstances precisely and meticulously.

Wedekind, however, refused to go along, and in his play *Die junge Welt* (1889), he ridiculed the dramatic technique of photographic faithfulness in reproducing the observed milieu. In addition, he attacked Gerhart Hauptmann, whom he considered the most characteristic representative of the naturalistic movement in Germany; Hauptmann had used material from Wedekind's life in the play *Das Friedensfest,* thereby incurring his wrath. Wedekind never shared the conviction that it was paramount to show how men and women are shaped by their social and political conditions in order to liberate them from their economic malaise. The naturalistic drama seemed to leave untouched the traditional moral conservatism of society, nor did it, in his view, depart drastically from the classical structure of the drama. Wedekind saw the reasons for the shortcomings of modern society in the willingness of man to accept, follow, and perpetuate a twisted and stagnant code of ethics, which is, strangely, proclaimed to be the guarantee of human happiness. Relief could come, Wedekind argued, only when man was made conscious of the reactionary bias upon which the entire culture rested.

Reasoning that sensuality and instinctual drives had to be recognized as the most powerful forces in life, he wanted to replace middle-class morality with a natural behavioral code. He questioned the assumption that human beings are primarily rationally and spiritually oriented, and he identified our egoistic, narcissistic nature as the source of our actions. An awareness of human nature and a morality more adequate than the prevailing one would bring emancipation to men and women and liberate society from prejudice. Wedekind's psychological and physiological studies confirmed his conviction for the need to define anew the condition of man in modern civilization, which both Nietzsche und Marx had thoroughly analyzed and critically assessed before him. Wedekind also expressed ideas that later were to be scientifically substantiated and systematized in the writings of Freud. All these men have in common a mode of imagination and consciousness that transcends the limitations of a taboo-ridden society.

We discover in Wedekind's writings a moral commitment that goes beyond the puritan spirit of his time. He shows, even exaggerates, the life of the senses, particularly our sexual impulse, in order to provoke and to unmask social reality. The theme of a genuinely human morality animates the characters of his dramas and their relations to one another. The failure of the individual who either tries to act according to human nature and become inevitably excluded from the social world, or rebels unsuccessfully against the pillars of society and their moral principles, represents an indictment as well as a failure of bourgeois society, which condemns and destroys the outsider and the rebel.

Lulu, the main character in *Erdgeist (Earth Spirit)* and *Die Büchse der Pandora (Pandora's Box)*, finds herself banished from middle-class propriety when she proclaims and indeed lives the maxim that love alone makes life relevant. She is treated like a whore, forced into open prostitution, and finally killed by a sex maniac. In spite of her obviously insatiable desires, Wedekind considers her to have been sacrificed by a society that negates the very nature of love and denies sexual freedom. As stated in the prologue to *Erdgeist*, Wedekind sees in Lulu the archetype and incarnation of beauty and hedonism.

Wedekind had a preference for the Sturm und Drang dramatists and their rebellion against tyranny and dramatic convention. He found himself closer in spirit to Lenz, Schiller, and above all Büchner than to his own contemporaries, and he proved to be as intensely individualistic and original for his time as they had been for theirs. He created a form of expression and action that contained what later came to be recognized as the early stylistic and dramatic features of literary Expressionism. In the twentieth century he gained the stature of "father" of the Expressionist movement, although he saw himself akin to neither the naturalists nor the early Expressionists. To present the side of human life not easily recognizable on the level of consciousness, he departed from the structure of the classical drama and its logical sequence of beginning, middle, and end. Instead of creating a controlled architectonic structure and adhering to the unities, he made use of elements that have since become essential parts of modern drama. The "open form" in the drama is characterized by its stress on scenes instead of acts, by the free handling of time and place, and by accidental arrangements of incidents. Wedekind presents dialogue as reflection and self-expression rather than as a means of communication. The language becomes increasingly aggressive, and the syntax is deliberately and progressively fragmented, thus producing the effect of everyday speech and revealing man's contradictory, often unintelligible reality. The imagery is chosen in an attempt to approximate the mental processes, fusing the poetic and the drastic. Sentences stop short at exclamations or trail off in uncertainty. The unreflected and dreamlike utterances that flow from subjective experiences are often counterbalanced by the satirical and grotesque. Thus the audience is brought to a sudden awareness and prevented from too closely indentifying with an illusionary world. As long as Wedekind was convinced that taboos and antiquated social mores precluded sensible, intelligent participation and that a regeneration of man was possible, an organic connection existed between his subject matter and his new technical devices, but obsession with the theme of the artist as an outcast and a dampening of his imagination later redirected Wedekind's aesthetic originality into more conventional channels.

Criticized at first for their content and structure, Wedekind's plays met countless obstacles before they could be performed. This was all the more disappointing to Wedekind, since he considered the very nature of the play to be revealed in the mise en scène and the acting. Wedekind repeatedly declined invitations to lecture on his works, because apart from the plays on the stage, nothing else could be communicated. He also opposed categorically any attempt by critics to see in him a propagator of abstract theories. He bitterly complained about the tendency to interpret *Spring Awakening* both as a serious tragedy and as a propaganda piece preaching sexual enlightenment.

Spring Awakening, written between 1890 and 1891, published in 1891, had a difficult start. Critics considered it pedantic, unsavory, even pornographic. Reinhardt first staged the play successfully in Berlin in 1906. It stands as an example of Wedekind's dramatic skill. The action takes place in a small German town around 1890 and shows the conflict between the generations. On the one hand the parents and teachers demand respect and unquestioning obedience; on the other, the young generation, troubled, unenlightened, sexually restless, yet sensitive to the underlying prudishness and hypocrisy in their environment, is aware that their elders have their own pleasures. The rigid atmosphere increases unrest and anxiety and finally leads to pregnancy, abortion, and the death of a girl; to suicide for one boy who is afraid of not being able to live up to parental demands; and to reform school for another.

We detect Wedekind's convictions when Melchior, in opposition to educational and religious doctrines, declares egoism and pleasure to be the source of human actions. Young people, still free from encroaching taboos, are what Freud was later to term "polymorphous perverse." At the same time, however, they feel guilty and bewildered. A genuine understanding and reconciliation between the old and the young is impossible. The established morality of the older generation is exposed by Moritz, who reappears after death with his head under his arm: "My morality hounded me to death. I used the murder because of my dear parents" (III, 7). Death is caused not by inexorable necessity but by parental and social pressure. At the very end of the play, however, an unknown man in a mask pleads for life against death at the moment when Melchior, beckoned by his dead friend Moritz, is tempted to follow him. The man in the mask leads Melchior back into life, and Wedekind the moralist has him define morality as the real product of two imaginary factors called "should and would" (III, 7). Life remains triumphant, leaving the young generation with an enervating doubt and a challenge to see it through sensibly and with a little more self-knowledge.

Wedekind called *Spring Awakening* a tragedy of childhood, but he was appalled by the heavy-handed, gloomy performances of his day and never ceased to emphasize the humor and playfulness of each scene, convinced the entire plot would be all the more gripping if acted out in a light and laughing manner. It is not surprising that Wedekind stressed the importance of individual scenes, for although the drama is divided into three acts the scenes stand almost by themselves, each carrying the meaning of the whole, the indeterminate and incongruous quality of real life. Not the unfolding plot but its fragmentation, raised to a principle, contributes to the unity of the play. In no other play has Wedekind so successfully blended such disparate components: erratic eruptions and silence itself, the lyrical and ironic in speech and metaphor. The characters speak a peculiarly stylized language in the original that has been modernized somewhat in the English version of the play.

The juxtaposition of the individual and society in a play that Wedekind thought among his best, *The Marquis of Keith* (1900), reveals Wedekind's ethical premises. Keith, adventurer, outsider, crook, and cynic tries to make a living in a saturated, corrupt bourgeois world. He is a failure because of his insouciance in a profit-oriented, calculating society. In the discourse between Keith the pragmatic sensualist and the idealistic moralist Scholz, juxtaposing a life of joyful pleasure and the rigid duty of a puritan, Scholz is being defeated and retreats to an insane asylum. Keith, in the end, opts for life although it is nothing but a slippery slope. The abdication of both the sensualist and the idealist reflects the corruption of a society that smugly and contentedly conducts business in the name of ambiguous morality. Actually, society finds itself in a much more critical state than the protagonist, who is at least conscious of the hypocritical behavior of himself and his fellow man. Wedekind was convinced of the ethical intent of his play. In his lifetime, however, many castigated Wedekind for supposedly undermining the moral order and stability of middle-class life. They called him a cynic and immoralist, ignoring his dramatic achievements, his psychological probings, and his enlightening morality. A few days after his death on March 9, 1918, Bertolt Brecht praised Wedekind as one of the great educators of modern Europe.

Ödön von Horváth (1901–38)

The years after World War I to the end of the Weimar Republic (1918–33) brought a revolutionary spirit and a host of aesthetic innovations to postwar German drama and the performing arts. Frank Wedekind had rejected the naturalist credo mirroring reality as objectively as possible in favor of a fragmented, associative dialogue, and the Expressionist playwrights Sternheim, Kaiser, Toller et al. (cf. The German Library, vol. 66) took a stand against the rules of classic dramatic structures, thereby developing a novel aesthetic and thematic discourse. The Austrian playwright Ödön von Horváth, as well as Marieluise Fleisser, and in his fashion Bertolt Brecht *(Puntila)*, revived the folk play to resurrect it from crude, sentimental entertainment. There had been, after all, a venerable tradition of Viennese playwrights who had supplied the popular suburban theater with comedies exposing the individual foibles and public shortcomings of their time. Ferdinand Raimund (1790–1836) had enriched the stage with his fairy-tale plays, his musical interventions, his constantly changing scenery, and his moral imperative of achieving a better world. Johann Nepomuk Nestroy (1801–62) (cf. The German Library, vol. 31) went one step further in transcending the local farces and musical tales. In his plays social reality was punctuated and unmasked and formal rigidity left behind. His comedies unfold in the discursive and instrumentalized language of characters who had clearly become the representatives of their class. Ödön von Horváth called his own early plays folk plays in the manner of this theatrical tradition of Johann Nepomuk Nestroy. However, Horváth also felt a close kinship to folk singers and comedians. His works have little in common with the shallow popular comedies that thrived at his time and that have survived in contemporary form in many television shows. Horváth envisioned a sociocritical folk play in which the affairs of ordinary people are dealt with in popular form. To achieve a synthesis of the real and the ironic mood he insisted that not a word of dialect should be spoken on the stage. In his plays the characters should converse in a stylized High German, recognizable as unfamiliar to them. Horváth depicts the problems of these people, exposing their animosity toward one another and toward the regulations and expectations of bureaucrats and their institutions. The lives of his characters are affected by the economic malaise after World War I and their unhappiness about their uprootedness. Far from glorifying the petty bourgeois, Horváth presents the discourse of desperate, hypocritical and frequently belligerent individuals. There are hints of what soon was to emerge in the cynical, brutal language and mood of the Nazi era in Germany and Austria.

Ödön von Horváth was born in Fiume, then part of Austria, of Hungarian parents in 1901. He became a freelance writer of plays, novels and short prose texts. Until 1934 he lived in Murnau near Munich. There followed a few years in Vienna, in the countryside near Salzburg and in Berlin, but when Hitler-Germany annexed Austria in 1938, he emigrated to Paris. A few months later, standing under a tree on the Champs Élysées he was killed instantaneously by a falling branch.

Horváth's first play *Revolte auf Cote 3018 (Revolt on Coast 3018)*, later published under the title *Die Bergbahn (1927–28) (The Mountain Train)*, was his first attempt to add a critical dimension to the popular comedies of his time. There followed *Sladek der schwarze Reichswehrmann (1929) (Sladeck, the Black Reich-Soldier)*. With the following three plays *Italienische Nacht (1930)*

(Italian Night), Geschichten aus dem Wienerwald (1931) (Tales from the Vienna Woods), and Kasimir und Karoline (1932) (Casimir and Caroline), Horváth reached the peak of his public career. His next drama Glaube Liebe Hoffnung (1933) (Faith Hope and Charity) never reached the stage until after World War II. Figaro lässt sich scheiden (1934) (Figaro Gets a Divorce), however, was produced the same year. Don Juan kommt aus dem Krieg (1935) (Don Juan Comes Back from the War), a dark renounciation of war, again had to wait many years to reach the stage. Der Jüngste Tag (1938) (Judgment Day) was not published until 1959. Horváth also finished three novels between 1930 and 1938: Der ewige Spiesser (The Eternal Philistine), Jugend ohne Gott (Youth without God) and Ein Kind unserer Zeit (A Child of Our Time). Today his plays have become part of the repertory theater in Germany and many of his works have been performed in America. In the seventies, a Horváth Renaissance set in. He influenced and was emulated by several contemporary German playwrights, such as Franz Xaver Kroetz, Martin Sperr, and Wolfgang Bauer. Peter Handke, Austria's most successful playwright of the post–World War II era, placed Horváth even above Bertolt Brecht.

Tales from the Vienna Woods takes place in 1931 during the depression and in the social milieu of small shopkeepers in Vienna. The old generation, authoritarian and mean-spirited, and the young generation, insecure and disillusioned, try to come to terms with each other, constantly fenced in by the banality of their lives. The carefree easy music of Johann Strauss serves as an ironic backdrop to the deteriorating relationships of two generations of the postwar era. Although all characters display the wasteland and the longing of their souls, the life and fate of Marianne, daughter of the toy shop owner on a quiet street in Vienna, exposes the hypocrisy of the time. She is engaged to the robust local butcher, falls in love with Alfred, a drifter and gambler, who dissipates the money of a civil service widow who is the owner of the tobacconist and newspaper shop in the same street. After a picnic in the Vienna Woods and the declaration of their Christian principles and racial prejudices, the small community of shopkeepers returns to Vienna. One year later Marianne, Alfred, and their young child live in humble circumstances in the neighborhood. Marianne is pushed into making money as a music-hall dancer. Although she submits to everything, Alfred leaves her nonetheless to return to his former lover. The child, deliberately neglected by Alfred's grandmother in the country, dies. Reconciled with her own father, Marianne in desperation attacks the old woman. Subdued and humiliated, she is humored by her former fiancé and readmitted to his life. She, however, feels her life is finished. At the end of the play it is evident that the tales from the Vienna Woods will continue unabated. The dialogue of the characters is a laconic vehicle to uncover the emptiness, desolation, and hidden violence of ordinary people.

Ödön von Horváth strove for a synthesis of realism and alienating irony. Dissatisfied with some productions of his plays, he published instructions on how to stress the dramatic dialogue to reveal the distorted consciousness of the petty bourgeoisie and their antisocial drives. He wanted to be a chronicler of his time and that meant showing the masses of people and their personal and public circumstances. To this day, his plays are an indictment of the dark recesses of the human psyche caught in mental and social pauperization of modern society. And last but not least, an indictment of the hierarchical structures and gender relations in Europe between two World Wars.

Marieluise Fleisser (1901–74)

Marieluise Fleisser was born in 1901 in the provincial town of Ingolstadt in Bavaria. Educated in a Catholic convent, she tried to escape the stultifying routine by reading, particularly the works of Strindberg. After graduation, she left for Munich to study theater arts, literature, and philosophy. Since this was against the wish of her father, however, she did not finish her studies and enter the teaching profession but persisted in her decision to become a writer. With mounting interest she had read the plays of young Bertolt Brecht, only three years older than she—*Baal, Drums in the Night,* and *In the Jungle of Cities*—and when eventually she was introduced to him by her friend and writer Lion Feuchtwanger, she was equally fascinated by the man. To the end of her life she would never doubt his superiority. Brecht advised and supported her but also manipulated her dramatic efforts to meet his standards. Her first play *Fegefeuer in Ingolstadt,* 1924, (originally *Die*

Fusswaschung), in translation *Purgatory in Ingolstadt,* was first performed in Berlin in 1926 with Brecht's assistance and met both with instant success as well as with criticism and rejection by conservative critics. Her next play *Pioniere in Ingolstadt (Engineers in Ingolstadt),* written the same year, was performed in Dresden in 1928. Brecht urged her to change the play by adopting his technique of epic style and structure and following his concepts of using the stage as a forum to present the contradictory nature of modern society, always with an eye on the necessity of change. The revised play, critical of the social and militarist pressures in a typical small garrison town during the Weimar Republic, caused a scandal in Berlin and elsewhere. Brecht had deliberately provoked this and shrugged it off as inconsequential. Marieluise Fleisser had to bear the unbounded rage of the people in her own town, the national press, and an open letter that denounced her as a shameless woman. Her close relationship with Brecht lasted for five years and when they finally parted, she resisted his influence and become a successful playwright, novelist, and story writer in her own right. Instead of Brecht's demand for a theater suited for the "scientific age," avoiding emotional identification and stressing an epic distance to eliminate "unsavory intoxication," she created a discourse focused on the internal, private passions and confusions of her characters in a narrow, provincial environment. Her experiences of the rigid life of shopkeepers, craftsmen, civil servants, clerks, and soldiers in her home town had shaped her imagination. Male authority and power coupled with inflexible moral and religious demands was a deadly combination for a woman who wanted to save her social independence and mental freedom. Moreover, Ingolstadt had been a military base for centuries surrounded by an idyllic landscape indifferent to human affairs. The harmless and harmonious lives of the citizens was deceptive. In 1933 a conservative, patriotic pride was to explode into a militant and nationalist mania bent on the persecution and destruction of the Other. Small wonder that Fleisser's preoccupation with the male and female psyche and the repressed discourse between men and women under local pressure became a significant and recurring subject of her works in the twenties looking forward to times to come.

She still spent time alternating between Munich, Berlin, and Ingolstadt. However, breaking up with Brecht pushed her into personal and artistic isolation. Briefly engaged to Josef Haindl, a tobacco wholesale merchant in Ingolstadt, she remained in Berlin and finally dissolved the liaison. Another partnership with the conservative and narcissistic journalist and writer Hellmut Draws Tychsen ended after three years. Her relationship with him had been a disaster, but for the first time in her life she traveled to foreign countries (Denmark, France, Andorra, Sweden). Back in Ingolstadt she ventured on one more trip to Berlin. Lonely and exhausted she tried to kill herself. Longing for protection and security and unable to survive as a writer she married the wholesale merchant Josef Haindl after all. The unhappy marriage lasted from 1935 to 1958. As a dependent housewife she also had to help run the business and could not muster time and energy to continue her writing. Shunned by the people who could neither forgive nor forget her for having exposed inhuman conditions in their town and openly discussed sexual drives, and overcome by her duties, she suffered a nervous breakdown and spent months in a sanatorium. Considered an enemy of the people by the Nazis after 1933, her books were burnt and with the exception of a few short articles she was not allowed to publish anything. Finally she began to write a play *Karl Stuart* but did not finish it and fell silent again. Her life as a writer seemed to be over and the public began to forget her. Politically suspect, she had to work as an untrained worker to support the war effort. To survive the pressure she finished *Karl Stuart* in 1944 and started on another play *Der Starke Stamm (The Strong Tribe)*. Only years after the end of the war, her husband dead and his business in ruins, was she to be acclaimed as a serious writer. Similar to the rediscovery of Ödön von Horváth, a renewed interest in her life and work developed after the war in the late nineteen-sixties. Although her best plays had originated during the Weimar Republic, she was now celebrated by critics as an original, sensitive writer. Post–World War II playwrights, such as Franz Xaver Kroetz, Martin Sperr, and Rainer Werner Fassbinder idolized Horváth and Fleisser as instigators of the modern folk play. Her observant realism and the fragmentary, laconic discourse of her characters shaped their own productions. She in turn called them "all my sons." After the war she was in touch again with her old friends Lion Feuchtwanger and Bertolt Brecht. Her plays were now being performed. One novel, a number of short stories, a few essays and articles, and her plays constitute her collected works. She was invited to give lectures and received several literary prizes. Marieluise Fleisser died in Ingolstadt in 1974.

The play *Purgatory in Ingolstadt* was first performed in 1926. After the Hitler years and long years of neglect, Fleisser revised the text in the late sixties to stress the social context of the play. The action of the play takes place in a small town. The private rivalries among family members disclose the antagonistic feelings between the older and younger generations as did so many plays of Expressionist playwrights of the twenties. The public meanness of young adults against anybody who does not adapt to the social norm, the religious demands of the church and the rule of the gang, are reflective of the repressive atmosphere at home, at school, and in church. The epic structure of the drama slowly reveals the ambiguous, contradictory emotions of the characters and their verbal and physical wrath. Olga, pregnant by a classmate and told by him to abort the child, is about to take her life when she is lured back by Roelle, an ungainly and abstruse young man, the most complex and disturbed character of the play. Convinced of his male superiority he saves her from drowning but wants to keep her in bondage, as "befits a woman." Their distorted relationship makes for their own private purgatory. Roelle, boasting about his imagined supernatural visions becomes the perfect victim of his classmates and the crowd who gather to demand that he perform a miracle as he had always boasted he could do. After his failure they throw stones at him and declare him an outcast. He offers to humiliate Olga in order to be again accepted by them. An object of scientific experiments by the local doctor, reminiscent of Büchner's Woyzeck, Roelle is denied a life of his own. He finally confesses his sin of being different. The prevailing sexual, social, and religious taboos and the deranged socialization of men and women perpetuate male power, female dependence, and public intolerance. Nobody can escape this purgatory. There can be no absolution, not from the family, school, or church, not even in death as long as private and public mores remain unchallenged. However, the play is not an open attack on institutions but a display of the discourse and contradictions of people trapped by their psychological impoverishment and the ruthless insensitivity and brutality of the crowd.

Comparable to those of Wedekind and Horváth, Fleisser's characters speak in a strangely controlled, ritualized language with quotes from and references to the Bible to catch the hypocritical and instrumentalized communication of their social environment. Provincial life becomes more transparent when listening to Marieluise Fleisser. *Purgatory in Ingolstadt* is a tragi-comedy of small-town people anywhere—or, as she believed herself, Ingolstadt *is* everywhere.

M. H.-S.

Frank Wedekind

Spring Awakening

Characters

This translation of *Spring Awakening* was first staged on May 24, 1974, at the National Theatre, with the following cast:

Children

MELCHIOR GABOR	Peter Firth
MORITZ STIEFEL	Michael Kitchen
HÄNSCHEN RILOW	Dai Bradley
ERNST RÖBEL	Gerard Ryder
OTTO	David Dixon
GEORG ZIRSCHNITZ	Keith Skinner
ROBERT	Martin Howells
LÄMMERMEIER,	Christopher Guard
WENDLA BERGMANN	Veronica Quilligan
MARTHA BESSEL	Jane Carr
THEA	Jenny Agutter
ILSE	Patti Love

Boys in the Reformatory

DIETER	Rupert Frazer
REINHOLD	Ian Mackenzie
RUPERT	James Smith
HELMUT	Glyn Grain
GASTON	Bryan Brown

Parents

HERR GABOR	Joseph O'Conor
HERR STIEFEL	James Mellor
FRAU GABOR	Susan Engel
FRAU BERGMANN	Beryl Reid
INA MÜLLER, Wendla's sister	Judith Paris

Teachers

HEADMASTER SUNSTROKE	William Squire
PROFESSOR GUTGRINDER	Kenneth Benda
PROFESSOR BONEBREAKER	Alex McCrindle
PROFESSOR TONGUETWISTER	Stephen Williams
PROFESSOR FLYSWATTER	Peter Needham
PROFESSOR THICKSTICK	Kenneth Mackintosh
PROFESSOR APELARD	Colin Fay

Other adults

THE MASKED MAN	Cyril Cusack
DR LEMONADE	Daniel Thorndike
DR PROCRUSTES	Alan Hay
REVEREND BALDBELLY	Pitt Wilkinson
FASTCRAWLER, the school porter	Alan Hay
FRIEND ZIEG (named GOAT in this text)	Glyn Grain
LOCKSMITH	Pitt Wilkinson
UNCLE PROBST	Peter Rocca

Directed by Bill Bryden

The action takes places in a provincial town in Germany, 1891–92.

Act 1

SCENE 1

Living room.

WENDLA: Why have you made my dress so long, Mother?

FRAU BERGMANN: You're fourteen today.

WENDLA: I'd rather not have been fourteen if I'd known you'd make my dress so long.

FRAU BERGMANN: Your dress isn't too long, Wendla. What next? Can I help it if my child is four inches taller every spring? A grown girl can't still go round dressed like a little princess.

WENDLA: At least the little princess's dress suits me better than this nightshirt. Let me wear it once more, Mother. One more long summer. Fourteen or fifteen, that's still soon enough for this sackcloth. Let's keep it till my next birthday. I'd only trip over the braid and tear it.

FRAU BERGMANN: I don't know what I should say. I'd willingly keep you exactly as you are, darling. Other girls are stringy or plump at your age. You're not. Who knows what you'll be like when they're grown up?

WENDLA: Who knows—perhaps I won't be anything anymore.

FRAU BERGMANN: Child, child, where d'you get these ideas?

WENDLA: Don't, Mommy. Don't be sad.

FRAU BERGMAN (*kisses her*): My precious.

WENDLA: They come to me in the evening when I can't sleep. It doesn't make me the least bit sad, and I go to sleep better then. Is it a sin to think about such things, Mother?

FRAU BERGMANN: Go and hang the sackcloth in the wardrobe. Put your little princess's dress on again and God bless you. When I get a moment I'll sew a broad flounce round the bottom.

WENDLA (*hanging the dress in the wardrobe*): No, I'd rather even be twenty than that. . . . !

FRAU BERGMAN: Only so that you don't catch cold! There was a time when this little dress was too long on you, but. . . .

WENDLA: Now, when summer's coming? O Mother, even children don't catch diphtheria in the knees! How can you be so fussy?

You don't feel cold when you're my age—least of all in your knees. Would it be better if I was too hot? You ought to thank God that early one morning your precious doesn't rip the sleeves off her dress and come to you before it's still light with no shoes and stockings on! When I wear my sackcloth I'll be dressed like a fairy queen underneath. Don't be cross, Mommy. No one can see it then.

SCENE 2

Sunday evening.

MELCHIOR: It's too boring. I give up.

OTTO: Then we'll all have to stop!—Have you done your homework, Melchior?

MELCHIOR: Go on playing!

MORITZ: Where are you going?

MELCHIOR: Walking.

GEORG: It'll be dark soon!

ROBERT: Have you done your homework already?

MELCHIOR: Why shouldn't I walk in the dark?

ERNST: Central America! Louis the Fifteenth ! Sixty verses of Homer! Seven quadratic equations!

MELCHIOR: Damned homework!

GEORG: If only the Latin essay wasn't wanted tomorrow!

MORITZ: You can't think of anything without homework getting in the way!

OTTO: I'm going home.

GEORG: And me, Homework!

ERNST: And me, and me.

ROBERT: 'Night, Melchior.

MELCHIOR: Sleep well!

They all go except MORITZ *and* MELCHIOR.

MELCHIOR: I'd like to know exactly what we're in this world for!

MORITZ: School makes me wish I was a cart horse! What do we go to school for? To be examined! And why are we examined? So we can fail. Seven have got to fail because the next class is only big enough for sixty.—I've felt so odd since Christmas. . . .

O hell, if it wasn't for papa I'd pack my things tonight and sign on board a ship.

MELCHIOR: Let's talk about something else.

They walk.

MORITZ: Look at that cat with its tail poking up in the air!

MELCHIOR: D'you believe in omens?

MORITZ: Don't really know. It came from over there. It's nothing.

MELCHIOR: In my opinion that's the Charybdis people fall into when they try to rise out of the Scylla of religious superstitition. Let's sit under this beech. The warm wind's blowing over the mountains. I'd like to be a little animal that's rocked and swayed in the tops of the trees the whole night.

MORITZ: Undo your waistcoat, Melchior.

MELCHIOR: O, the way the wind blows your clothes!

MORITZ: God, it's getting pitch dark, you can't see a hand stuck up in front of you. Where are you, actually?—Melchior, don't you also think that man's sense of shame is just a product of his education?

MELCHIOR: I was thinking about that the other day. It seems to me, at least, it's deeply rooted in human nature. For example, suppose you had to completely strip off in front of your best friend. You wouldn't do it, not unless he does it at the same time.—But then perhaps it's all just a question of whatever happens to be in good taste.

MORITZ: I've already decided when I have children I'll let them sleep together in the same room, in the same bed if possible—boys and girls. I'll let them help each other to dress and undress morning and night, and when it's hot the boys and the girls will both wear nothing all day except a white woolen tunic and a leather belt. I think that then when they grow up they won't be as tense as most of us are.

MELCHIOR: I'm sure of it! The only question is, what about when the girls have babies?

MORITZ: Why have babies?

MELCHIOR: I believe in a definite instinct in these things. For example, suppose you keep two cats—a tom and a bitch—shut up together from when they're kittens. You keep them away from all contact with the outside world so they've only got their instincts left. Sooner or later the cat will become pregnant, even though they had no example to follow.

MORITZ: With animals that must finally happen by itself.

MELCHIOR: Even more so with men I think! Listen, Moritz, when your boys are sleeping in the same bed with your girls and suddenly they feel their first masculine itch—I'll take a bet with anyone that—

MORITZ: You may be right. But still.

MELCHIOR: And I'm sure it would be just the same with the girls! Not that girls actually—obviously one can't speak definitely—but at least you can surmise—and their natural curiosity would do the rest!

MORITZ: By the way, I've got a question.

MELCHIOR: What?

MORITZ: But you will answer?

MELCHIOR: Of course?

MORITZ: Promise!

MELCHIOR: My hand on it. Well, Moritz?

MORITZ: Have you really done your homework?

MELCHIOR: Come on, you can tell me. There's no one else here.

MORITZ: Of course, my children will have to work all day in the farm or the garden—or play games that are good for their bodies. Riding, gymnastics, climbing—and certainly no sleeping on soft beds like us. We're terribly weak. I don't believe you'd ever have dreams if you slept on a hard bed.

MELCHIOR: From now till after the harvest I'm only going to sleep in my hammock. I've put my bed away. It folds up. . . . Last winter I dreamed I whipped our Rufus so long he couldn't move. That's the worst thing I've dreamed.—Why are you staring at me like that?

MORITZ: Have you already felt it?

MELCHIOR: What?

MORITZ: How you said.

MELCHIOR: The masculine itch?

MORITZ: H-hm.

MELCHIOR: And how!

MORITZ: Me too.

MELCHIOR: I've been able to for a long time. Almost a year now.

MORITZ: It was like being struck by lightning.

MELCHIOR: Did you have a dream?
MORITZ: But only very short—some legs in bright blue ballet tights climbing over the teacher's desk or at any rate I thought they wanted to climb over—I only caught a glimpse.
MELCHIOR: Georg Zirnschnitz dreamed about his *mother!*
MORITZ: Did he tell you that?
MELCHIOR: Out on Hangman's Hill.
MORITZ: If you knew what I've gone through since that night!
MELCHIOR: Bad conscience?
MORITZ: Bad conscience? *Fear of death!*
MELCHIOR: My God!
MORITZ: I thought I was incurable. I believed I was suffering from an internal defect. In the end I only quietened down when I started to write my memoir. Yes, yes, Melchior, the last three weeks have been a Golgotha to me.
MELCHIOR: I was more or less all set for it. I felt a bit ashamed. But that was all.
MORITZ: And you're almost a whole year younger than me!
MELCHIOR: I shouldn't give it another thought, Moritz. In my experience there isn't a set age for the first time these feelings turn up. You know that tall Lammermeier with the blond hair and hooked nose? He's three years older than me. Hänschen Rilow says he still dreams about apple tart and custard.
MORITZ: Chuck it, Melchior, how can Hänschen Rilow know?
MELCHIOR: He asked him.
MORITZ: He asked him? I wouldn't dare ask anyone.
MELCHIOR: You just asked me.
MORITZ: Good Lord, yes! Perhaps Hänschen also wrote his Last Will! The games they play with us! And we're supposed to be grateful. I don't remember ever wanting that sort of excitement! Why couldn't I just sleep in peace till it was all over? My poor parents could have had a hundred better children than me. But I came, I don't know how, and then it's my fault I didn't stay away! Haven't you ever thought about that, Melchior, exactly how we came into this madhouse?
MELCHIOR: You don't even know that, Moritz?
MORITZ: How should I! I see how hens lay eggs, and I hear mother's supposed to have carried me under her heart! Is that enough? And I remember that when I was five I was already

embarrassed when anyone turned up the Queen of Hearts with the low-cut dress. That feeling's gone. But now I can't even speak to a girl without something I ought to be ashamed of coming into my head and—I swear to you, Melchior—I don't know *what*.

MELCHIOR: I'll tell you everything. I got it partly from books, partly from illustrations, partly from looking at nature. You'll be surprised. It turned me into an atheist. I've already told Georg Zirnschnitz! He wanted to tell Hänschen Rilow, but he'd already had it from his governess when he was a kid.

MORITZ: I've gone through the encyclopaedia from A to Z. Words—nothing but words, words! Not one single straight-forward explanation. O this feeling of shame! What good is an encyclopaedia if it doesn't answer the first questions about life?

MELCHIOR: Have you ever seen two dogs running across the street?

MORITZ: No! You'd better not tell me now, Melchior. I've got to face Central America and Louis the fifteenth! As well as sixty verses of Homer, seven quadratic equations, the Latin essay— I'd just get into hot water with everyone again tomorrow. When you have to study like a cart horse you must be as docile and stupid as a donkey.

MELCHIOR: Come back to my room. In three quarters of an hour I'll do the Homer, the equations, and *two* essays. I'll decorate yours with a few simple mistakes, and the ball's in the hole! Mother will make us some more lemonade and we'll have a pleasant chat about reproduction.

MORITZ: I can't. I can't have a pleasant chat about reproduction. If you want to do me a favor give me some written instructions. Write down all you know. Write it as simply and clearly as possible and stick it in my book during PT tomorrow. I'll take it home without knowing it's there. I'll come across it sometime when I'm not expecting to. I won't be able to stop my weary eyes running over it. . . . If it's absolutely unavoidable you can go as far as a few diagrams in the margin.

MELCHIOR: You're like a girl. Well, have it your own way! It'll be rather interesting homework. One thing, Moritz.

MORITZ: Hn?

MELCHIOR: Have you seen a girl?

MORITZ: Yes!

MELCHIOR: Everything?
MORITZ: The lot.
MELCHIOR: And me! So you won't need many diagrams.
MORITZ: At the fair. In the cubicle at the back of the wax works.
If I'd been caught I'd have been chased out of school! So beautiful—and O! as clear as daylight.
MELCHIOR: Last summer I was with Mama at Frankfurt. . . . Are you going already, Moritz?
MORITZ: Homework. 'Night.
MELCHIOR: Good night.

SCENE 3

THEA, WANDLA *and* MARTHA *come along the street arm in arm.*

MARTHA: How the water gets into your shoes!
WENDLA: How the wind blows in your face!
THEA: How your heart thumps!
WENDLA: Let's go to the bridge. Ilse said the river's full of trees and bushes. The boys have taken a raft out on the water. They say Melchior Gabor was nearly drowned last night.
THEA: O, he can swim!
MARTHA: Of course he can, brat!
WENDLA: If he couldn't swim he could easily have been drowned!
THEA: Your plait's coming undone, Martha! Your plait's coming undone!
MARTHA: O—let it come undone! It annoys me day and night. I mustn't have short hair like you, I mustn't have natural hair like Wendla, I mustn't have a fringe, I even have to go round the house with it done up—all to please my aunts!
WENDLA: Tomorrow I'll bring some scissors to Bible class. While you recite "Blessed is the man who walks not in the counsel of the wicked" I'll cut it off.
MARTHA: For God's sake, Wendla! Papa beats me till I'm crippled and mama locks me up in the coal cellar for three nights at a time.
WENDLA: What does he beat you with, Martha?
MARTHA: Sometimes I think they'd miss something if they didn't have a disgraceful brat like me!

THEA: But, Martha!

WENDLA: And they wouldn't let you thread a bright blue ribbon through the top of your petticoat like us?

THEA: Pink satin! Mama insists pink satin goes with my pitch black eyes.

MARTHA: Blue looked so well on me! Mama pulled me out of my bed by my plait. Well—I fell head first flat on the floor. You see, Mother comes up to pray with us every evening. . . .

WENDLA: If I was you I'd have run far away long ago.

MARTHA: "There you are, see what it'll come to! Yes, there you are! But she'll learn—O, she'll soon learn! At least I'll never be able to blame my mother when anything goes wrong—"

THEA: Hoo hoo!

MARTHA: D'you know what my mother meant by that, Thea?

THEA: No. Do you, Wendla?

WENDLA: I'd have asked her.

MARTHA: I lay on the floor and screamed and roared. Then Papa comes. Rip—petticoat down. I'm out through the door. "There you are! Now I want to go out on the street like that!—"

WENDLA: But that wasn't true, Martha!

MARTHA: I was freezing. I'd got the street door open. I had to sleep in a sack all night.

THEA: I couldn't sleep in a sack to save my life!

WENDLA: I'd like to sleep in your sack for you once.

MARTHA: If only they wouldn't beat me.

THEA: But you'd suffocate in it!

MARTHA: Your head's free. They tie it under your chin.

THEA: And then they beat you?

MARTHA: No. Only when it's something special.

WENDLA: What do they beat you with, Martha?

MARTHA: O, whatever they lay their hands on. Does *your* mother maintain it's indecent to eat bread in bed?

WENDLA: No, no.

MARTHA: I always think, they have their pleasure—even though they never talk about it. When I have children I'll let them grow up like the weeds in our rose garden. No one looks after them but they grow tall and strong—and the roses get weaker every summer and hang down on their stems.

THEA: When I have children I'll dress them all in pink—pink hats, little pink dresses, pink shoes. Only the stockings—stockings pitch black. When I go for a walk I'll let them all trot along in front of me. What about you, Wendla?

WENDLA: D'you already know you'll get some?

THEA: Why shouldn't we get some?

MARTHA: Aunt Euphemia hasn't got any.

THEA: Goose! Because she's not *married*!

WENDLA: Aunt Bauer was married three times—and she hasn't got even one.

MARTHA: If you do get some, Wendla, what d'you want: boys or girls?

WENDLA: Boys! Boys!

THEA: And boys for me!

MARTHA: And me. I'd rather have twenty boys than three girls.

THEA: Girls are boring.

MARTHA: If I wasn't already a girl I know I wouldn't want to become one.

WENDLA: That's a matter of taste, Martha. I'm happy because I'm a girl. Believe me I wouldn't change places with a king's son.— But I still only want boys!

THEA: That's stupid, so stupid, Wendla!

WENDLA: But surely, child, it must be a thousand times more ennobling to be loved by a man than a girl!

THEA: You're not claiming that Herr Pfalle the junior Afforestation Officer loves Melli more than she loves him?

WENDLA: Of course I do, Thea. Pfalle has pride. He's proud of being a Junior Afforestation Officer—because that's all he's got! But Melli has *bliss*—because she's got a million times more than she had when she was on her own!

MARTHA: Aren't you proud of yourself, Wendla?

WENDLA: That would be silly.

THEA: Watch how she walks—how she looks—how she holds herself, Martha! If that's not pride!

WENDLA: But why? I'm just so happy at being a girl. If I wasn't a girl I'd kill myself so that next time. . . .

MELCHIOR *passes and greets them.*

THEA: He's got such a wonderful head.

MARTHA: He makes me think of the young Alexander going to school with Aristotle.

THEA: O God, Greek history! All I remember is that Socrates lay in a barrel while Alexander sold him a donkey's shadow.

WENDLA: I heard he's third in his class.

THEA: Professor Bonebreaker says he could be first if he wanted.

MARTHA: He's got a beautiful forehead, but his friend's got soulful eyes.

THEA: Moritz Stiefel? That doormouse, always asleep.

MARTHA: I've always found him very interesting company.

THEA: He puts you in a compromising situation everytime you meet. At the Rilow's Children's Ball he offered me some chocolates. Imagine, Wendla, they were warm and soft. Isn't that—? He said they'd been in his trousers too long.

WENDLA: What d'you think: Melchior Gabor once told me he didn't believe in anything—not in God, the afterworld—hardly in anything in this world!

SCENE 4

Park in front of the Grammar School.

MELCHIOR, OTTO, GEORG, ROBERT, HÄNSCHEN RILOW, LAMMERMEIER.

MELCHOR: D'you know where Moritz Stiefel's got to?

GEORG: He'll catch it! O, he'll catch it!

OTTO: He goes too far, he'll trip up one day!

LAMMERMEIER: God knows I wouldn't like to be in his shoes now!

ROBERT: Impertinence! Disgraceful!

MELCHIOR: What—what is it?

GEORG: What is it? I'll tell you what it is. . . .

LAMMERMEIER: I don't want to be involved.

OTTO: Nor me—God, no.

MELCHIOR: If you don't tell me immediately. . . .

ROBERT: It's very simple, Moritz Stiefel is burglaring the staff room.

MELCHIOR: The staff room!

OTTO: The staff room. Straight after Latin.

GEORG: He was last. He stayed behind on purpose.
LAMMERMEIER: When I went down the corridor I saw him open the door.
MELCHIOR: I'll be damned!
LAMMERMEIER: No—he'll be!
GEORG: They probably forgot the key.
ROBERT: Or Moritz carries a skeleton key.
OTTO: I wouldn't put that past him!
LAMMERMEIER: He'll be lucky if all he gets is detention.
ROBERT: It'll go on his report.
OTTO: If the governors don't just kick him out.
HÄNSCHEN: There he is.
MELCHIOR: White as a sheet.

> MORITZ *comes in in frantic excitement.*

LAMMERMEIER: Moritz, Moritz, what have you done now!
MORITZ: Nothing—nothing. . . .
ROBERT: You're shaking.
MORITZ: With excitement—with happiness—with luck.
OTTO: Were you copped?
MORITZ: I've passed! Melchior, I've passed! O now the world can go to hell! I've passed! Who thought I'd pass? I still can't believe it! I read it twenty times! I couldn't believe it! O God it was still there! Still there! *I've passed!* (*Smiles.*) I don't know—it's so funny—the floor's going round—Melchior, Melchior, if you knew what it was like!
HÄNSCHEN: Congratulations, Moritz. Just be grateful you got away.
MORITZ: You can't know, Hänschen, you can't imagine the risk! For three weeks I crept by that door as if it was the gates of hell. And today a crack, the door was open. I think if someone had offered me a fortune—nothing, O nothing could have stopped me! I stood in the middle of the room. I pulled the files open— tore through the pages—there it is!—and the whole time . . . I'm shuddering.
MELCHIOR: And the whole time . . . ?
MORITZ: The whole time the door was wide open behind me. How I got out—how I got down the stairs I'll never know.
HÄNSCHEN: Has Ernst Röbel passed?

MORITZ: O yes, Hänschen! Ernst Röbel passed too!

ROBERT: Then you didn't read it right. If you don't count the dunces, then we and you and Röbel make sixty-one, and the next class only holds sixty.

MORITZ: I read it perfectly clearly. Ernst Röbel goes up as well as me—of course at the moment we're both only provisional. Next term they'll decide which of us has to give way. Poor Röbel! God knows I'm not worried about myself now. I've been too near the abyss already.

OTTO: I bet five marks you have to give way.

MORITZ: You haven't got it. I don't want to clean you out. O Lord, I'll work like a slave after this. I can tell you now—I don't care if you believe me—it doesn't matter anymore—I—I know how true it is: if I hadn't passed I'd have shot myself.

ROBERT: With a peashooter!

GEORG: Yellow belly!

OTTO: I'd like to see you shoot!

LAMMERMEIER: Clip his ear and see what he does!

MELCHIOR (*hits* LAMMERMEIER): Come on, Moritz. Let's go to the forester's hut.

GEORG: You don't believe that rubbish!

MELCHIOR: Would it bother you? Let them chatter, Moritz, we'll go—out of this town!

PROFESSORS GUTGRINDER *and* BONEBREAKER *go by.*

BONEBREAKER: Beyond my comprehension, my dear fellow, how my best student can feel himself drawn toward precisely my very worst.

GUTGRINDER: Beyond mine too, my dear chap.

SCENE 5

A sunny afternoon.

MELCHIOR *and* WENDLA *meet each other in the forest.*

MELCHIOR: Is it really you, Wendla? What are you doing up here on your own? I've been wandering through the forest for three hours without meeting a soul, and now suddenly you come toward me out of the trees.

WENDLA: Yes, it's me.

MELCHIOR: If I didn't know you were Wendla Bergmann I'd think you were a wood nymph that's fallen out of the branches.

WENDLA: No, no, I'm Wendla Bergmann. Where have you come from?

MELCHIOR: I've been thinking.

WENDLA: I'm collecting woodruff. Mama uses them for spring wine. She *was* coming with me but Aunt Bauer turned up at the last moment. She doesn't like climbing so I came on my own.

MELCHIOR: Have you got the woodruff?

WENDLA: A whole basket full! It's as thick as clover over there under the beeches. Now I'm trying to find a path. I seem to have gone wrong. Perhaps you could tell me what time it is?

MELCHIOR: Just after half past three. When are you expected?

WENDLA: I thought it was later. I lay down quite a while on the moss by the stream and dreamed. Time went so quickly. I was afraid evening was already coming.

MELCHIOR: If you're not expected, let's stay here a little bit longer. My favorite spot's under the oak. If you lean your head back against the trunk and stare through the branches up at the sky, it hypnotises you. The ground's still warm from the sun this morning. I've wanted to ask you something for weeks, Wendla.

WENDLA: But I must be home by five.

MELCHIOR: We'll go together. I'll carry the basket and we'll go along the river bed and be on the bridge in ten minutes. When you lie like this with your head propped in your hands you have the strangest ideas. . . .

Both are lying under the oak.

WENDLA: What did you want to ask me, Melchior?

MELCHIOR: I know you often visit the poor, Wendla, and take them food and clothes and money. D'you go because you want to or does your mother send you?

WENDLA: Mostly Mother sends me. They're poor working-class families with too many children. Often the man can't find work so they're cold and hungry. We've got a lot of left-over things lying about in cupboards and drawers, we'll never use them now. What made you think of that?

MELCHIOR: Are you pleased when your mother sends you?

WENDLA: O very pleased! How can you ask!

MELCHIOR: But the children are dirty, the women are sick, the rooms are crowded with filth, the men hate you because you don't have to work. . . .

WENDLA: That's not true, Melchior. And if it were true I'd go even more.

MELCHIOR: Why even more, Wendla?

WENDLA: I'd go to them even more. It would give me far more happiness to be able to help them.

MELCHIOR: So you go to the poor to make yourself happy?

WENDLA: I go to them because they're poor.

MELCHIOR: And if it didn't make you happy you wouldn't go?

WENDLA: Can I help it if it makes me happy?

MELCHIOR: And for that you go to heaven! I was right, I've been going over this for a month! Can a miser help it if visiting dirty, sick children doesn't make him happy?

WENDLA: O, I'm sure it would make you very happy!

MELCHIOR: And yet because of that he suffers eternal damnation! I'll write an essay and send it to the Reverend Baldbelly. He put all this in my head! Why does he drivel on at us about the joys of sacrificing yourself for others? If he can't answer, I'm not going to any more confirmation classes and I won't be confirmed.

WENDLA: Don't make your poor parents miserable over that! Let them confirm you. They don't cut your head off. If it wasn't for our dreadful white dresses and your baggy trousers we might even get some fun out of it.

MELCHIOR: There is no self-sacrifice! There is no selflessness! I watch the good enjoying themselves while the bad tremble and groan—I watch you shaking your curls and laughing, Wendla Bergmann, and it all makes me feel as lost as an outcast—Wendla, what did you dream about when you were on the grass by the stream?

WENDLA: Nonsense—silly things. . . .

MELCHIOR: With your eyes open?

WENDLA: I dreamed I was a poor, poor beggar girl. I was sent out on the streets every morning before five. I had to beg from brutal, heartless people, all day in the storm and rain. And when I came home at night, shivering with hunger and cold, and when I didn't have all the money my father wanted, I was beaten . . . beaten . . .

MELCHIOR: I understand, Wendla. You get that from silly children's books. I promise you there aren't brutal people like that any more.

WENDLA: O no, Melchior, you're wrong. Martha Bessel is beaten night after night and you can see the weals next day. O what she must suffer! It makes me hot when she tells us about it. I pity her so much. I often have to cry in my pillow in the middle of the night. I've been thinking for months how I can help her. I'd happily take her place just for one week.

MELCHIOR: The father should be reported immediately. Then they'd take the child away.

WENDLA: I haven't been hit in my whole life, Melchior—not even once. I can hardly imagine what it's like to be beaten. I've beaten myself to find out what it does to you. It must be a horrifying feeling.

MELCHIOR: I don't believe it ever makes a child better.

WENDLA: What?

MELCHIOR: Being beaten.

WENDLA: With this switch for example. Ugh, how springy and thin.

MELCHIOR: That would draw blood.

WENDLA: Would you like to beat me with it once?

MELCHIOR: Who?

WENDLA: Me.

MELCHIOR: What's the matter, Wendla?

WENDLA: There's no harm in it.

MELCHIOR: O be quiet! I won't beat you.

WENDLA: But if I let you do it!

MELCHIOR: No, Wendla.

WENDLA: But if I ask you for it, Melchior!

MELCHIOR: Are you out of your mind?

WENDLA: I've never been beaten in my whole life!

MELCHIOR: If you can ask for something like that. . . .

WENDLA: Please, please!

MELCHIOR: I'll teach you to ask! (*He hits her.*)

WENDLA: O God—I don't feel it at all. . . .

MELCHIOR: Of course not—through all your skirts.

WENDLA: Then beat my legs!

MELCHIOR: Wendla! (*He hits her harder.*)

WENDLA: You're only stroking me! Stroking me!
MELCHIOR: You wait, you bitch, I'll thrash the hide off you!

He throws the stick away and hits out at her with his fists. She bursts into a terrible scream. He takes no notice and punches at her in fury. Heavy tears stream down his face. He jumps up, grips his head and runs into the wood sobbing with misery.

Act 2

SCENE 1

Evening in MELCHIOR's *study.*

The window is open, the lamp burns on the table, MELCHIOR *and* MORITZ *sit on the sofa.*

MORITZ: I'm quite lively again now, just a bit on edge. But I slept all through Greek. I'm surprised old Tonguetwister didn't twist my ears. I just scraped in on time this morning. My first thought when I woke up was irregular verbs. Damnation-hell-and-fireworks, I conjugated all through breakfast and all the way to school, till everything was green in front of my eyes . . . I must have gone blank about three. The pen made one more blot in my book. When Mathilde woke me up the lamp was smoking and the blackbirds were singing their hearts out in the lilac under the window—suddenly I felt so completely miserable again. I fastened my collar and put a brush through my hair—but you feel satisfied when you've forced something out of yourself.
MELCHIOR: May I roll you a cigarette?
MORTIZ: Thanks, I'm not smoking.—If I can only keep it up! I'll work and work till my eyes drop out. Ernst Röbel's already failed six times since the holidays: three times in Greek, twice with Bonebreaker, the last time in literary history. I've only been in that pitiful condition five times, and it's definitely not happening again! Röbel won't shoot himself! Röbel's parents didn't sacrifice everything for him. He can become a mercenary whenever he likes, or a cowboy or a sailor. If *I* fail my father will have a heart attack and my mother go into a madhouse. I'd never survive it. Before the exams I prayed like Christ in the

garden, I implored God to let me catch consumption so that this bitter cup would pass. It passed—but I'm still afraid to look up day or night. The halo that floats over it is winking at me from the distance. Well now I've got the bull by the horns I'm going to climb on its back. Then if I fall I have an infallible guarantee that I'll break my neck.

MELCHIOR: Life is always unexpectedly mean. I rather incline to hanging myself from a tree. What's keeping mama with the tea?

MORITZ: Tea will do me good. I'm actually shaking, Melchior! I feel so strangely disembodied. Please touch me. I see—I hear—I feel much more clearly—and yet it's all in a dream—O, so strange. The garden's lying down there in the moonlight, so still and deep, as if it's lying in eternity. There are veiled figures coming out of the ground under the bushes. They hurry over the clearings—busy and breathless—and vanish in the dusk. It's as if a meeting's gathering under the chestnut trees. Shouldn't we go down, Melchior?

MELCHIOR: After tea.

MORITZ: The leaves are rustling like little insects! It's as if my dead grandmother was telling me the story of "The Queen with No Head." There was a beautiful queen, as beautiful as the sun, more beautiful than all the other girls. But unfortunately she came into the world with no head. She couldn't eat, or drink, or see, or laugh, or even kiss. She could only make the court understand her by her soft little hands, and she tapped out declarations of war and death sentences with her pretty little feet. One day she was defeated by a king who happened to have two heads. They got in each other's hair all the time and quarrelled so much that neither of them could get a word in. The top wizard took the smaller head and put it on the queen. There, it fits marvellously. So the king married the queen, and instead of getting in each other's hair they kissed: on their foreheads, their cheeks, their mouths—and lived happily ever after. All rubbish! Since the holidays I can't get the headless queen out of my mind. When I see a beautiful girl, I see her with no head—and I keep suddenly seeing myself with no head. . . . Perhaps one day someone will put a head on me.

FRAU GABOR *brings tea and puts it on the table in front of* MORITZ *and* MELCHIOR.

FRAU GABOR: There, boys, drink your tea. Good evening, Herr Stiefel, how are you?

MORITZ: Thank you, Frau Gabor.—I'm watching the dance down there.

FRAU GABOR: You don't look too well. D'you feel all right?

MORITZ: It's nothing. I've been going to bed a bit late the last few nights.

MELCHIOR: Imagine, he worked through the whole night.

FRAU GABOR: You shouldn't, Herr Stiefel. You must look after yourself. Think of your health. School can't give you your health back again. Brisk walks in the fresh air. That's worth more at your age than perfect grammar.

MORITZ: Yes—brisk walks! While you're walking you can work in your head! Why didn't I think of that?—But I'd still have to do the written work indoors.

MELCHIOR: Do the written stuff with me. That'll make it easier for both of us. Mother, you know Max von Trenk went down with nervous exhaustion? Well, Hänschen Rilow came straight from Trenk's deathbed lunch-time today and told the Head Trenk had just died in his presence. The Head said "Indeed. haven't you still got two hours detention owing from last week? Here's a note for your Form Master. Get it sorted out. The whole class will assist at his funeral." Hänschen could hardly move.

FRAU GABOR: What's your book, Melchior?

MELCHIOR: *Faust*.

FRAU GABOR: Have your read it?

MELCHIOR: Not all of it.

MORITZ: We're just in the Walpurgis Night.

FRAU GABOR: If I were you I'd have waited a year or two for that.

MELCHIOR: I haven't come across any other book that I think is so beautiful, mother. Why shouldn't I read it?

FRAU GABOR: Because you don't understand it.

MELCHIOR: You can't know that, mother. Of course, I know I don't understand its deepest meaning . . .

MORITZ: We always read together. That makes it incredibly easier to understand.

FRAU GABOR: You're old enough to know what's good for you and what's bad for you, Melchior. Do whatever you feel able to answer for to your own conscience. I shall be the first to ac-

knowledge it if you never give me any cause to forbid you anything. I only want to make you aware that even the best can
work harm when one lacks the maturity to know how to use it.
But I shall always put my trust in you, rather than in some vague
doctrine of education. If you need anything else, boys, come and
call me, Melchior. I'm in my bedroom. *(Goes.)*

MORITZ: Your mother meant the business with Gretchen and the
baby.

MELCHIOR: Did we even pause over it?

MORITZ: *Faust* couldn't have treated it more cold-bloodedly!

MELCHIOR: A common little scandal like that can't be the summit
of such a masterpiece! Suppose Faust had just promised to marry
her and then walked off! That would have been just as bad.
There'd been no baby—but Gretchen could still have died of a
broken heart. When you see how frantically they all pounce on
that one incident you'd think the whole world revolved round
penis and vagina.

MORITZ: Frankly, Melchior, since reading your essay I feel it does.
It fell out on the floor when I was reading a history book. I
bolted the door and went through your lines like an owl flying
through a burning wood. I think I read most of it with my eyes
shut. It was like listening to your own forgotten memories—a
song you hummed to yourself when you played as a child, and
then hearing it again when you're lying down to die, coming out
of someone else's mouth and breaking your heart. What moved
me most was the part you wrote about the girl. I can't get it out
of my mind. Honestly, Melchior, I'd rather suffer wrong than
do wrong. To have to be overpowered by such a gentle force,
and still be innocent—that seems the greatest sort of happiness
to me.

MELCHIOR: I don't want to be given happiness like a beggar!

MORITZ: Why not?

MELCHIOR: I don't want anything I didn't have to fight for!

MORITZ: But would that still be happiness, Melchior? Melchior,
the girl enjoys it like someone in heaven. It's a girl's nature to
protect herself, to keep herself free from all bitterness till the last
moment—so that she can feel all heaven falling on her at once.
A girl is afraid of hell even at the moment she steps into paradise.
Her feelings are as fresh as a stream when it breaks from the

rocks. The girl lifts up a chalice that no earthly mouth has touched, a cup of flaming sparkling nectar and gulps it down—I think the satisfaction a man gets out of it must be cold and flat.

MELCHIOR: Think what you like but shut up. I don't like to think about it. . . .

SCENE 2

FRAU BERGMANN *wearing a hat and cape, and with a beaming face, comes through the middle door. She carries a basket on her arm.*

FRAU BERGMANN: Wendla! Wendla!

WENDLA *appears in petticoat and stays at the side door right.*

WENDLA: What is it, Mother?

FRAU BERGMANN: You're up already, precious? What a good girl!

WENDLA: You've been out this early?

FRAU BERGMANN: Get dressed quickly. You must go down to Ina. You must take her this basket.

WENDLA *(gets dressed during the following)*: You've been to Ina's? How was Ina? Won't she ever get better?

FRAU BERGMANN: You'll never guess, Wendla, last night the stork was with her and brought her a little boy.

WENDLA: A boy! A boy! O that's wonderful! That's what her chronic influenza was!

FRAU BERGMANN: A perfect boy!

WENDLA: I must see him, Mother! Now I'm an aunt three times—aunt to one girl and two boys!

FRAU BERGMANN: And what boys! That's what happens when you live so close to the stork! It's only two years since she walked up the aisle in her white dress.

WENDLA: Were you there when he brought him?

FRAU BERGMANN: He'd just flown off again. Don't you want to pin on a rose?

WENDLA: Why didn't you get there a bit sooner, Mother?

FRAU BERGMANN: I believe he might have brought you something too—a brooch perhaps.

WENDLA: It's such a pity.

FRAU BERGMANN: Now I told you he brought you a brooch.

WENDLA: I've got enough brooches.

FRAU BERGMANN: Then be contented, child. What more do you want?

WENDLA: I would very much like to have known whether he flew in through the window or down the chimney.

FRAU BERGMANN: You must ask Ina. O yes, you must ask Ina that, precious. Ina will tell you exactly. Ina spoke to him for a good half hour.

WENDLA: I shall ask Ina when I get there.

FRAU BERGMANN: And don't forget, precious. I shall be very interested myself to know if he came in through the window or the chimney.

WENDLA: Or perhaps I'd better ask the chimney sweep. The chimney sweep's bound to know if he used the chimney.

FRAU BERGMANN: Not the chimney sweep, dear. Not the chimney sweep. What does the chimney sweep know about storks? He'll tell you all sorts of nonsense he doesn't believe himself. What—what are you staring at in the street?

WENDLA: Mother, a man—as big as three horses, with feet like paddle-steamers!

FRAU BERGMANN *(running to the window)*: I don't believe it! I don't believe it!

WENDLA *(at the same time)*: He's holding a bed-stead under his chin and playing "Watch on the Rhine" on it—he's just gone round the corner.

FRAU BERGMANN: You'll always be a child! Frightening your silly old mother. Go and get your hat. I sometimes wonder if you'll ever get any sense in your head. I've given up hope.

WENDLA: So have I, mother, so have I. There's not much hope for my head. I've got a sister who's been married two and a half years, and I'm an aunt three times, and I've no idea how it all happens. . . . Don't be cross, Mommy, don't be cross! Who in the world should I ask but you? Please, Mommy, tell me. Tell me, dear. I feel ashamed of myself. Do tell me, Mommy! Don't scold me for asking such things. Answer me—what is it?—how does it happen? You can't really insist that now I'm fourteen I still have to believe in the stork?

FRAU BERGMANN: But good lord, child, how funny you are! What ideas you get! I really cannot do such a thing.

WENDLA: Why not, Mother? Why not? It can't be anything ugly if it makes you all so happy.

FRAU BERGMANN: O—God help me! I would deserve to be . . . Go and get dressed, Wendla. Get dressed.

WENDLA: I'll go . . . and what if your child goes to the chimney sweep to ask?

FRAU BERGMANN: But this will send me out of my mind! Come here, Wendla, come to me. I'll tell you! I'll tell you everything! O Almighty Father!—Only not now, Wendla. Tomorrow, the day after tomorrow, next week—whenever you like, my precious.

WENDLA: Tell me today, Mother! Tell me now! This moment. I can never stop asking now I've seen you so frightened.

FRAU BERGMANN: I can't Wendla.

WENDLA: O why can't you, Mommy? I'll kneel at your feet and lay my head in your lap. Put your apron over my head and talk and talk as if you were sitting alone in your room. I won't flinch or cry out. I'll be patient and bear it whatever it is.

FRAU BERGMANN: Heaven knows none of this is my fault. Wendla! Heaven sees into my heart. I'll put myself into God's hands, Wendla—and tell you how you came into this world. Now listen to me, Wendla.

WENDLA *(under the apron)*: I'm listening.

FRAU BERGMANN *(ecstatically)*: But I can't, child! I can't be responsible! I'd deserve to be put in prison—to have you taken away from me. . . .

WENDLA *(under the apron)*: Be brave, Mother!

FRAU BERGMANN: Well, listen!

WENDLA *(under the apron, trembling)*: O god, O God!

FRAU BERGMANN: To have a child—you understand me, Wendla?

WENDLA: Quickly, Mother—I can't bear it anymore.

FRAU BERGMANN: To have a child—the man—to whom you're married—you must—*love*—love, you see—as you can only love your husband. You must love him *very much with your whole heart*—in a way that can't be put into words! You must *love* him, Wendla, in a way that you certainly can't love at your age . . . Now you know.

WENDLA *(getting up)*: Well, good heavens!

FRAU BERGMANN: Now you know what a testing time lies before you!

WENDLA: And that's all?

FRAU BERGMANN: As God is my witness! Now take that basket and go to Ina. She'll give you some chocolate to drink, and some cake too. Come on, let me look at you once more—boots laced up, silk gloves, sailor suit, rose in your hair . . . your little skirt really is getting too short for you, Wendla!

WENDLA: Have you bought the meat for lunch, Mommy?

FRAU BERGMANN: God bless you. I must sew a broad flounce round the bottom.

SCENE 3

HÄNSCHEN RILOW (*with a light in his hand, he bolts the door behind him and lifts the lid*): Have you prayed tonight Desdemona?

He takes a reproduction of the Venus of Palma Vecchio from the inside pocket of his jacket.

You don't look like the Lord's Prayer, darling—contemplating the coming moments, the lovely moments of coming ecstasy—still just as when I first saw you lying in the window of that little corner shop, just as alluring with those smooth limbs, this soft curve of the hips, these young, tense breasts—O, how drunk the Great Master must have been when the fourteen-year-old original lay stretched out before him on the studio couch!

Will you come to me in my dreams now and then? I'll welcome you with outstretched arms and kiss your breath away. You'll take me over like an heiress moving back into her deserted palace. Gates and doors fly open with unseen hands, and down below in the park the fountain begins to splash happily. . . .

It is the cause! It is the cause! The terrible hammering in my breast proves I'm not murdering you for a whim! My throat goes dry when I think of the lonely nights ahead. And I swear to you, woman, it's not the disgust that comes from over indulgence! Who'd flatter himself by being disgusted with you? No— you suck the marrow from my bones, bend my back, take the sparkle from my young eyes. Your inhuman modesty is too demanding, your motionless limbs, too exhausting! It's me or you!

And I've won!

If I counted them all—all the others I fought this battle with on this same spot! Ruben's Venus—bequeathed to me by that waspish-thin governess Miss Hatherley-Brown, the rattlesnake in my nursery paradise! Correggio's Io. Titian's Galathea. J. van Beer's Ada. Cupid by Bourguereau—the Cupid I abducted from the secret drawer in papa's desk and locked up in my harem. A quivering, trembling Leda by Makart I came across in my brother's exercise books. *Seven,* O, lovely candidate for death, have gone before you down the path to Tartarus. Let that console you and don't make my torments unbearable with those imploring looks!

You don't die for *your* sins but *mine*! With a bleeding heart I've murdered seven wives in self-defense. There's something tragic in the role of Bluebeard. All his wives put together didn't suffer as much when he strangled them as he did each time!

But my conscience will be at peace, my body will get stronger when you no longer dwell in the red silk cushions of my jewelry box. Now I shall open my opulent pleasure dome to portraits of The Puritan Maid, Mary Magdalene. The Respectable Farmer's Wife—and then I'll get over you sooner. Perhaps in another three months, my angel, your naked flesh-pot would have started to gnaw my brains like the sun melting butter pudding. It's time we were granted a decree!

Ugh, I feel a Heliogabalus rising in me! *Moritura me salutat!* Girl, girl why d'you press your knees together—even now when you stand before eternity? *One* tremble, and I'll set you free! *One* feminine wriggle, *one* flicker of lust, of pity, woman! I'd let you lie in a gold frame over my bed! Don't you know it's your respectability that drives me to my debaucheries? Alas, alas, so much inhumanity! One always notices her sort had a good upbringing! It's exactly the same with me! Have you prayed tonight, Desdemona?

My heart breaks. Rot! Even St. Agnes had to die for her virginity, and she wasn't half as naked as you! One last kiss on your blooming body, your girlish, budding breasts, your sweet curved—your cruel knees. . . .

It is the cause, it is the cause, my soul! Let me not name it to you, you chaste stars! It is the cause!

The picture falls into the depths. He shuts the lid.

SCENE 4

A hayloft.

MELCHIOR *lies on his back in fresh hay.* WENDLA *comes up the ladder.*

WENDLA: *Here's* where you've crept to! They're all looking for you. The hay wagon's gone out again. You've got to help. There's a storm coming.

MELCHIOR: Go away. Go away.

WENDLA: What is it? Why are you hiding your face?

MELCHIOR: Get out! I'll throw you down on the threshing floor!

WENDLA: Now I certainly won't go. (*Kneels beside him.*) Come out in the fields with me, Melchior? It's sticky and gloomy here. It doesn't matter to us if we get soaked!

MELCHIOR: The hay smells so good. The sky outside must be as dark as the grave. All I can see is the bright poppy on your breast—I can hear your heartbeat. . . .

WENDLA: Don't kiss me, Melchior! Don't kiss me!

MELCHIOR: Your heart—listen to it beating.

WENDLA: You love each other—when you kiss—no, no!

MELCHIOR: O, believe me, there's no such thing as *love*! It's all self, all ego. I don't love you anymore than you love me.

WENDLA: Don't! Don't, Melchior!

MELCHIOR: Wendla!

WENDLA: O, Melchior! Don't, don't.

SCENE 5

Frau Gabor sits and writes.

FRAU GABOR: Dear Herr Stiefel,
  After twenty-four hours of thinking and thinking over what you have written to me, I take up my pen with a heavy heart. I cannot, I give you my solemn word, obtain the cost of a passage to America for you. Firstly, I do not have that much at my disposal, and secondly, if I had, it would be the greatest

possible sin to put into your hands the means of carrying out a recklessness so fraught with consequence. You would do me a grave injustice, Herr Stiefel, if you found in this refusal a sign of any lack of love on my part. On the contrary, it would be a grave offense to my duty as a motherly friend if I also were to lose my head and, influenced by your momentary desperation, abandon myself to first impulses. I will gladly, should you so wish, write to your parents and try to persuade them that throughout this term you have done all that lay in your power, and exhausted your strength—so much so that any rigorous condemnation of your failure would not only be unjust but might very well be detrimental to your physical and spiritual health.

The threat hinted at in your letter—that if your escape were not made possible you would take your life—does to be frank, Herr Stiefel, somewhat surprise me. Be a misfortune never so undeserved, one should not allow oneself to stoop to underhand methods. The method by which you seek to make me, who have always been kind to you, responsible for any ensuing tragedy, smacks somewhat of that which in the eyes of ill-disposed persons might well be taken as an attempt at extortion. I must own that, least of all from you, who otherwise know so well the respect one owes oneself, was the above mentioned to be expected. However, I am convinced that you were still suffering from the effects of first shock and therefore unable to understand the nature of your conduct. And so I confidently trust that these my words will reach you in an already more composed frame of mind. Take things for what they are. In my opinion it is quite wrong to judge a young man by his examination results. We have too many instances before us of bad scholars who became remarkable men, and, contrariwise, of splendid scholars who did not especially prove themselves in later life. Be that as it may, I give you my assurance that, so far as lies within my power, your misfortune shall in no way alter your relations with Melchior. It will always afford me joy to watch my son's intercourse with a young man who, let the world judge him how it may, will always be able to command my fullest sympathy. And therefore, head up, Herr Stiefel. These crises come to us all in one form or another and must be seen through. If we immediately resort to dagger and poison there will very soon be no one left in the world. Let me hear a line from you before long. The very best wishes of your staunch devoted motherly friend Fanny G.

SCENE 6

The BERGMANNS' *garden in morning sunlight.*

WENDLA: Why did you slip out of the room? To pick violets! Because Mother sees me smiling. Why can't you close your lips anymore? I don't know. I really don't know, I don't know the words. . . .
The path's like a soft carpet. No stones, no thorns. My feet don't touch the ground . . . . O how I slept last night!
They were here. I feel as solemn as a nun at communion.
These beautiful violets! Hush, mother, I'll wear my sackcloth.
O God, if only someone could come and I could throw my arms round his neck and tell!

SCENE 7

Evening, dusk.

The sky is lightly clouded, the path winds between low bushes and reeds. The river is heard a little way off.

MORITZ: The sooner the better. I don't belong here. Let them kick each other to bits. I'll shut the door behind me and walk away into freedom. Why should I let them push me about? I didn't force myself on them. Why should I force myself on them now? I haven't got a contract with God. Look at it from any angle you like, they forced me. I don't blame my parents. Still, they were old enough to know what they were doing. I was a baby when I came in the world—or I'd have had enough sense to come as someone else!
I'd have to be off my head: someone gives me a mad dog, and when he won't take his mad dog back *I* play the gentleman and. . . .

I'd have to be off my head!

You're born by pure chance and after mature reconsideration you mustn't . . . ? I could die laughing! At least the weather cares. It looked like rain all day and now it's cleared. The strange stillness everywhere. Nothing harsh or loud. The whole world like a fine cobweb. Everything so calm and still. The landscape is a beautiful lullabye. "Sleep, little prince, go to sleep." Fräulein Hectorina's song. A pity she holds her elbows awkwardly! The last time I danced it was the feast of St. Cecilia. Hectorina only dances with young toffs. Her dress was cut so low at the back and the front. Down to the hips at the back, and in front down to—you mustn't think about it. She couldn't have had a bodice on. . . . That might keep me here. More out of curiosity. It must be a strange sensation—like being dragged over maelstroms. I won't tell anyone I've come back half-cocked. I'll behave as if I've done everything. It's shameful to have been a man and not known the most human thing. You come from *Egypt,* dear sir, and you've never seen the pyramids?

I don't want to cry anymore. Or think about my funeral. Melchior will lay a wreath on my coffin. Reverend Baldbelly will console my parents. The Head will cite examples from history. I don't suppose I'll get a tombstone. I'd have liked a snow-white marble urn on a black syenite column—luckily I won't miss it. Monuments are for the living not the dead. It would take at least a year to go through everyone in my head and say good-bye. I don't want to cry now. I'm glad I can look back without bitterness. The beautiful evenings with Melchior!—under the willows, the forester's hut, the old battleground with the five lime trees, the quiet ruins of the castle. When the moment comes I'll think with my whole being of whipped cream. Whipped cream won't stop me. It leaves behind a pleasant aftertaste, it doesn't end up in your trousers. . . . And then I've always thought people were worse than they are. I've never met one who didn't try his best. I felt sorry for them because they had me to deal with.

I go to the altar like an ancient Etruscan youth. His death rattles bring his brothers prosperity for the year ahead. Drop by drop I drink the dregs. The secret shudders of crossing over. I weep with the sadness of my lot. Life gave me the cold shoulder. From the other side solemn, friendly faces beckon me: the headless queen, the headless queen—compassion, waiting for me, with open arms. . . . The laws of this world are for children, I've earned my pass. The balance sinks, the butterfly rises and flies away. The painted veil no longer blinds me. Why should I play this mad game with Illusion? The mists part! Life is a question of taste.

ILSE, *in torn clothes and with a colored scarf on her head, taps his shoulder from behind.*

ILSE: What have you lost?
MORITZ: Ilse?
ILSE: What are you looking for?
MORITZ: Why did you frighten me?
ILSE: What are you looking for? What have you lost?
MORITZ: Why did you frighten me like that?
ILSE: I've just come from town. I'm going home.
MORITZ: I don't know what I've lost.
ILSE: No use looking for it then.
MORITZ: Blast! Blast!
ILSE: I haven't been home for four days.
MORITZ: Creeping about like a cat.
ILSE: I've got my dancing shoes on. Mother's eyes will pop out. Walk back to our house with me.
MORITZ: Where have you been this time?
ILSE: With the Phallustics!
MORITZ: Phallustics!
ILSE: With Hohl, Karl, Paganini, Schiller, Rank, Dostoevsky— with anyone I could! O, mother will jump!
MORITZ: Do you sit for them?
ILSE: Karl's painting me as an eremite. I stand on a Corinthian column. Karl's off his head, believe me. Last time I trod on his tube of paint. He wiped his brush in my hair. I boxed his ears. He threw his palette at me. I knock the easel down. He chases me with is paint stick over the divan, tables, chairs, round and round the studio. There's drawing by the fire. Behave or I'll tear it! He says he'll behave and then ends up kissing me terribly— terribly, believe me.
MORITZ: Where d'you spend the nights when you're in town?

ILSE: Yesterday at Nohl's—the day before at El Greco's—Sunday with Bojokewitsch. We had champagne at Paganini's. Velazquez sold his Plague Sufferer. Adolar drank out of the ashtray. Schiller sang "The Mother who Murdered her Child" and Adolar beat hell out of the guitar. I was so drunk they had to put me to bed. You're still at school, Moritz?

MORITZ: No, no—this is my last term.

ILSE: That's right. O, time passes much better when you're earning. D'you remember how we played bandits? Wendla Bergmann and you and me and the others. You all came to our place in the evenings and drank the goat's milk while it was still warm. What's Wendla up to? Last time I saw her was at the flood. What does Melchior Gabor do? Does he still look so solemn? We used to stand opposite each other in music.

MORITZ: He's a philosopher.

ILSE: Wendla was at our place a while back and brought mother some stewed fruit. I was sitting for Isidor Landauer then. He wants me for the Virgin Mary mother of God with the baby Jesus. He's an idiot and disgusting. Ugh, never settles. Have you got a hangover?

MORITZ: From last night. We knocked it back like hippopotamuses. I staggered home at five.

ILSE: You've only got to look at you! Were there any girls?

MORITZ: Arabella. We drank beer out of her slipper. She's Spanish, you know. The landlord left us alone with her the whole night.

ILSE: You've got only to look at you, Moritz! I don't know what a hangover is! Last carnival I didn't go to bed or get out of my clothes for three days and nights! From Fancy Dress Balls to the cafés, lunch on the lake, cellar revues in the evenings, nights back to the Fancy Dress Balls. Lena was with me and that fat Viola. Heinrich found me on the third night.

MORITZ: Was he looking for you?

ILSE: He tripped over my arm. I was lying unconscious on the street in the snow. Afterward I went back to his place. I couldn't get away for two weeks—that was a terrible time! Every morning I had to pose in his Persian dressing gown, and every evening walk round his rooms in a black page-boy tunic. White lace, cuffs, collar and knees. He photographed me in a different way

every day—once as Adriadne on the arm of the sofa, once as
Leda, once as Ganymede, and once on all fours as a female
Nobobycanesor. He was also squirming on about murder, shooting, suicide, drugs and fumes. He brought a pistol in bed every
morning, loaded it with shot, and pushes it into my breast: one
twitch and I press. O, he would have pressed, Moritz, he would
have pressed. Then he put the thing in his mouth like a pea
shooter. It's supposed to be good for the self-preservation instinct. Ugh—the bullet would have gone through my spine!

MORITZ: Is Heinrich still alive?

ILSE: How should I know? There was a big mirror in the ceiling
over the bed. The little room looked as tall as a tower, as bright
as an opera house. You saw yourself hanging down alive from
the sky. I had terrible dreams, God, O God, if only the day
would come. Good night, Ilse. When you're asleep you're so
beautiful I could murder you.

MORITZ: Is this Heinrich still alive?

ILSE: No, please God. One day he was fetching absinthe and I
threw my coat on and slipped out in the street. The carnival was
over. The police picked me up. What was I doing in men's
clothes? They took me to the station. Then Nohl, Karl, Paganini,
Schiller and El Greco, all the Phallustics, came and stood bail
for me. They carried me home in a posh cab. Since then I've
stuck to the crowd. Karl's an ape, Nohl's a pig, Berlioz's a goat,
Dostoevsky's a hyena, El Greco's a bear—but I love them, all of
them together, and I wouldn't trust anyone else even if the world
was full of saints and millionaires.

MORITZ: I must go home, Ilse.

ILSE: Come back to my place.

MORITZ: Why? Why . . .?

ILSE: To drink warm goat's milk. I'll curl your hair and hang a
bell round your neck. Or there's a rocking-horse you can play on.

MORITZ: I must go home. I've still got the Sassanids, the sermon
on the mount, and the Parallelepipedon on my conscience. Good
night, Ilse.

ILSE: Sleep tight! Do you still play in the wigwam where Melchior
Gabor buried my tomahawk? Ugh! Before you're ready I'll be in
the dustbin. (*She hurries away.*)

MORITZ (*alone*): One word! That's all it needed! (*Calls.*) Ilse! Ilse! Thank God she can't hear. I'm not in the mood. You have to be clear-headed and relaxed for that. Pity, pity—a wasted chance. I'll say I had huge crystal mirrors over my beds and reared an untamed colt and let it prance round me on carpets in long black silk stockings and shiny black boots and long black kid gloves and black velvet round its throat and in an insane frenzy I took the pillow and smothered it—I will smile when they talk of lust— I will—scream!—Scream—! To be you, Ilse! Phallic! Unselfconscious! That's what takes my strength away! That happy child, that child of nature—that little whore on my path of misery! (*In the bushes on the bank.*) I've come here again without knowing it . . . the grass bank. The rods of the bulrushes look taller since yesterday. The view through the willows is the same. The river passes as slowly as melted lead. I mustn't forget . . . (*He takes* FRAU GABOR's *letter from his pocket, and burns it.*) How the sparks float . . . here and there, round and round—souls! Shooting stars! Before I made the flame I could see the rushes and a line on the horizon. Now it's dark. I shan't go home now.

Act 3

SCENE 1

Staff room.

Portraits of Pestalozzi and J. J. Rousseau. Gaslamps burn over a green table. At the table sit PROFESSORS APELARD, THICKSTICK, GUTGRINDER, BONEBREAKER, TONGUETWISTER *and* FLYSWATTER. HEADMASTER SUNSTROKE *sits at the head of the table on a raised chair. The School Porter* FASTCRAWLER *huddles by the door.*

SUNSTROKE: Would any gentleman care to add any further remarks? Gentlemen! We cannot for the gravest of reasons abstain from asking the Minister of State for Cultural Affairs for the expulsion of our guilt-laden student. We cannot abstain so as to atone for the disaster that has already befallen us, and no less we cannot so as to secure our Institution against similar blows.

We cannot abstain so as to chastise our guilt-laden student for the demoralising influence he has borne over his fellow students, and no less we cannot so as to prevent the further bearing of that demoralising influence. We cannot abstain—and here, gentlemen, might lie our most compelling reason, whereby whatsoever objections that are raised may be utterly crushed—so as to protect our Institution from the devastation of a suicide epidemic which had already come to pass in other Institutions and which has rendered, until now, our scholarly task of uniting our scholars by means of the fruits of scholarly instruction to the fruition of the life of scholarship, ridiculous. Would any gentlemen care to add any further remarks?

THICKSTICK: I can no longer close my mind to the conviction that the time has come when the opening of a window should be permitted somewhere.

TONGUETWISTER: The at-atmosphere here is dom-dominated by a resemblance to the subterranean cat-catacombs of a medieval a-a-a-ssize!

SUNSTROKE: Fastcrawler!

FASTCRAWLER: Present, sir!

SUNSTROKE: Open a window. Thanks to God we have sufficient atmosphere outside. Would any gentlemen care to add any further remarks?

FLYSWATTER: Should any of my colleagues wish to permit the opening of a window I for my part raise no objection. I would merely request that the window permitted to be open is not immediately in the back of my neck!

SUNSTROKE: Fastcrawler!

FASTCRAWLER: Present, sir!

SUNSTROKE: Open the other window. Would any gentlemen care to add any further remarks?

GUTGRINDER: Without in any way wishing to complicate the issue I would ask you to recall that since the long holidays the other window has been bricked up.

SUNSTROKE: Fastcrawler!

FASTCRAWLER: Present, sir!

SUNSTROKE: Let the window be shut. I see myself forced, gentlemen, to put the matter to a vote. I call upon those colleagues who are in favor of permitting the opening of the only window that now comes into question, to rise from their seats. (*He counts.*) One, two, three. Fastcrawler!

FASTCRAWLER: Present, sir!

SUNSTROKE: Leave the other window shut as well. For my part I hold to my conviction that the atmosphere here leaves nothing to be desired. Would any gentlemen care to add any further remarks? Gentlemen! Let us suppose that we were to abstain from requesting the Minister of State for Cultural Affaires for the expulsion of our guilt-laden student—then *we* would be held responsible for the disaster that has befallen us. Of the various schools plagued by suicide epidemics the Minister has already shut down those in which the devastion has claimed a sacrifice of twenty-five percent. It is our duty as guardians and defenders of our Institution to defend it against so shattering a blow. It deeply pains us, my dear colleagues, that we find ourselves in no position to take into account the mitigating features presented by our guilt-laden student. An indulgent approach that left us blameless in our handling of our guilt-laden student would *not* leave us blameless in our handling of the at present highly probable threat to the existence of our Institution. We see ourselves forced to judge the guilty so as not to be judged guilty ourselves! Fastcrawler!

FASTCRAWLER: Present, sir!

SUNSTROKE: Fetch him up.

FASTCRAWLER *goes.*

TONGUETWISTER: If the dom-dominating at-at-atmosphere officially leaves nothing to be desired might I then pro-propose the motion that the other window also be bricked u-u-u-u-u-u-u-u-u-u-u-up?

FLYSWATTER: Should it appear to our respected colleague that our room is not sufficiently ventilated, might I propose the motion that he has a ventilator bored in the top of his head?

TONGUETWISTER: I do-do-don't have to put up with that! I do-do-don't have to put up with rudeness! I'm in possession of all my f-f-f-f-five senses!

SUNSTROKE: I must call upon our colleagues Flyswatter and Tonguetwister for a show of decorum. Our guilt-laden student stands at the door.

FASTCRAWLER *opens the door, and* MELCHIOR *steps in front of the meeting. He is pale but composed.*

SUNSTROKE: Step closer to the table. After the respectable landlord Herr Stiefel had been informed of his late son's unseemly misconduct, that bewildered father searched, in the hope that he might come across the cause of this disgusting crime, in the remaining effects of his son Moritz and found, in an at the moment irrelevant place, a handwritten document which, without in any way making this disgusting crime at all comprehensible, does afford us an, alas, all too clear insight into the criminal's state of moral chaos. I refer to a handwritten document in dialogue-form entitled *"On Copulation,"* replete with life-size illustrations, and crammed with obscenities so shameless that they might well satisfy the utmost demands for depravity that a degenerate lecher could make on obscene literature.

MELCHIOR: I have. . . .

SUNSTROKE: You have to be silent. After Herr Stiefel had put the document in question into our hands and we had given the bewildered father our solemn word to at all costs ascertain its author, the handwriting was compared with the handwriting of every fellow student of the deceased malpractiser and matched, according to the unanimous verdict of the whole faculty and in complete agreement with the expert opinion of our honoured colleague the Professor of Calligraphy, yours.

MELCHIOR: I have. . . .

SUNSTROKE: You have to be silent. Notwithstanding the overwhelming evidence of this identification, acceded to by such unimpeachable authorities, we believe ourselves able to refrain from precipitate action for the moment, and to instead impartially interrogate you about the crime against morality of which you stand accused and which served as an incitement to self-destruction.

MELCHIOR: I have. . . .

SUNSTROKE: You have to answer the precisely phrased questions, which I shall put to you one after the other, with a simple and respectful yes or no. Fastcrawler!

FASTCRAWLER: Present, sir!

SUNSTROKE: The file. I request our secretary, Herr Flyswatter, to take down the protocol from now on word for word as exactly as possible. (*To* MELCHIOR.) Do you know this document?

MELCHIOR: Yes.

SUNSTROKE: Do you know what this document contains?

MELCHIOR: Yes.

SUNSTROKE: Is the handwriting in this document yours?

MELCHIOR: Yes.

SUNSTROKE: Does this obscene document owe its manufacture to you?

MELCHIOR: Yes. Sir, I ask you to show me one obscenity in it.

SUNSTROKE: You have to answer the precisely phrased questions, which I shall put to you, with a simple and respectful yes or no.

MELCHIOR: I've written no more and no less than everyone of you knows to be a fact.

SUNSTROKE: This insolent puppy!

MELCHIOR: I ask you to show me one offence against morality in that paper!

SUNSTROKE: Do you imagine that I will stand here and let myself become the butt of your jests? Fastcrawler!

MELCHIOR: I have. . . .

SUNSTROKE: You have as little respect for the dignity of your assembled masters as you have for mankind's sense of shame when confronted with the moral order of the universe. Fastcrawler!

FASTCRAWLER: Present, sir!

SUNSTROKE: This is the definitive text on how to learn Esperanto in three easy months without a master!

MELCHIOR: I have. . . .

SUNSTROKE: I call upon our secretary to close the protocol.

MELCHIOR: I have. . . .

SUNSTROKE: You have to be silent. Fastcrawler!

FASTCRAWLER: Present, sir!

SUNSTROKE: Put him down.

SCENE 2

Churchyard in pouring rain.

REVEREND BALDBELLY *stands in front of the open grave with an umbrella in his hand. On his right* HERR STIEFEL, *his friend* GOAT

and UNCLE PROBST. *On the left* HEADMASTER SUNSTROKE *and* PRO-
FESSOR BONEBREAKER. STUDENTS *make up the rest of a circle. Some
distance off* MARTHA *and* ILSE *stand by a half-fallen gravestone.*

BALDBELLY: Whosoever spurns the grace with which the Eternal
Father blesses all who are born in sin, he shall die the death of
the spirit. And whosoever in flesh and pride denies the worship
owed to God and lives and serves evil, he shall die the death of
the body. But whosoever sacrilegeously casts aside the cross with
which the Almighty inflicts this life of sin, verily, verily I say
unto you, he shall die the eternal death. *(He throws a shovel of
earth into the grave.)* But we who go forth on the path of thorns,
let us praise the Lord, the All Merciful, and thank him for his
unsearchable gift of predestination. For as surely as this died the
three-fold death, as surely will Lord God lead the righteous to
salvation and eternal life. Amen.

HERR STIEFEL *(with tear-choked voice as he throws a shovel of
earth into the grave):* That boy wasn't mine. That boy wasn't
mine. I had my doubts about that boy since he was a tot.

SUNSTROKE *(throws a shovel of earth into the grave):* While suicide is the greatest conceivable offense against the moral order
of the universe, it is at the same time the greatest conceivable
proof *of* the moral order of the universe, in that the suicide spares
the moral order of the universe the necessity of pronouncing its
verdict and so confirms its existence.

BONEBREAKER *(throws a shovel of earth into the grave):* Dila-
tory—dissipated—debauched—dissolute—and dirty!

UNCLE PROBST *(throws a shovel of earth into the grave):* I would
not have believed my own mother if she'd told me a child would
treat its parents so basely.

FRIEND GOAT *(throws a shovel of earth into the grave):* To do
that to a father who for twenty years cherished no other thought
from morning till night than the welfare of his son!

BALDBELLY *(shaking* HERR STIEFEL'S *hand):* We know that they
who love God make all things serve the best. Corinthians I,
14:12. Think of the comfortless mother and try to replace her
loss by redoubled love.

SUNSTROKE *(shaking* HERR STIEFEL'S *hand):* And after all it's clear
that we might well not have been able to promote him anyway.

BONEBREAKER *(shaking* HERR STIEFEL's *hand):* And if we had promoted him he'd certainly have been left standing next spring.

UNCLE PROBST *(shaking* HERR STIEFEL's *hand):* It's your duty to think of yourself before everything else now. You are head of a family. . . .

FRIEND GOAT *(shaking* HERR STIEFEL's *hand):* Take my arm. Cat's-and-dogs weather, enough to wring the bowels. If we don't all immediately perform the vanishing trick with a glass of hot punch we'll catch a heart condition!

HERR STIEFEL *(blowing his nose):* That boy wasn't mine. That boy wasn't mine.

HERR STIEFEL *is lead away by* PASTOR BALDBELLY, HEADMASTER SUNSTROKE, PROFESSOR BONEBREAKER, UNCLE PROBST *and* FRIEND GOAT. *The rain lessens.*

HÄNSCHEN *(throws a shovel of earth into the grave):* Rest in peace, poor sod. Give my regards to my dead brides—and put in a word for me to God, you poor fool. You're so innocent they'll have to put something on your grave to scare the birds off.

GEORG: Did they find the pistol?

ROBERT: There's no point in looking for a pistol.

ERNST: Did you see him, Robert?

ROBERT: Rotten, blasted swizz! Who saw him? anyone?

OTTO: That's the mystery! They threw a cloth over him.

GEORG: Did his tongue hang out?

ROBERT: The eyes! That's why they threw the cloth over him.

OTTO: Horrible!

HÄNSCHEN: Are you sure he hanged himself?

ERNST: They say he's got no head now.

OTTO: Rubbish! All talk!

ROBERT: I had the rope in my hand. They always cover up a hanged man.

GEORG: He couldn't have chosen a more small-minded way of going off.

HÄNSCHEN: What the hell, hanging's supposed to be fun!

OTTO: The fact is, he still owes me five marks. We had a bet. He swore he'd be promoted.

HÄNSCHEN: It's your fault he's down there. You said he was bragging.

OTTO: Rot! I have to slave through the nights too. If he'd learned his Greek history he wouldn't have had to hang himself.

ERNST: Have you done your essay, Otto?

OTTO: Only the start.

ERNST: I don't know what we're supposed to write about.

GEORG: Weren't you there when Apelard gave it out?

HÄNSCHEN: I'll stick together some bits of Democritus.

ERNST: I'll get something out of the reference library.

OTTO: Have you done tomorrow's Virgil?

The STUDENTS *go.* MARTHA *and* ILSE *come to the grave.*

ILSE: Quick, quick! The gravediggers are coming over there.

MARTHA: Shouldn't we wait?

ILSE: What for? We'll bring fresh ones. Always fresh, fresh! They grow everywhere!

MARTHA: That's right, Ilse. *(She throws an ivy wreath into the grave.* ILSE *opens her apron and lets a stream of fresh anemones fall onto the coffin.)* I'll dig up our roses. I get beaten anyway. They'll grow so well here.

ILSE: I'll water them every time I go by. I'll bring forget-me-nots from the brook and irises from home.

MARTHA: It'll become a marvel!

ILSE: I'd already crossed the bridge when I heard the bang.

MARTHA: Poor thing.

ILSE: And I know why, Martha.

MARTHA: Did he tell you something?

ILSE: He was on parallelepipedon! Don't tell.

MARTHA: Cross my heart.

ILSE: Here's the pistol.

MARTHA: That's why they couldn't find it.

ILSE: I took it straight out of his hand when I went by.

MARTHA: Let's have it, Ilse! Let's have it, please!

ILSE: No, it's my keepsake.

MARTHA: Ilse, is it true he's down there with no head?

ILSE: He must have loaded it with water. His blood was spattered round and round on the bulrushes. His brains were hanging all over the willows.

SCENE 3

HERR *and* FRAU GABOR.

FRAU GABOR: . . . They needed a scapegoat. The accusations were getting louder and they couldn't wait for them to die down. And because Melchior had the misfortune to cross those pedants just at this moment, shall I, his mother, help the hangmen to finish their work? God keep me from such a thing!

HERR GABOR: For fourteen years I've silently observed your imaginative methods of rearing children. They contradicted my own convictions. I have always lived by the conviction that a child isn't a toy. A child has a right to our solemn seriousness. But I told myself, if spirit and grace can replace serious principles, then they might be preferable to serious principles. I'm not blaming you, Fanny. But don't stand in my way when I try to make amends for the wrong you and I have done the boy.

FRAU GABOR: I'll stand in your way as long as there's a drop of human blood in me! My child would be lost in a reformatory. A natural criminal might be made better in such an institution. I don't know. But a decent nature will be made criminal just as a plant dies when it's taken from the light. I'm not aware of any wrong. I thank God now, as I always have, for showing me how to make my child decent and honest. What has he done that's so terrible? It would never enter my head to make excuses for him—but it's not his fault he's been hounded out of school! And if it had been his fault he's certainly paid for it! You may understand these things better than I do. Theoretically you may be perfectly right. But I will not allow my son to be brutally hounded to his death!

HERR GABOR: That doesn't depend on us, Fanny, that's the risk that went with our happiness. He who's too weak falls by the wayside. And in the end it's not the worst if the inevitable comes on time. May heaven spare us that! Our duty now is to strengthen the waverer, so long as reason shows us how. It's not his fault they hounded him out of school. If they hadn't hounded him out that wouldn't be his fault either! You're too easy going. You see minor peccadillos when we are faced with fundamental defects of character. Women aren't called on to judge these things. Whoever can write what Melchior wrote must be contaminated in his innermost core. The marrow is effected. Even a nature only half-sound couldn't bring itself to that! None of us are saints, we all stray from the way. But his document is grounded in Principle. It doesn't suggest one accidental false step, it documents with terrifying clarity an openly cherished talent, a natural propensity, for the Immoral for the sake of the Immoral. It shows that rare spiritual corruption we lawyers call "moral insanity." Whether anything can be done about his condition, it's not for me to say. If we wish to preserve one glimmer of hope, and above all keep our consciences unsullied as the parents of the culprit, then we must act with resolution and determination. Don't let's quarrel anymore, Fanny! I know how hard this is for you. You worship him because he matches your own generous nature so well. Rise above yourself! For once act unselfishly in your relations with your son.

FRAU GABOR: O God—how can one fight against it! Only a man can talk like that. Only a man can be so blinded by the dead letter he can't see what's staring him in the face! I've handled Melchior responsibly and carefully from the beginning. Are we to blame for this coincidence? Tomorrow a tile could fall on your head and your friend comes—your father, and instead of tending your wounds he treads on you! I will not let my child be taken out and murdered in front of my eyes. That's what his mother's for!—I cannot understand it. It's beyond belief. What in the world has he written? Isn't it the clearest proof of his harmlessness, his silliness, his child-like innocence, that he *can* write something like that? You don't need to know much about people—you must be an utterly soulless bureaucrat or totally shrivelled up, to see moral corruption in that! Say what you like. When you put Melchior in a reformatory, I shall divorce you! And then I shall see if somewhere in the world I can't find help to save my son from destruction.

HERR GABOR: You will have to give in—if not today then tomorrow. It's not easy for any of us to discount our misfortunes. I shall stand by you when your courage fails, I shall begrudge no effort or sacrifice to lighten your burden. I see the future so gray, so overcast—it only needs you to be lost to me now.

FRAU GABOR: I'll never see him again. I'll never see him again. He can't bear vulgarity. he can't live with filth. He'll lose all restraints—that terrible example is before his eyes! And if I saw him again—O God, God, that heart full of spring—that bright laughter—all, all—his young determination to fight for everything that's good and just—as bright and fresh as the morning sky—that boy I cherished as my highest good! Take me if his crime cries out for retribution! Take me! Do what you want with me! Let me bear the guilt! But keep your terrible hand away from my child.

HERR GABOR: He has offended!

FRAU GABOR: *He has not offended!*

HERR GABOR: *He has* offended! I would have given anything to spare your boundless love for him. This morning a woman came to me, like a ghost, hardly able to speak, with *this* letter in her hand—a letter to her fifteen year-old daughter. Out of silly curiosity she's opened it—her daughter was not at home. In the letter Melchior explains to the fifteen year-old child that his conduct gives him no peace, he has wronged her etcetera etcetera. She is not to worry, even if she suspects consequences. He is already taking steps to find help, his expulsion makes that easier. The earlier wrong may yet lead to their happiness—and more of the same meaningless chatter.

FRAU GABOR: I don't believe it!

HERR GABOR: The letter is forged. It's an attack. Someone trying to use an expulsion that's already known to the whole town. I haven't yet spoken to the boy—but kindly look at the hand. Look at the writing.

FRAU GABOR: An unheard of, shameless infamy!

HERR GABOR: I fear so!

FRAU GABOR: No, no—never.

HERR GABOR: Then all the better for us. The woman stood wringing her hands and asking me what she should do. I told her not to let her fifteen-year-old daughter climb about in haylofts. As luck would have it she left the letter with me. If we send Melchior away to another school, where he wouldn't even be under parental supervision, we'll have another incident within three weeks—another expulsion—his spring-like heart is already getting used to it. Tell me, Fanny, where shall I put the boy?

FRAU GABOR: In the reformatory.

HERR GABOR: The . . . ?

FRAU GABOR: Reformatory.

HERR GABOR: Above all, he'll find there what he was unjustly denied at home: iron discipline, principles and a moral force under which he must at all times subordinate himself. By the way, the reformatory isn't the chamber of horrors you imagine.

It lays its main emphasis on developing Christian thinking and sensibility. The boy will finally learn there to put the good before the interesting, and to act not according to his nature but according to the rules. Half an hour ago I had a telegramme from my brother, which confirms the deposition of that woman. Melchior has confided in him and asked for money for their flight to England. . . .

FRAU GABOR *(covers her face):* God have mercy on us!

SCENE 4

Reformatory. A corridor.

DIETER, REINHOLD, RUPERT, HELMUT, GASTON *and* MELCHIOR.

DIETER: Here's a coin.

REINHOLD: What for?

DIETER: Drop it on the floor. Spread yourselves out. The one who hits it, keeps it.

RUPERT: Coming in, Melchior.

MELCHIOR: No thanks.

HELMUT: Git!

GASTON: He can't anymore. He's here for the rest cure.

MELCHIOR *(to himself):* It's clever to stay out. They're all watching me. I'll join in—or I've had it. Being shut up makes them suicidal. If you break your neck it's all right! If you get out it's all right! You can only win! Rupert looks friendly, he'll show me round. I'll teach him about the Bible—how Lot got drunk and slept with his daughters and offered them to other men, how David was a Peeping Tom who slept with a soldier's wife and warmed his bed with a beautiful virgin called Abishay the Shunnamite. He's got the unluckiest face in my squad.

RUPERT: Coming!

HELMUT: I'm coming too.

GASTON: Day after tomorrow if you're lucky!

HELMUT: Hold on! Now! Jesus—Jesus.

ALL: Altogether now!—Ten out of ten!

RUPERT *(taking the coin):* Ta, very much.

HELMUT: That's mine, pig!

RUPERT: Animal!

HELMUT: They'll top you!

RUPERT *(hits him in the face)*: For that? *(Turns and runs away.)*

HELMUT *(chasing him)*: I'll kick your head off!

THE OTHERS *(chasing him)*: Get him, after him! Get him! Get him! Get him!

MELCHIOR *(alone, turns to the window)*: That's where the lightning conductor goes down. You'd have to wrap a handkerchief round. . . . When I think of her the blood goes to my head, and Moritz is like a chain round my feet. I'll try the newspapers. Become a hack. They pay by the hundred lines. News, gossip, articles—ethics—psychology. You can't starve now! Soup kitchens, hostels.—This building is sixty feet high and the plaster's falling off. . . . She hates me—I took her freedom away. Whatever I do now, it's still rape. But later on perhaps she'll. . . . I must hope. The new moon in eight days. I'll grease the hinges. Find out who has the key. On Sunday night I'll have a fit in the chapel. I hope to God no one else is ill! I'll slip over the sill— swing—grab—but you must wrap a handkerchief round. . . . Here comes the Grand Inquisitor. *(Goes off left)*.

DR. PROCRUSTES *comes on right with a* LOCKSMITH.

PROCRUSTES: Undoubtedly the windows are on the fourth floor, and I've planted stinging nettles underneath. But what are stinging nettles to degenerates? Last winter one of them climbed out of the skylight. We had all the fuss of fetching, carrying, interning. . . .

LOCKSMITH: Would you like the grating in wrought iron?

PROCRUSTES: Wrought iron—and since you can't build it into the wall, rivet it.

SCENE 5

A bedroom.

FRAU BERGMANN, INA MULLER *and* DR. LEMONADE. WENDLA *in bed.*

DR. LEMONADE: How old are you actually?

WENDLA: Fourteen and a half.

DR. LEMONADE: I've prescribed purgative pills for fifteen years and in a large number of cases witnessed the most dazzling success. I place them above codliver oil and iron tonic. Start with three or four pills a day and increase the dosage just as fast as you can tolerate them. I advised Fräulein Elfriede Baroness von Witzleben to increase the dose by one pill every third day. The baroness misunderstood me and increased the dose by three pills every day. After barely three weeks the baroness could already proceed with her lady mother to an exclusive spa in the mountains. I excuse you from all fatiguing walks and special diets. But you must promise me, dear child, to keep moving and not be too shy to ask for food as soon as the desire for it returns. Then this wind round the heart will go away, and the headaches, the shivering, the dizzyness—and our terrible indigestion. Only eight days after starting the cure Fräulein Elfriede Baroness von Witzleben could already eat a whole roast chicken with new boiled potatoes for breakfast.

FRAU BERGMANN: May I offer you a glass of wine, Doctor?

DR. LEMONADE: Thank you kindly, dear Frau Bergmann. My patients await me. Don't take it too much to heart. In a few weeks our charming little patient will once more be as fresh and lively as a sprite. Rest assured. Good day, Frau Bergmann. Good day, dear child. Good day, ladies. Good day.

FRAU BERGMANN *goes to show him out.*

INA (*at the window*): The leaves on your plane-trees are changing colour. Can you see it from the bed? They come and go, a short glory, hardly worth being happy about. I must go too. Herr Müller's meeting me at the post office, and before that I have to go to the dressmaker. Mucki's getting his first trousers, and Karl's going to get a new jersey suit for the winter.

WENDLA: Sometimes I'm so happy—there's so much joy and the sunshine is so bright. I want to go out, and walk over the fields when it's dusk, and look for primroses and sit and dream by the river. And then this *toothache* starts, and I think that tomorrow is the day I shall die. I feel hot and cold, everything goes dark, and the monster flutters in. . . . Whenever I wake up Mother's crying. O that hurts so much. . . . I can't tell you, Ina.

INA: Shall I lift your pillow?

FRAU BERGMANN *comes back.*

FRAU BERGMANN: He thinks the vomiting will stop and then it will be safe for you to get up. I think you should get up soon, too, Wendla.

INA: Perhaps next time I come to see you you'll be jumping round the house again. Bless you, mother. I really must go to the dress-maker. God bless you, Wendla, dear. (*Kisses her.*) Soon, soon better!

WENDLA: Thank you, Ina. Bring me some primroses next time you come. Good-bye. Say hello to the boys for me.

INA *goes.*

WENDLA: What did he say outside, Mother?

FRAU BERGMANN: Nothing. He said Fräulein von Witzleben also tended to faint. Evidently it almost always happens with anemia.

WENDLA: Did he say I have anemia, Mother?

FRAU BERGMANN: When your appetite returns you're to drink milk and eat fresh vegetables.

WENDLA: O Mother, Mother, I don't think I have anemia.

FRAU BERGMANN: You have anemia child. Be quiet, Wendla, be quiet. You have anemia.

WENDLA: No, Mother, no! I know it! I can feel it! I haven't got anemia. I've got dropsy.

FRAU BERGMANN: You have anemia. He said you have anemia. Be quiet, Wendla. It will get better.

WENDLA: It won't get better. I have dropsy. I'm going to die, mother, O mother, I'm going to die.

FRAU BERGMANN: You won't have to die, Wendla. You won't have to die. . . . Merciful heaven, you won't have to die.

WENDLA: Then why d'you cry so much?

FRAU BERGMANN: You won't have to die, child! You haven't got dropsy. You have a baby, Wendla! You have a baby! O, why have you done this to me?

WENDLA: I haven't done anything to you. . . .

FRAU BERGMANN: O don't keep lying, Wendla! I know everything. I couldn't say it before. Wendla, Wendla. . . .

WENDLA: But it's just not possible, Mother. I'm not even married.

FRAU BERGMANN: God in heaven—that's just it, you're not married! That's what's so terrible! Wendla, Wendla, Wendla, what have you done?

WENDLA: O God, I don't know anymore. We were lying in the hay—I've never loved anyone in the world except you, you, mother!

FRAU BERGMANN: My precious!

WENDLA: O Mother, why didn't you tell me everything?

FRAU BERGMANN: Child, child, don't let's make each other more unhappy. Keep calm. Don't give up hope, my dear! Tell that to a fourteen-year-old girl? No, I'd sooner have believed the sun could go out! I did nothing to you my dear mother hadn't done to me! O let us put our trust in the dear lord, Wendla. Let us hope in his mercy, and do our part. Look, so far nothing's happened. And if only we don't become timid now—God's love will not abandon us. *Be brave, be brave, Wendla.* . . . Once before I sat with my hands in my lap and stared out of the window, and in the end everything turned out well—and now suddenly the world falls to pieces and my heart breaks . . . why are you shaking?

WENDLA: Someone knocked.

FRAU BERGMANN: I didn't hear anything, my precious. (*Goes to the door and opens it.*)

WENDLA: O I heard it so clearly. Who's outside?

FRAU BERGMANN: No one. Mr. Schmidt's mother from Garden Street. You're just on time, Mrs. Schmidt.

SCENE 6

MEN *and* WOMEN *working in a hillside vineyard.*

The sun sets behind the mountains. The clear-toned notes of bells come up from the valley. HÄNSCHEN RILOW *and* ERNST RÖBEL *loll in the dry grass at the top of the vineyard, under overhanging rocks.*

ERNST: I've worked too hard.

HÄNSCHEN: We mustn't be sad. Time passes so quickly.

ERNST: The grapes hang there. You can't even reach out for them. And tomorrow they're crushed.

HÄNSCHEN: Being tired is as bad as being hungry.

ERNST: O no more.

HÄNSCHEN: That big one.

ERNST: I can't stretch.

HÄNSCHEN: I could bend the branch till it swings between our mouths. We needn't move. Just bite the grapes and let the branch swing back.

ERNST: You only have to make up your mind—and all your old energy gushes up.

HÄNSCHEN: And the flaming sky—the evening bells—I don't hope for much more out of life.

ERNST: Sometimes I already see myself as a dignified parson— a cheerful little housewife, big library, all sorts of honors and decorations. Six days shalt thou labor and on the seventh open your mouth. When you're out walking schoolchildren greet you politely, and when you get home the coffee's steaming, there's homemade cake on the table, and the girls are bringing in the apples through the garden door. Can anything be better?

HÄNSCHEN: Half-shut eyelashes, half-open mouths, and Turkish pillows. I don't believe in the Sentimental. You know, the old people wear dignified faces to hide their stupidity. Among themselves they call each other fools just as we do. I know it. When I'm a millionaire I'll erect a great monument to God. Think of the future as bread and milk and sugar. Some people drop it and howl, others stir it till they sweat. Why not just cream off the top? Or don't you think you can?

ERNST: Let's cream off the top.

HÄNSCHEN: And throw the rest to the chickens. I've already slipped my head out of so many nooses.

ERNST: Let's cream off the top. Why are you laughing?

HÄNSCHEN: You're off again!

ERNST: Someone's got to start!

HÄNSCHEN: In thirty years when we look back to this evening, I suppose it could seem incredibly beautiful.

ERNST: And now it just happens!

HÄNSCHEN: Why not?

ERNST: If I was on my own—I might even cry.

HÄNSCHEN: We mustn't be sad. (*Kisses his mouth.*)

ERNST: (*Kissing him*). When I left home I only meant to speak to you and then go back.

HÄNSCHEN: I was waiting for you. Virtue looks good but it only suits imposing figures.

ERNST: It's several sizes too big for us. I'd have been on edge if I hadn't met you. I love you, Hänschen, I've never loved anyone like this—

HÄNSCHEN: We mustn't be sad! Perhaps when we look back in thirty years we'll jeer—but now everything is beautiful. Glowing mountains, grapes hanging down in our mouths, the evening wind stroking the rocks like a little kitten playing. . . .

SCENE 7

Bright November night.

Dry leaves rustle on bushes and trees. Torn clouds chase each other over the moon. MELCHIOR *climbs over the churchyard wall.*

MELCHIOR (*jumping down inside*): That pack won't follow me here. While they search the brothels, I'll get my breath and sort myself out. . . . Jacket in shreds, pockets empty. I couldn't defend myself against a child. I'll keep moving through the woods during the day. . . . I knocked a cross down—the frost's killed all the flowers anyway. Everything's bare! The kingdom of death! This is worse than climbing out of the skylight! Like falling and falling and falling into nothing! I wasn't prepared for this! I should have stayed where I was!

Why her and not me? Why not the guilty? Providence or a riddle? I'd break stones, starve—how can I even walk upright? One crime leads to another: I'll sink in a swamp. I haven't got the strength to finish it. . . . It was not wrong! It was not wrong! It was not wrong!

No one's ever walked over graves and been so full of envy. No— I wouldn't have the courage! O, if I could go mad—tonight! The new ones are over there. The wind whistles on each gravestone in a different key—listen, the voices of pain! The wreaths are rotting on the marble crosses. They fall to pieces and jog up and down on their long strings. There's a forest of scarecrows over the graves. Taller than houses. Even the devil would run away. The gold letters flash so coldly. That's a willow tree groaning. Its branches are like a giant's fingers feeling over the epitaphs.

A stone angel. A tablet. That cloud's thrown its shadow on everything. How it races and howls! Like an army rushing up to the east! And no stars. There's evergreen round this one. Evergreen? A girl.

> *Here rests in God*
> *Wendla Bergmann*
> *Born May 5, 1878,*
> *Died of anemia*
> *October 27, 1892,*
> *Blessed are the pure in heart*

And I murdered her. I am her murderer. Now there's nothing. I mustn't cry here. I must go away. I must go.

MORITZ STIEFEL, *with his head under his arm, comes stamping across the graves.*

MORITZ: One moment, Melchior! This chance won't come again so soon. You can't know how much depends on time and place. . . .

MELCHIOR: Where have you come from?

MORITZ: Over there by the wall. You knocked my cross down. I lie by the wall. Give me your hand, Melchior.

MELCHIOR: You are *not* Moritz Stiefel!

MORITZ: Give me your hand. I know you'll be grateful. It will never be so easy for you again. This is a very lucky meeting. I came up especially . . .

MELCHIOR: Don't you sleep?

MORITZ: Not what you call sleep. We sit on church towers, on the roofs of houses—wherever we like. . . .

MELCHIOR: At peace?

MORITZ: For pleasure. We ride on the wooden horses at fairs, and float round empty churches. We fly over great assemblies of people, over scenes of disaster, gardens, festivals. We crouch in the corners of people's houses, and wait by their beds. Give me your hand. The dead are alone, we don't go with each other, but we see and hear everything that happens in the world. We know that it's all vanity, the things men do and strive after, and we laugh at it.

MELCHIOR: What help is that?

MORITZ: What use is help? Nothing touches us now, for good or bad. We stand high above earthly things—each alone for himself. We don't go with each other because it's boring. None of us has anything it would hurt him to lose. We are infinitely above all despair and rejoicing. We are content with ourselves, and that is all. We despise the living so much we can hardly pity them. They amuse us with their pretensions—and if they will live they don't deserve to be pitied. We smile at their tragedies—each to himself—and watch. Give me your hand! When you give me your hand you'll fall over laughing at what happens then—

MELCHIOR: Doesn't that disgust you?

MORITZ: We stand too high for that. We smile! At my funeral I stood among the mourners. I quite enjoyed myself. That is serenity, Melchior, the sublime! I howled more than anyone and tottered to the wall holding my belly with laughing. Our serenity is simply the attitude that allows us to swallow the dregs. They laughed at me too, before I raised myself up to their height.

MELCHIOR: I don't want to laugh at myself.

MORITZ: The living are the last who deserve to be pitied! I admit I'd never have thought it. But now I don't know how men can be so naïve. I see through the fraud so clearly and no more doubts are left. How can you still hesitate, Melchior? Give me your hand! In less time than it takes to twist a chicken's neck you'll rise high over yourself. Your life is a sin of omission—

MELCHIOR: Can you forget?

MORITZ: We can do anything. Give me your hand! We can sorrow for youth because it takes its anxieties for ideals, and old age because stoical resolution breaks its heart. We see the emperor quake with fear at the street ballad, and the clown at the last trumpet. We see through the comedian's make-up, and watch the poet put on his mask in the dark. We look at the satisfied in all their destitution, and the capitalists toiling and groaning. We watch lovers blush before each other, when they already know they'll betray and be betrayed. We see parents bringing children into the world to be able to shout at them: how lucky you are to have such parents—and we see the children go off and do the same. We know about the innocent in their lonely passions, and we hear Schiller in the mouth of a ten-minute whore. We see god and the devil exposing themselves to ridicule in front of each other, and hold in us the unshakable conviction that they're both drunk. . . . Peace, rest, Melchior! Just give me your little finger. You can be as white as snow before this moment comes again.

MELCHIOR: If I throw in my lot with you, Moritz, I do it out of self-disgust. I'm a pariah. Everything that gave me courage is in the grave. I'm incapable of any ideals—and I can see nothing, nothing that can stand in my path to the bottom. I think I'm the most disgusting creature in creation. . . .

MORITZ: Why hesitate?

A MASKED MAN *comes in.*

MASKED MAN (*To* MELCHIOR): You're shivering with hunger. You're certainly in no state to decide anything. (*To* MORITZ) Get out!

MELCHIOR: Who are you?

MASKED MAN: That will be made clear. (*To* MORITZ) Hop it! What are you up to? Why aren't you wearing your head?

MORITZ: I shot myself.

MASKED MAN: Then stay where you belong. You're finished! Don't pester us with the stench of your grave. Incredible—look at your fingers! Filthy brute! It's already rotting.

MORITZ: Please, don't send me away—

MELCHIOR: Who are you?

MORITZ: Don't send me away. Please. Let me stay with you a little longer. I won't contradict you. It's terrible under there.

MASKED MAN: Then why all this bragging about serenity and the sublime? You know very well that's humbug—sour grapes. Why must you lie so persistently?—you—you wraith! If it means so much to you, stay as far as I'm concerned. But stop all this huffing and puffing, young man—and please don't stick your rotting thumb in my pie!

MELCHIOR: Will you tell me who you are?

MASKED MAN: No. I'll make you a proposition: put yourself in my hands. For a start, I'll do something about your present mess.

MELCHIOR: You're my father!

MASKED MAN: Wouldn't you know your dear father from his voice?

MELCHIOR: No.

MASKED MAN: Your father is at this moment seeking comfort in the strong arms of your mother. I'll open the world for you. Your temporary despair is caused by your miserable condition. With a hot dinner inside you you'll joke about it.

MELCHIOR: *(to himself)* Only *one* of them can be the devil! *(Aloud)* After the things I've done, a hot dinner won't give me peace again!

MASKED MAN: It depends on the dinner. One thing I will tell you, your little girl would have given birth marvellously. She was built ideally. Unfortunately, she was put down—entirely by Mother Schmidt's abortion methods. I'll take you out into the world. I'll give you the chance to widen your horizon in astonishing ways. I'll introduce you to every single interesting thing in the world.

MELCHIOR: Who are you? Who are you? I can't put myself in the hands of someone I don't know!

MASKED MAN: You only learn to know me *by* putting yourself in my hands.

MELCHIOR: Is that true?

MASKED MAN: It's a fact. And by the way, you have no choice.

MELCHIOR: I can give my hand to my friend whenever I like.

MASKED MAN: Your friend is a charlatan. No one smiles while he's still got a penny to spend in his pocket. The sublime humorist is the most miserable, pitiful creature in creation.

MELCHIOR: The humorist can be what he likes! Tell me who you are, or I'll give him my hand.

MASKED MAN: Now?

MORITZ: He's right, Melchior, I was trying it on. Take his invitation, and get everything you can out of him. It doesn't matter how well he's masked—at least he's *something*!

MELCHIOR: Do you believe in God?

MASKED MAN: Depends.

MELCHIOR: Well, tell me who invented gunpowder.

MASKED MAN: Berthold Schwarz—a Franciscan monk at Freiburg im Breisgau about 1330.

MORITZ: What wouldn't I give if he hadn't!

MASKED MAN: You'd only have hanged yourself.

MELCHIOR: What are your views on morality?

MASKED MAN: Son—am I a schoolboy?

MELCHIOR: How do I know what you are!

MORITZ: Don't quarrel. Please, don't quarrel. What's the use of that? Why sit here in the churchyard—two living and one dead— at two o'clock in the morning, if all we can do is quarrel like drunks? It will be a pleasure for me to be present at these discussions. If you want to quarrel, I'll take my head and go.

MELCHIOR: You're still the same old drag!

MASKED MAN: The ghost isn't wrong. One should never lose one's dignity. By morality I understand the real product of two imaginary forces. The imaginary forces are *should* and *would*. The product is called Morality, and no one is allowed to forget that's real.

MORITZ: If only you told me that before! My morality hounded me to death. I used the murder weapon because of my dear parents. "Honour thy father and mother and thy days shall be long." The Bible certainly came unstuck over me.

MASKED MAN: You shouldn't be carried away by appearances, my boy. Your parents would no more have died than you needed to. Looked at clinically, they'd have raged and stormed simply for the good of their health.

MELCHIOR: That might be true. But I can certainly tell you that if I'd given my hand to Moritz just now, sir, that would have been purely and simply because of my morality!

MASKED MAN: And that's exactly where you're not Moritz!

MORITZ: I don't think there's much difference—not so much that you shouldn't have been allowed to pop up for me. I walked slowly enough along that alder plantation with the pistol in my pocket.

MASKED MAN: Then you don't remember me? Even in your last moments you were still standing undecided between life and death. But I think this is really not the best place to prolong such a profound discussion.

MORITZ: It's certainly getting chilly. They dressed me up in my Sunday suit but they didn't put anything on underneath.

MELCHIOR: Good-bye, Moritz. I don't know where this man will take me. But *he* is alive. . . .

MORITZ: Don't hold it against me for trying to kill you, Melchior. It was only my old devotion. I'd spend a whole lifetime of tears and misery, if I could walk by your side again.

MASKED MAN: In the end everyone has his part—*you* the comforting knowledge of having nothing—*you* the tormenting doubt of everything. Good-bye.

MELCHIOR: Good-bye, Moritz. Thank you for coming back once more. The happy, good times we had together in those fourteen years! I promise you whatever happens in the years to come, if I change ten times, and go up or down, I'll never forget you . . .

MORITZ: Thank you, thank you. You were my only friend.

MELCHIOR: . . . and one day if I'm old and my hair's gray, perhaps then you'll be closer to me again than all the people who shared my life.

MORITZ: Thank you. Good luck on the journey, gentlemen. Don't let me keep you any longer.

MASKED MAN: Come on, young man. (*He takes* MELCHIOR's *arm and disappears with him over the graves.*)

MORITZ (*alone*): I sit here with my head in my arm. The moon covers its face, the veil falls away and it doesn't look any wiser. So I go back to my place. I straighten my cross after that clumsy idiot's kicked it over, and when everything's in order I lie down on my back again, warm myself in my rotting decay and smile.

Translated by Edward Bond

The Marquis of Keith

Characters

CONSUL CASIMIR *a merchant*
HERMANN CASIMIR *his son, fifteen years old*
THE MARQUIS OF KEITH
ERNST SCHOLZ
MOLLY GREISINGER
ANNA, COUNTESS WERDENFELS *a widow*
SARANIEFF *a painter*
ZAMRIAKI *a composer*
SOMMERSBERG *a writer*
RASPE *a police inspector*
OSTERMEIER *proprietor of a brewery*
KRENTZL *a master builder*
GRANDAUER *a restaurateur*
FRAU OSTERMEIER
FRAU KRENTZL
BARONESS VON ROSENKRON *a divorcée*
BARONESS VON TOTLEBEN *a divorcée*
SASHA
SIMBA
A BUTCHER'S HELPER
A BAKERY WOMAN
A PORTER
PATRONS OF THE HOFBRÄUHAUS

Scene

The place of the action is in Munich, late summer, 1899.

Act 1

[A *study, the walls of which are covered with pictures. In the rear wall to the right there is a door leading into the hallway, and to the left a door leading into a waiting room. A door in the right wall leads into the living room. Downstage left is a writing table on which unrolled plans are lying; on the wall beside the writing table is a telephone. There is a divan downstage right, with a smaller table in front of it; somewhat upstage is a larger table. Bookcases with books; musical instruments, bundles of notes and documents. The* MARQUIS OF KEITH *is seated at the writing table engrossed in one of the plans. He is a man of about twenty-seven, medium height, slender and bony; he would have an exemplary figure if not for the limp in his left leg. His features are vigorous, though at the same time nervous and hard. He has piercing gray eyes, a small blond mustache. His unmanageable short, straw-blond hair is carefully parted in the middle. He is dressed in a suit well chosen for its social elegance, but by no means foppish. He has the rough, red hands of a clown.* MOLLY GREISINGER *enters from the living room and places a covered tray on the table in front of the divan. She is a plain sort of creature, brunette, somewhat shy and harassed, wearing a plain house dress, but at the same time she possesses large, black, soulful eyes.*]

MOLLY: There you are, my dear. Tea, caviar and cold cuts. Did you know you were up at nine this morning?

KEITH [*without moving*]: Thank you, my dear.

MOLLY: You must be starved. Any word yet on the Fairyland Palace? Will it be built?

KEITH: Can't you see I'm busy?

MOLLY: Mm. Always when I come in, too. It seems I know you only from the gossip of your lady friends.

KEITH [*without turning in his chair*]: I knew a woman once who covered both ears whenever I talked business. "Come and tell me when you've *done* something!" she would say.

MOLLY: Unlucky me—your knowing all kinds of women.

[*A bell rings.*]

MOLLY: Now who could that be? [*Goes into the hall to open the door.*]

KEITH [*to himself*]: Poor creature!

MOLLY [*returns with a card*]: A young gentleman to see you. I told him you were busy.

KEITH [*having read the card*]: Just who I wanted to see!

[MOLLY *brings in* HERMANN CASIMIR *and goes off into the living room.*]

HERMANN [*a fifteen-year-old student in an extremely elegant cycling costume*]: Good morning, Baron.

KEITH: To what do I owe the honor?

HERMANN: I suppose I should come right out with it. I was at the Café Luitpold last night with Saranieff and Zamriaki. I told them I absolutely had to have a hundred marks. Saranieff suggested I come to you.

KEITH: All Munich thinks I'm an American railroad tycoon.

HERMANN: Zamriaki said you always have cash on hand.

KEITH: I patronize Zamriaki because he's the greatest musical genius since Richard Wagner. But these highway robbers are not proper company for you.

HERMANN: I find them interesting nonetheless. I discovered them at a meeting of the Anarchists.

KEITH: Ah, revolutionary gatherings. Fine way to start your life. Your father must be delighted.

HERMANN: Why doesn't my father let me leave Munich!

KEITH: Because you're not old enough.

HERMANN: At my age I can learn more from *real experience* than from scooting around on a *school bench!*

KEITH: Real experience deprives you of your natural abilities. And in your situation especially. The son of our greatest German financial genius. What does your father think of me?

HERMANN: My father never speaks to me.

KEITH: But he does speak to others.

HERMANN: That may be. I'm at home as little as possible.

KEITH: That's unfortunate. I've followed your father's financial operations since before my days in America. Your father rejects the possibility that there's anyone as clever as himself. It's why he refuses to join my enterprise.

HERMANN: I could never lead a life like my father's. I'd be miserable.

KEITH: Suppose your father just doesn't know how to interest you in his profession?

HERMANN: The important thing isn't merely to live; but to learn everything about life and the world.

KEITH: A desire that will lead you to ruination. Take my word for it. What you must learn is to live within the circumstances of your birth. It will guard you against degrading yourself quite so cheerfully.

HERMANN: By pumping you for money? Is wealth the highest value, then?

KEITH: Theoretically, perhaps. These values are called "higher" because they're founded on money. And they're *possible* only *because* of money. You, of course, are free to devote yourself either to an artistic or a scientific profession because your father has already made a fortune. If in doing so, however, you disregard the world's guiding principle, then you are deliberately dropping your inheritance into the hands of swindlers.

HERMANN: If Jesus Christ had chosen to act according to this guiding principle. . . .

KEITH: Just bear in mind that Christianity liberated two-thirds of mankind from slavery. Not a single idea—social, scientific or artistic—revolves around anything other than property. That's why the Anarchists are the sworn enemies of ideas. And don't expect the world to change in this regard. Man adjusts or man is eliminated. [*He has sat down at the writing table.*] I'll give you the hundred marks. But do come around sometime when you aren't in need of money. How long since your mother died?

HERMANN: Three years this spring.

KEITH [*handing him a sealed note*]: Take this note to Countess Werdenfels, Brienner Strasse 23. Give her my best regards. I haven't any cash on me today.

HERMANN: Thank you, Baron.

KEITH [*showing him out; as he closes the door behind him*]: Thank you, it was my pleasure. [*With this he returns to the writing table, rummaging in the plans.*] His old man treats me like a dog-catcher. Hm, I must arrange a concert as soon as possible. Public opinion will then force him into joining my enterprise. If worst comes to worst, I will simply have to do without him. [*A knock at the door.*]. Come in!

[ANNA, THE WIDOWED COUNTESS WERDENFELS *enters. She is a voluptuous beauty of thirty: white skin, turned-up nose, sparkling eyes, luxuriant chestnut-brown hair.*]

KEITH [*going to meet her*]: So, here you are, my queen! I've just sent young Casimir to you with a small request.

ANNA: So that was the young Casimir, was it?

KEITH [*after kissing her hastily on the mouth, which she has offered to him*]: He'll be back if he doesn't find you.

ANNA: He doesn't in the least resemble his father.

KEITH: Let's forget about his father, shall we? I've approached some people whose social ambitions assure me of their enthusiasm for my enterprise.

ANNA: But everyone knows that old Casimir loves to patronize young artists—especially if they are female.

KEITH [*devouring* ANNA *with his eyes*]: One look at you, Anna, and I'm another person. You're the living pledge of my good fortune. But won't you have some breakfast? There's tea, caviar and cold cuts.

ANNA [*sits on the divan and eats*]: I have a lesson at eleven. I dropped in for only a moment. Madame Bianchi tells me that in a year's time I could be Germany's leading Wagnerian soprano.

KEITH [*lighting a cigarette*]: Perhaps in a year you'll be doing so well that the greatest Wagnerian sopranos will be seeking *your* patronage.

ANNA: Fine, yes! But it's difficult for me, with my limited woman's intelligence, to imagine reaching the heights so soon.

KEITH: I quite agree with you. Personally, I allow myself to be pulled along without resistance till I can comfortably say: "This is where I will build!"

ANNA: And in that, my dear, I shall be your most faithful accomplice. For some time now my delirious love of life has brought me to thoughts of suicide.

KEITH: One man steals what he wants, the other receives it as a gift. When I went out into the world, my boldest aspiration was to end up a village school master in Upper Silesia.

ANNA: And little did you dream that one day Munich would lie at your feet.

KEITH: All I knew of Munich was from a geography class. If my reputation isn't exactly spotless, remember the depths I rose out of.

ANNA: I pray fervently every night for some infusion of your energy.

KEITH: Energy? Me? Nonsense.

ANNA: You couldn't live without constantly battering your head through one stone wall after another.

KEITH: Unfortunately, I can't breathe in a bourgeois atmosphere. It's the major limitation to my talent. If that explains my achievement, then I take no credit for it. Then, of course, there are those who find themselves rooted on a certain social plan where they vegetate without ever coming into conflict with the world.

ANNA: You, of course, emerged full-blown from the heavens.

KEITH: But a bastard nonetheless. Intellectually my father was a prominent man, especially in mathematics and the other exact sciences, and my mother was a gypsy.

ANNA: If I had your skill in reading people's faces, I could grind their noses into the dust with the tip of my toe.

KEITH: Gifts of that sort cause more distrust than they're worth, and bourgeois society has always secretly despised me for it. It's society's very timidity—quite against its own will—that has made my reputation. The higher I climb, the more they trust me. One day the crossing of the philosopher with the horse-thief will be fully appreciated.

ANNA: The only topic of conversation these days is your Fairyland Palace.

KEITH: The Fairyland Palace is a rallying point for my powers, nothing more. I have no intention of auditing account books for the rest of my life.

ANNA: And what about me? Do you think I want to take singing lessons the rest of my life? You said the Fairyland Palace was to be built for me.

KEITH: For you to dance around on your hind legs the rest of your life and be crucified by those nitwits of the press? What you need are a few more highlights in your past.

ANNA: Well, I certainly can't pull a family-tree from my hat like the Mesdames von Rosenkron and von Totleben.

KEITH: Nor would I envy them for it, my dear.

ANNA: I certainly hope not! What feminine charms *should* I envy them for?

KEITH: I inherited these ladies when I took over the concert agency. Once I'm established they can peddle radishes or write novels for all I care.

ANNA: I care more about the shine on my shoes than about any feelings you may have for me. And do you know why? Because you are the most inconsiderate creature I've every known. All you care about is your own sensual gratification. If you were to leave me, I'd feel only pity for you. Just take care *you* aren't the one who gets left.

KEITH [*caressing* ANNA]: My life has a long history of sudden reversals, and now I'm seriously considering building a house—a house with high ceilings, a park, and a broad flight of stairs leading to the entrance. Ah! and with a contingent of beggars in the driveway to complete the picture. The past is over for me and I won't be turning back. It's too often been a life-and-death struggle. I wouldn't advise a friend to take my career as a model.

ANNA: You're indestructible.

KEITH: Yes, and I attribute that to everything I've achieved up to now. You know, Anna, if we'd been born in two separate worlds, we'd have had to find one another.

ANNA: I'm not exactly destructible myself.

KEITH: Even if Providence hadn't destined us for each other because of our similarity of tastes, there's one thing we have in common . . .

ANNA: A robust constitution.

KEITH [*sits beside her and caresses her*]: As far as women are concerned, intelligence, health, sensitivity and beauty are inseparable, any one of which leads inevitably to the other three. If these traits are intensified in our children . . .

[SASHA, *a thirteen-year-old errand boy in livery jacket and knee breeches, enters from the hallway and places an armful of newspapers on the center table*].

KEITH: What has Councilor Ostermeier to say?

SASHA: The Councilor gave me a letter. It's there with the news-papers. [*He goes off into the waiting room.*]

KEITH [*having opened the letter*]: I can thank your being with me here for this! [*Reads*] ". . . I have frequently been told about your plans and am extremely interested. I shall be at the Café Maximilian at noon today. . . ." The world has just now been placed in the palm of my hand! And if old Casimir decides to come along, I can simply turn him my backside. With these "worthy" gentlemen on my side, my power is absolute.

ANNA [*has risen*]: Could you give me a thousand marks?

KEITH: Broke again?

ANNA: The rent is due.

KEITH: That can wait till tomorrow. Don't worry about it.

ANNA: Whatever you say. Count Werdenfels prophesied on his deathbed that one day I would learn about life's less agreeable side.

KEITH: If he had appreciated you more he might still be alive.

ANNA: His prophecy has yet to be fulfilled.

KEITH: You'll have the money tomorrow at noon.

ANNA [*while* KEITH *accompanies her out*]: No please. I'll come for it myself.

[*The stage remains empty for a moment. Then* MOLLY GREISINGER *enters from the living room and clears away the tea things.* KEITH *returns from the hallway.*]

KEITH [*calling*]: Sasha! [*Removes one of the pictures from the wall*]. This will have to see me through the next two weeks.

MOLLY: Do you really think we can continue living this way?

SASHA [*enters from the waiting room*]: Baron?

KEITH [*gives him the picture*]: Go over to Tannhäuser's. Tell him to put this Saranieff in his window. He can have it for three thousand marks.

SASHA: Very good, Baron.

KEITH: I'll be along in five minutes. Wait! [*He takes a card from his writing table on which "3000 M" is written and slips it into the picture frame.*] Three thousand marks! [*Goes to the writing table.*] But first I must dash off a newspaper article about it.

[SASHA *goes off with the picture.*]

MOLLY: I'd just once like to see the smallest result from all this big talk!

KEITH [*writing*]: "The Aesthetic Ideal in Modern Landscape Painting."

MOLLY: If Saranieff could paint, you wouldn't have to write newspaper articles about him.

KEITH [*turning around*]: I beg your pardon?

MOLLY: I know, you're busy.

KEITH: You were saying?

MOLLY: I received a letter from Bückeburg.

KEITH: From your mama?

MOLLY [*finds the letter in her pocket and reads*]: "You are both welcome at any time. You could move into the two front rooms on the third floor. That way you could wait quietly until your transactions in Munich are completed."

KEITH: Can't you understand, my dear, that these little letters of yours are undermining my credit?

MOLLY: There's no bread for tomorrow.

KEITH: Then we'll dine out. The Hotel Continental?

MOLLY: I wouldn't be able to swallow a bite for fear the bailiff was here attaching our beds.

KEITH: He's still working on that. Why can that little head of yours think only about food and drink? Life would be so much happier if only you saw its brighter side. You have the most incorrigible fascination with misfortune.

MOLLY: No, *you!* Other people breeze through life without a worry. They live for one another in comfortable houses with no threat to their happiness. And here *you* are, with all your talents, running around like a madman, ruining your health, and still we're penniless.

KEITH: When have you ever gone hungry! Is it *my* fault you never spend anything on clothes? When I've finished writing this article, I'll have three thousand marks. Take a cab, buy everything you can think of on the spur of the moment.

MOLLY: He'll as likely pay three thousand marks for that picture as I am to wear silk stockings for you!

KEITH [*rises unwillingly*]: You're a jewel!

MOLLY [*throws her arms around his neck*]: Have I hurt you, darling? Forgive me! Please! But I honestly believe what I just said.

KEITH: If the money doesn't last beyond tomorrow, I won't regret the sacrifice.

MOLLY [*wailing*]: I know it was hateful of me. Beat me!

KEITH: The Fairyland Palace is as good as built.

MOLLY: Then at least let me kiss your hand. Please let me kiss your hand.

KEITH: I hope I can maintain my composure over the next few days.

MOLLY: Why won't you let me? How can you be so inhuman?

KEITH [*pulls his hand out of his pocket*]: It's time you took stock of yourself, my dear; otherwise you might be in for a big surprise.

MOLLY [*covering his hand with kisses*]: Why won't you beat me? I know I deserve it!

KEITH: You're cheating yourself of happiness with all the devices a woman has at her disposal.

MOLLY [*jumps up indignantly*]: I'm not frightened by these flirtations of yours! We're too close, you and I. Once that bond breaks, you're free; but as long as you're down on your luck, you're mine.

KEITH: Fearing my good fortune more than death will be your undoing, Molly. If tomorrow my hands are free, you won't stay another moment.

MOLLY: Good! As long as you know.

KEITH: But I'm not *down* on my luck!

MOLLY: Just let me work here only till your hands are free.

KEITH [*sits again at the writing table*]: Very well, do as you will. But you know how I dislike women who work.

MOLLY: I refuse to be a monkey or parrot for your sake. And I can't very well ruin you by standing over a washtub, instead of running around with you, half-naked, to fancy dress balls.

KEITH: This doggedness of yours is really quite superhuman.

MOLLY: It's certainly beyond *your* comprehension.

KEITH: Even if I *did* understand, it still wouldn't help you.

MOLLY [*triumphantly*]: There's no need to rub your nose in it, my dear. But I *will* spell it out to you, if you like. I wouldn't be one bit happier if I thought myself better than God made me—*just because you love me!*

KEITH: That goes without saying.

MOLLY [*triumphantly*]: Because you can't live without my love. Keep your hands as free as you like. Whether I stay is up to me entirely. All that's required is that I leave you a few remnants of love for your other women. Let them deck themselves out as vulgarly as they please; it saves me the boredom of going to comedies. You and your ideals! I know all about that. If it ever came to your carrying any of them out—and fat chance there is of that!—I'd gladly be buried alive.

KEITH: You should learn to take what fortune offers you.

MOLLY [*tenderly*]: Just what *does* it offer me, my love? We had these same endless fears in America, too. And in the end everything always fell apart. In Santiago you weren't elected president, and you were nearly sentenced to death when on the decisive evening we failed to have brandy on the table. Do you remember how you shouted: "A dollar, a dollar, a republic for a dollar!"?

KEITH [*jumps up enraged and goes to the divan*]: I was born into this world a cripple, but I refuse to condemn myself to be a slave because of it. And just because I was born a beggar, I *will not* deny myself life's most extravagant luxuries as my rightful inheritance.

MOLLY: You'll never do more than look at them from the outside, no matter how long you live.

KEITH: Only death can change what I've just said. And death would think twice before coming, afraid of making a fool of himself. If I die without having lived, I'll come back as a ghost.

MOLLY: Your trouble is a swelled head.

KEITH: But *I am justified!* When you were fifteen and an irresponsible child, you left school and ran off with me to America. If we part now, and you are left to your own devices, you'd come to the worst end possible.

MOLLY [*throws her arms around his neck*]: Then come to Bückeburg with me! My parents haven't seen their Molly for three years. They'll give you half their money, they'll be so happy! And how well we could live there together.

KEITH: In Bückeburg?

MOLLY: All troubles end sometime.

KEITH [*freeing himself*]: I'd rather pick up cigar butts in cafés.

SASHA [*returns with the picture*]: Herr Tannhäuser says he can't put the picture in his window. Herr Tannhäuser says he already has a dozen pictures by Herr Saranieff.

MOLLY: So what else is new.

KEITH: That's why I keep you here. [*Goes to the writing table and tears up the piece of paper.*] At least I needn't write a newspaper article about it.

[SASHA *goes into the waiting room after placing the picture on the table.*]

MOLLY: These Saranieffs and Zamriakis are people of another cut entirely. They know how to turn people's pockets inside out. The two of us are just too simple for the great world.

KEITH: Your kingdom is not yet come. Leave me alone. Bückeburg will just have to wait.

MOLLY [*as the bell rings in the corridor, claps her hands maliciously*]: The bailiff!

[*She hurries to open the door*].

KEITH [*looks at his watch*]: What else can we sacrifice to fortune?

MOLLY [*accompanies* ERNEST SCHOLZ *into the room*]: The gentleman refuses to give me his name.

[ERNEST SCHOLZ *is a slender, extremely aristocratic figure of about twenty-seven; black wavy hair, a Vandyke beard, and under his strong elongated eyebrows large water-blue eyes with an expression of helplessness.*]

KEITH: Gaston! Where have you come from?

SCHOLZ: Your welcome is a good sign. I've changed so that I presumed you'd never recognize me.

[MOLLY, *after looking at* SCHOLZ, *decides against removing the breakfast dishes for fear of disturbing the two men. She goes into the living room without the dishes.*]

KEITH: You seem worn out. But then life never really was a game.

SCHOLZ: At least not for me. That's precisely why I've come. It's on your account that I'm here in Munich.

KEITH: Thank you. Whatever I have left over from my business is yours.

SCHOLZ: I know how bitter a struggle life is for you. But now I want to get to know you personally. I would like to place myself under your spiritual guidance for a time; but only on one condition: that you permit me to put my financial resources at your disposal.

KEITH: But why? I'm just about to become director of a gigantic corporation. And I assume you're not doing badly yourself. If I'm not mistaken, we last saw each other four years ago.

SCHOLZ: At the legal convention in Brussels.

KEITH: You had just passed your state examination.

SCHOLZ: And you were writing for every newspaper around. You may recall how I reproached you for your cynicism at the ball in the Palace of Justice.

KEITH: You had fallen in love with the daughter of the Danish ambassador, and you broke out in a rage when I maintained that women are by nature a far more materialistic breed than men, even after experiencing the finest of luxuries.

SCHOLZ: I see you're no different now from when we were children—an unscrupulous monster. And you were absolutely right.

KEITH: I've never been more flattered.

SCHOLZ: I'm a broken man. However much I may detest your view of life from the depths of my soul, as of this moment I entrust you with the riddle of my existence—which, by the way, I consider to be insoluble.

KEITH: Good God! I see you're finally shaking off melancholy and coming out from under your cloud!

SCHOLZ: This is no cowardly capitulation on my part. I've done all in my power to solve this riddle and failed every time.

KEITH: At least it's behind you now. During the Cuban Revolution I was to be shot with twelve conspirators. Naturally I fell down at the first shot and played "dead" until they came to bury me. From that day on I felt myself master of my fate. [*Jumping up.*] We assume no obligations at birth, and we have nothing to throw away except our life. Living on after death is outside the rules.— That time in Brussels, I believe, you intended going into the civil service?

SCHOLZ: I decided on the Ministry of Railroads.

KEITH: I never understood why, with your enormous wealth, you never chose to live the life of a great lord, in accord with your tastes.

SCHOLZ: I intended, first, to become a useful member of human society. Had I been born the son of a day-laborer it would have happened as a matter of course.

KEITH: One can help one's fellow men best by working to one's own advantage. The further my interests extend, the greater the number of people I can provide with the means of livelihood. Whoever imagines that by doing his job and feeding his children he's accomplishing something useful is merely pulling the wool over his own eyes. The children would be grateful if they'd never been born, and a hundred poor devils are struggling for the same job.

SCHOLZ: I could see no reason why I should stroll through the world, a worthless idler, just because I was rich. I have no artistic talent, and I didn't think myself insignificant enough to be satisfied with a happy marriage and the raising of children.

KEITH: Then you've given up the civil service?

SCHOLZ [hangs his head]: Because I was the cause of a terrible disaster while I still held office.

KEITH: On my return from America, someone who had met you the year before in Constantinople said you'd been traveling for two years, but were back and soon to be married.

SCHOLZ: I broke the engagement three days ago. I've never been more than half a man. Since the day I came of age, I've been convinced that I couldn't enjoy my existence until I'd justified it through honest work. This point of view has led me to seek pleasure out of a sheer sense of duty, nothing else, as though I were doing penance. But every time I intended to open my arms to life, I became paralyzed by the memory of the unfortunate souls who lost their lives horribly because of my exaggerated conscientiousness.

KEITH: What *is* all this?

SCHOLZ: I changed one of the railroad's regulations. There was the constant danger that it couldn't be carried out to the letter. Naturally my fears were exaggerated, but with every day I saw the disaster draw nearer. I lack the intellectual equilibrium of people who come from homes worthy of human beings. The day after my regulation was introduced, two express trains collided. Nine men, three women and two children lost their lives. I had to inspect the scene myself. It isn't my fault I'm still alive after seeing it.

KEITH: And then you traveled.

SCHOLZ: I went to England, to Italy, but still felt cut off from human activity. In pleasant, happy surroundings, amid deafening music, I suddenly hear a piercing cry, because I am unexpectedly reminded of the disaster. Even in the Orient I lived like a frightened owl. To be quite honest, ever since the day of the disaster I've been convinced that I can buy back my joy in living only through self-sacrifice. But to do so I must have access to life. I had hoped to find that access a year ago when I became engaged to a lovely girl of lower-class origins.

KEITH: You intended her to become Countess Trautenau?

SCHOLZ: I am no longer Count Trautenau. I don't expect you to understand that. The press did everything possible to contrast my name and rank with the disaster I had caused. I felt bound by duty to my family to assume another name. For two years now I have been Ernst Scholz. That way my engagement could arouse no surprise; but disaster would have come from that as well. In her heart, no spark of love; in mine, only the need for self-sacrifice; our association, an endless chain of trivial misunderstandings. I've given the girl an ample dowry to make her a desirable match for someone of her station. She was so happy with her new-won freedom that she could scarcely express herself. And now, finally, I must learn the difficult art of forgetting myself. We can look death in the eye with clear consciousness; but no one can really live till he has forgotten himself.

KEITH [*throws himself into a chair*]: My father would turn over in his grave if he knew that you . . . were asking for my advice.

SCHOLZ: It's called: life contradicting bookish wisdom. Believe me, your father contributed his share toward my one-sided development, too.

KEITH: My father was as selfless and conscientious as the mentor and tutor of a Count Trautenau had to be. You were his model student, I his whipping-boy.

SCHOLZ: Don't you remember how our chamber maids at the castle used to kiss you, and even more passionately when I was around? [*Rising*] The next two to three years will be spent—

with no exception—[*tears in his voice*] teaching myself to be
a sensualist.

KEITH: Let's go to the dance this evening out at Nymphenburg!
That's as gauche as anything our kind can possibly do. But with
all the rain and sleet pouring down on my head I feel enticed to
bathe myself in the mire again.

SCHOLZ: I'm not eager for the yells and cries of the marketplace.

KEITH: There won't be a loud word spoken. Just a hollow roar
like the ocean uprooted from its depths. Munich is Arcadia and
Babylon simultaneously. The silent Saturnalian frenzy that grips
the soul at every turn has a fascination for even the most jaded.

SCHOLZ: Jaded? How? I've never in my life had a moment's
pleasure.

KEITH: We'll have to keep the crowd at a distance. My appearance
in such places attracts them like flies to carrion. But I promise
you, you'll forget yourself, all right. Not just tonight, but three
months from now when you think back on this evening.

SCHOLZ: I've even asked myself whether it's not my tremendous
wealth that's at the root of my misfortune.

KEITH [*indignant*]: That's blasphemy!

SCHOLZ: I've seriously considered renouncing my wealth as I have
my title. That would benefit my family only during my lifetime,
of course. In any case, I can dispose of my property on my
deathbed; which is to say, after it has ruined my life. If from my
youth onward, given my moral earnestness and industry, I'd had
to struggle for my livelihood, I would now be in the middle of
a brilliant career instead of an outcast.

KEITH: On the other hand, you might be wallowing with your
lower-class girl in the most common sort of trashy lovemaking
and then be cleaning the dirty boots of your "fellow men."

SCHOLZ: I'd make that exchange anytime, and gladly.

KEITH: Just don't fantasize that this railroad disaster is what's
keeping you from enjoying life. You feed off these memories
only because you're too dull to arrange for more delicate
nourishment.

SCHOLZ: You may be right. It's why I've come to you for spiritual guidance.

KEITH: We'll find something to sink our teeth into tonight. I'm
afraid I can't invite you to breakfast with me. I have a business

meeting at twelve with a local bigwig. But I'll give you a few lines to take to my friend Raspe. Spend the afternoon with him; we'll meet at six tonight at the Hofgarten Café [*He has gone to the writing table and writes a note*].

SCHOLZ: What sort of business are you in?

KEITH: I'm an art dealer, I write for the newspapers, and I have a concert agency—none of it worth talking about. You've come just at the right time to see the founding of a gigantic concert hall being built exclusively for my artists.

SCHOLZ [*takes the picture from the table and examines it*]: You have a nice picture gallery.

KEITH [*jumping up*]: I wouldn't take ten thousand marks for that. A Saranieff. [*Turning it around.*] You hold it this way.

SCHOLZ: I know nothing about art. While traveling, I didn't set foot inside a museum.

KEITH [*gives him the note*]: The gentleman is an international authority on crime; so don't be too open with him at first. Really a charming man. People never know whether they ought to keep an eye on me, or whether I'm here to keep an eye on them.

SCHOLZ: Thank you for your kind reception. At six tonight, then, the Hofgarten Café.

KEITH: Then off to Nymphenburg. And thank you for finally having confidence in me.

[KEITH *accompanies* SCHOLZ *out. The stage is empty for a moment. Then* MOLLY GREISINGER *enters from the living room and clears the tea service from the table.* KEITH *returns immediately.*]

KEITH [*calling*]: Sasha! [*Goes to the telephone and rings.*] Seventeen thirty-five. Inspector Raspe!

SASHA [*enters from the living room*]: Baron?

KEITH: My hat! My overcoat!

[SASHA *hurries into the hall.*]

MOLLY: Please, I beg of you, you mustn't have anything to do with this patron. He wouldn't be here unless he wanted to exploit us.

KEITH [*speaking into the telephone*]: Thank God you're there! Just wait ten minutes. You'll see for yourself. [*To* MOLLY, *while* SASHA *helps him into his overcoat.*] I must hurry to the newspaper offices.

MOLLY: What should I answer mama?

KEITH [*to* SASHA]: A carriage!

SASHA: At once, Baron. [*Goes off.*]

KEITH: Give her my deepest regards. [*Goes to the writing table.*] The plans—the letter from Ostermeier—tomorrow morning all Munich must know that the Fairyland Palace will be built.

MOLLY: Then you're not coming to Bückeburg?

KEITH [*the plans rolled up under his arm, he takes his hat from the table, center, and puts it on at a rakish angle*]: Can you imagine him a sensualist! [*Goes off hurriedly.*]

Act 2

[*In the Marquis of Keith's study the center table is laid with breakfast: champagne and a large dish of oysters. The* MARQUIS OF KEITH *leans against the writing table with his left foot on a stool, while* SASHA, *kneeling in front of him, buttons his shoes with a buttonhook.* ERNST SCHOLZ *stands behind the divan as he strums on a guitar he has taken from the wall.*]

KEITH: What time did you get back to your hotel this morning?

SCHOLZ [*with a radiant smile.*] Ten.

KEITH: Wasn't I right to leave you alone with that charming creature?

SCHOLZ [*smiling blissfully*]: After last night's discussions about art and modern literature, I wonder if I shouldn't start taking lessons from the girl. I was even more amazed when she asked to wait on your guests at your garden party that you say will astonish all of Munich.

KEITH: She considers it an honor. But let's not talk about the garden party now. I'm leaving for Paris tomorrow for a couple of days.

SCHOLZ: This comes at a most inopportune time for me.

KEITH: Come along then. One of my artists is to sing for Madame Marquesi before making her debut here.

SCHOLZ: And relive the mental torments I suffered in Paris?

KEITH: I thought last night's experience might help you over that hurdle? All right, then, spend your time during my absence with Saranieff. We're bound to run into him somewhere today.

SCHOLZ: The girl last night said Saranieff's studio was a chamber of horrors, full of every abomination known to man. And then she ran on in the most delightful way about her childhood; how when she was a girl in the Tyrol she spent all summer sitting in cherry trees, and how on winter evenings, till dark came on, she'd go sleighing with the village children. How can such a girl consider it an honor to serve at your party?

KEITH: It allows her the opportunity to fight the unspeakable contempt that bourgeois society has for her.

SCHOLZ: But how do they justify such contempt? How many hundreds of women in the best social circles have their lives ruined because the wellspring of life has dried up in them! Whereas in her it overflows it banks. This young girl's joy in life is no sin. Not like the soul-stifling discord my parents endured during twenty years of marriage!

KEITH: What is sin!

SCHOLZ: Yesterday I was so certain I knew. But today I can confess openly what thousands upon thousands of respectable people like me have experienced: that the man whose life is an empty failure is bitterly envious of the creature who has wandered from the path of the virtuous.

KEITH: The happiness of these creatures wouldn't be so despised were it not the most unprofitable business imaginable. Sin is nothing more than a mythic name for bad business. Good business is simply the way of the existing social order. No one knows that better than I. I, the Marquis of Keith, despite my reputation in Munich, despite my European reputation, am just as much outside the boundaries of society as that girl. Why else would I be giving the garden party? You have no idea how it pains me not to be able to receive the poor thing as one of my guests. It will be in far better taste if she comes as hired help.

SASHA [*has risen*]: Shall I call a carriage for the Baron.

KEITH: Yes.

[SASHA *goes off.*]

KEITH [*stamping his feet securely into his boots*]: You've read, I suppose, that the Fairyland Palace Company was established yesterday?

SCHOLZ: How could I have seen a newspaper since yesterday?

[*They both take their places at the breakfast table.*]

KEITH: It all depends on a brewer, a master builder, and a restaurateur. They are the caryatids that must support the pediment of the temple.

SCHOLZ: Incidentally, your friend Raspe, the police official, is a charming person.

KEITH: He's a scoundrel; I like him for quite another reason.

SCHOLZ: He's told me he was originally a theology student, but too much studying cost him his faith, and he tried getting it back the same way as the prodigal son.

KEITH: He sank lower and lower till finally the arm of the law caught him up and returned him to his faith by detaining him for two years under lock and key.

SCHOLZ: The girl absolutely failed to understand why I'd never learned to ride a bicycle. She thought it very reasonable of me not to have ridden a bicycle in Asia and Africa because of wild animals. But she thought I ought certainly to have begun in Italy.

KEITH: I'll warn you again, my friend: don't be too open with people. Truth is our most priceless possession and we can never be too sparing with it.

SCHOLZ: Is that why you assumed the title "Marquis of Keith"?

KEITH: I have as much right to be called "Marquis of Keith" as you have to be called "Ernst Scholz." I'm the adopted son of Lord Keith, who in the year 1863. . . .

SASHA [*enters from the hall, announcing*]: Professor Saranieff.

[SARANIEFF *enters. He wears a black Prince Albert coat with sleeves somewhat too long, light trousers which are somewhat too short, thick shoes and glaring red gloves. His rather long, unruly black hair is cut straight all the way around; on a black ribbon in front of his eyes that are filled with anticipation he wears a pincenez à la Murillo. His profile is expressive, and he sports a small Spanish mustache. After greeting them he hands his top hat to* SASHA.]

SARANIEFF: From the bottom of my heart, dear friend, I wish you the best of good fortune. The cables at last are cut and the balloon free to rise.

KEITH: The command of my enterprise awaits me: I'm afraid I can't invite you to breakfast.

SARANIEFF [*sitting down at the table*]: Then I shall release you from the obligation.

KEITH: Sasha, set another plate!

[SASHA *has hung up the hat in the hall and goes off into the living room.*]

SARANIEFF: I'm surprised the great Casimir's name isn't included on the board of directors of the Fairyland Palace.

KEITH: The reason is that I don't wish to waive credit for being the creator of my own work. [*Introducing them.*] Saranieff, the painter—Count Trautenau.

SARANIEFF [*taking a glass and plate and helping himself; to* SCHOLZ]: Count, I already know you inside and out. [*To* KEITH.] Simba was just with me; she's sitting this very moment for a Boecklin.

KEITH [*to* SCHOLZ]: Boecklin was a great artist himself. [*To* SARANIEFF.] You really needn't boast about these tricks of yours!

SARANIEFF: Make me famous, and I'll have no need for such tricks. I'll pay you thirty percent for life. Consider Zamriaki for a moment. His mind is already tottering like a rotting fence post. And why? Because he insists on immortality by honorable means.

KEITH: My only concern is his music. For the genuine composer the mind is always a hindrance.

SCHOLZ: To want immortality requires an extraordinary love of life.

SARANIEFF [*To* SCHOLZ]: Incidentally, our Simba described you to me as a most interesting person.

SCHOLZ: Yes, I can well imagine she doesn't meet old grumpusses like me every day.

SARANIEFF: She categorized you as a Symbolist. [*To* KEITH]. Then she raved on about some upcoming party with a gigantic fireworks display for the Fairyland Palace.

KEITH: You don't dazzle dogs with fireworks, but rational men feel insulted if you refuse them. In any case, I'm going to Paris for a few days first.

SARANIEFF: They've asked your opinion on a joint German-French mutual aid treaty, have they?

KEITH: Just keep it to yourself!

SCHOLZ: I had no idea you were also active in politics!

SARANIEFF: Is there anything the Marquis of Keith isn't active in?

KEITH: I won't have it said I took no interest in my own times.

SCHOLZ: Aren't your own affairs enough to keep you occupied if you take life seriously?

SARANIEFF: I'd say you take life too *damned* seriously! Did some washer woman in the village of Gizeh, at the foot of the pyramids, manage to give you the wrong collar by mistake?

SCHOLZ: You appear to have been fully informed about me. May I visit you someday in your studio?

SARANIEFF: If you like, we can have our coffee there right now. You'll even find your Simba there.

SCHOLZ: Simba?—Simba? What's all this talk about Simba? She told me her name was Kathi!

SARANIEFF: Her real name is Kathi; but the Marquis of Keith dubbed her Simba.

SCHOLZ [*to* KEITH]: Undoubtedly because of her stunning red hair.

KEITH: I'm sorry, but I have no information on the subject.

SARANIEFF: She's made herself comfortable on my Persian divan and is just now sleeping off her hangover from yesterday.

[MOLLY GREISINGER *enters from the living room and lays a place for* SARANIEFF.]

SARANIEFF: My heartiest thanks, dear madam; but as you can see, I've already finished. You'll pardon me, I hope, if I haven't taken the opportunity of kissing your hand.

MOLLY: Save your compliments for more worthy occasions!

[*The bell rings in the corridor;* MOLLY *goes to answer it.*]

KEITH [*looks at his watch and rises*]: You will have to excuse me, gentlemen. [*Calls.*] Sasha!

SARANIEFF [*wiping his mouth*]: Ah, but we'll go with you, of course. [*He and* SCHOLZ *rise.*]

[SASHA *enters from the waiting room with the coats and helps* KEITH *and* SCHOLZ *put theirs on.*]

SCHOLZ [*to* KEITH]: Why didn't you tell me you were married?

KEITH: Here, let me straighten your tie. [*He does so.*] You must give more attention to your outward appearance.

[MOLLY *returns from the hall with* HERMANN CASIMIR.]

MOLLY: The young Herr Casimir wishes to see you.

KEITH [to HERMANN]: Did you deliver my kind regards yesterday?

HERMANN: The Countess herself was waiting for money from you!

KEITH: Wait here just a moment. I'll be right back. [To SCHOLZ and SARANIEFF.] Gentlemen?

SARANIEFF [takes his hat from SASHA]: With you through thick and thin!

SASHA: The carriage is waiting, Baron.

KEITH: Sit with the driver!

[SCHOLZ, SARANIEFF, KEITH and SASHA go off.]

MOLLY [gathering the breakfast dishes together]: What can you possibly want in this madhouse! You'd be much more sensible to stay home with your mama!

HERMANN: [wanting to leave the room at once]: My mother happens not to be alive, dear lady; but I wouldn't want to bother you.

MOLLY: Oh, for heaven's sake, don't go! You're not bothering anyone. I just don't understand how parents can be so inhuman as not to protect their children from associating with these highway robbers. I once had a happy home like yours, and at the same age, and no wiser, without even thinking, I took a leap straight into the bottomless pit.

HERMANN [considerably agitated]: My God, I must find a way! I'll be ruined if I stay in Munich any longer! But the Marquis is bound to refuse me his help if he even suspects what I have in mind. Please, madam, please, don't betray me!

MOLLY: If only you guessed my state of mind right now, you wouldn't be in the least worried about my concern with your problems! I just hope you don't end up in a worse fix than me. If my mother had let me work, as I am now, instead of sending me ice-skating every free afternoon, I'd still have a life of happiness ahead of me!

HERMANN: But—if you're so miserable and you know—well, that you could still be happy, why—why don't you get a divorce?

MOLLY: Oh, God! Don't talk about things you don't understand! To get a divorce, you have to be married first.

HERMANN: I'm sorry, I—I thought you were.

MOLLY: God knows, I don't want to complain about anyone! But to get married in this world you first need papers. And having papers is beneath his dignity! [*A bell rings in the corridor.*] Morning till night, this place is like a post office! [*Goes off into the hall.*]

HERMANN [*pulling himself together*]: Why do I go shooting my mouth off like that!

[MOLLY *leads in the* COUNTESS WERDENFELS.]

MOLLY: You may wait here for my husband if you like. He should be back very soon. May I introduce you?

ANNA: Thank you. We've met.

MOLLY: Of course! Then I won't be needed. [*Goes into the living room.*]

ANNA [*sits down on the bench of the writing table beside* HERMANN *and places her hand on his*]: Tell me now, my dear, what you do at school that you need so much money?

HERMANN: I won't.

ANNA: But I'd like very much to know.

HERMANN: I can believe that!

ANNA: You're very stubborn.

HERMANN [*pulls his hands from hers*]: I will not be bargained with!

ANNA: Who's bargaining? Don't flatter yourself. You see, I divide human beings into two large classes. The young and interesting and the old maids.

HERMANN: In your opinion, of course, I'm an old maid.

ANNA: Well, unless you can tell me why you need all that money . . .

HERMANN: But how can I? I'm an old maid!

ANNA: On the contrary. I could tell from the first that you were young and interesting.

HERMANN: And I am, too; or I'd be content to stay here in Munich.

ANNA: But you're dying to get out into the world!

HERMANN: And now, I suppose, you want to know where. Paris—London.

ANNA: Paris is quite unfashionable these days.

HERMANN: I don't really care about going to Paris.

ANNA: Then why not stay here in Munich?—You have a father with more money than. . . .

HERMANN: Because there's nothing here to experience! I'll die if I stay in Munich, especially if I have to spend more time at school. An old school friend writes me from Africa that when you're unhappy in Africa you're ten times happier than when you're in Munich.

ANNA: Let me tell you something. Your friend is an old maid. Don't go to Africa. Stay here in Munich with us and *really* experience something.

HERMANN: But that's impossible here!

[MOLLY *shows in* POLICE INSPECTOR RASPE. RASPE, *in his early twenties, is dressed in a light-colored summer suit and straw hat and has the innocent childlike features of an angel by Guido Reni; short blond hair, the beginnings of a mustache. When he feels himself being watched he clamps his blue pince-nez onto his nose.*]

MOLLY: My husband will be back shortly, if you would care to wait. May I introduce you. . . .

RASPE: I really don't know, dear madam, if it would be of any real service to the Baron if you introduce me.

MOLLY: All right then!—Goodness! [*She goes into the living room.*]

ANNA: May I say that your precautions are quite superfluous? We have met.

RASPE [*seating himself on the divan*]: Hm—I'm afraid I shall have to recollect. . . .

ANNA: When you have sufficiently recollected yourself, then I should like to ask you not to introduce me either.

RASPE: How is it I've never heard you spoken of here?

ANNA: What's in a name? I was told that you spent two years in total solitude.

RASPE: And you, of course, revealed to no one that you knew me in my glory days.

ANNA: Whom haven't we known in his glory days!

RASPE: You're quite right. Pity is blasphemy. What could I do? I was the sacrifice of the insane confidence everyone had in me.

ANNA: And now you're young and interesting again?

RASPE: I now make use of that same insane confidence everyone had in me for the well being of my fellow men. By the way, can you tell me something more specific about this sensualist?

ANNA: I'm terribly sorry; he hasn't been put through his paces for me yet.

RASPE: It's really quite astonishing. A certain Herr Scholz—wants to train here in Munich to become a sensualist.

ANNA: And for that reason the Marquis of Keith introduces him to a police official?

RASPE: He's quite harmless. Scarcely knowing what to do with him, for his education's sake I took him to the Hofbräuhaus. It's quite near.

[MOLLY *opens the entrance door and shows in* CONSUL CASIMIR. *He is a man in his middle forties, rather heavy set, dressed in opulent elegance; a full face with luxuriant black beard, powerful mustache, bushy eyebrows, and hair parted carefully down the center.*]

MOLLY: My husband is not at home. [*Off.*]

CASIMIR [*without greeting anyone, goes straight toward* HERMANN]: There is the door! To think I have to hunt you down in this den of thieves!

HERMANN: You'd never have come looking for me here if it didn't look bad for your business!

CASIMIR [*threatening him*]: Will you be quiet! Move! Or do I have to show you how!

HERMANN [*pulls out a pocket revolver*]: Don't touch me, papa! Don't touch me! I'll shoot myself if you touch me!

CASIMIR: You'll pay for this when I get you home!

RASPE: Why should he let himself be treated like an animal?

CASIMIR: Must I be insulted here as well?

ANNA [*approaches him*]: Please, sir, this is bound to cause an accident. Calm down first. [*To* HERMANN.] Be reasonable now; go with your father.

HERMANN: There's nothing to go home *for!* If I drank myself into a stupor because I don't know why I'm alive, he'd never even notice!

ANNA: Then calm down and tell him what you have in mind. Just don't threaten your father with that revolver. Give me that thing.

HERMANN: Is that what you thought I wanted?

ANNA: You won't regret it. I'll give it back to you when you've quieted down. Do you take me for a liar?

[HERMANN *hesitantly gives her the revolver.*]

ANNA: Now ask your father to forgive you. If you have a spark of honor in you, you can't expect your father to take the first step.

HERMANN: But I will not be destroyed!

ANNA: First ask his forgiveness. You'll know then that he can be reasoned with.

HERMANN: I—I beg you to. . . . [*He sinks to his knees and sobs.*]

ANNA [*trying to raise him*]: Aren't you ashamed of yourself! Look your father in the eye!

CASIMIR: He has his mother's nerves!

ANNA: Prove to your father that he can have confidence in you. Go home now, and when you've quieted down you will tell your father all about your plans and your wishes. [*She leads him out.*]

CASIMIR [*to* RASPE]: Who is this woman?

RASPE: This is the first time in two years I've seen her. At the time she was a saleswoman in a shop on Perus Strasse. Her name was Huber, if I'm not mistaken. If you'd care to know anything further. . . .

CASIMIR: Thank you. At your service! [*Goes off.*]

[MOLLY *enters from the living room to remove the breakfast dishes.*]

RASPE: Excuse me, madam. Did the Baron really intend to return before dinner?

MOLLY: For God's sake, don't ask me such ridiculous things!

ANNA [*returns from the hall; to* MOLLY]: May I help you with that?

MOLLY: You ask if you can help. . . . [*She puts the serving tray back down on the table.*] Let whoever wants to clear the table! I didn't eat off it! [*Goes off into the living room.*]

RASPE: That bit with the boy was extremely well done.

ANNA [*sits down at the writing table*]: I envy him the carriage his father is taking him home in.

RASPE: Tell me, whatever became of that Count Werdenfels who used to give one champagne party after another two years ago?

ANNA: That happens to be *my* name now.

RASPE: I should have guessed! Would you convey to the Count my sincerest congratulations on his choice.

ANNA: I'm afraid that's no longer possible.

RASPE: Obviously then you've separated.

ANNA: Yes, obviously. [*Voices are heard in the hallway.*] I'll explain it to you some other time.

[KEITH *enters with* HERR OSTERMEIER, HERR KRENTZL, *and* HERR GRANDAUER, *all of them more or less large-bellied, bleary-eyed Munich Philistines.* SASHA *follows.*]

KEITH: What a remarkable stroke of luck! I can introduce you at once to one of our leading artists. Sasha, remove this mess!

[SASHA *goes into the living room with the breakfast dishes.*]

KEITH [*introducing them*]: Herr Ostermeier, the brewery proprietor; Herr Krentzl, the master builder; Herr Grandauer, the restaurateur: the caryatids of the Fairyland Palace—Countess Werdenfels. But your time is limited, gentlemen, and you did come to see the plans. [*Takes the plans from the writing table and unrolls them on the center table.*]

OSTERMEIER: Take your time, my friend. Five minutes one way or the other won't matter.

KEITH [*to* GRANDAUER]: Would you hold this, please—What you see here is the large concert hall with its retractable ceiling and skylight, so that in the summer it can serve as an exhibition palace. Next to it here is a smaller theater, one I intend to make a popular venue by decorating it in the most modern taste, something, shall we say, that is a cross between a dance hall and a mortuary. Modernity is always the cheapest and the most effective way to advertise.

OSTERMEIER: Hm—you haven't forgotten the lavatories, eh?

KEITH: Here you see detailed sketches of the cloak room and the toilet facilities.—And here, Herr Krentzl, is the façade: driveway, pediment and caryatids!

KRENTZL: I sure wouldn't want to be one of them caryatids!

KEITH: Just a joke, sir, just a joke.

KRENTZL: What'd my old lady have to say if I let myself be chiseled into one of them caryatids way up there, and even worse, on a Fairyland Palace!

GRANDAUER: As you know, my main concern for the restaurant is space.

KEITH: We have proposed, my dear Herr Grandauer, to devote the entire ground floor to the restaurant.

GRANDAUER: You can't go crowding folks into a place for eats and drinks like you can for listening to that music.

KEITH: And for afternoon coffee, Herr Grandauer, you will find we have a terrace on the mezzanine with a magnificent view of the grounds along the Isar.

OSTERMEIER: Begging your pardon, old friend, do you think we could have a look at your preliminary expense sheet.

KEITH [*producing a sheet of writing*]: Four thousand shares at five thousand comes to approximately twenty million marks.—I'm operating on the assumption, gentlemen, that each of us subscribes for forty preferred shares, and that we pay for them at once. The estimated dividend, as you can see, is extraordinarily low.

KRENTZL: Looks like all we need is the go-ahead from the local authorities.

KEITH: That's why, in addition to the shares, we are going to issue a number of interest-drawing bonds and place a portion of them at the city's disposal for worthy purposes.—The proposal is that the members of the governing board receive ten percent of the net profit before deductions for depreciation and reserves.

OSTERMEIER: Quite right. Can't ask for more than that.

KEITH: As far as the stock market is concerned, we'll need to work some on that. I'm going to Paris tomorrow for that very purpose. Two weeks from today we will celebrate with our founders' party at my villa on Brienner Strasse.

[ANNA *winces.*]

OSTERMEIER: Sure would be nice to get Consul Casimir to join up by the time the party comes along!

KRENTZL: That's the best idea yet, you know? With Casimir with us the authorities *couldn't* say no—not to *anything!*

KEITH: It is my hope, gentlemen, to call a general meeting of the board before the party. At that time you will see how I have taken into consideration your suggestions regarding Consul Casimir.

OSTERMEIER [*shakes his hand*]: So, have a pleasant trip to Paris, my friend. Let's hear from you. [*Bowing to* ANNA.] I take my leave, madam. My compliments.

GRANDAUER: With all respects. I wish you a good afternoon.

KRENTZL: Best regards. Good day!

[KEITH *leads the gentlemen out.*]

ANNA [*after he has returned*]: What can you possibly be thinking of, announcing your founders' party at my house?!

KEITH: I'll have a dress made for you in Paris that will render it quite unnecessary for you to be able to sing [*To* RASPE.] And you, sir—I will expect that at the founders' party you will utilize all your charm to bewitch the wives of our three caryatids.

RASPE: I doubt the ladies will be disappointed.

KEITH [*giving him some money*]: Here are three hundred marks. I'm bringing fireworks back from Paris, the likes of which the city of Munich has never seen.

RASPE [*to* ANNA]: He got it from the sensualist.

KEITH: I use every mortal according to his talents, and I must recommend a certain degree of caution in regard to my very dear friend, Herr Raspe.

RASPE: When a man looks, as you do, as though he'd been cut from the gallows, making his way honestly through life is no art. I'd be curious to know where you'd be today if you had my angelic face!

KEITH: With a face like yours, I'd have married a princess.

ANNA [*to* RASPE]: If I'm not mistaken, you had a French name when we were first introduced.

RASPE: Having become a useful member of human society, I no longer indulge in French names.—Permit me to pay you my respects. [*Goes off.*]

ANNA: My serving staff is simply not large enough to handle big suppers!

KEITH [*calls*]: Sasha!

SASHA [*enters from the waiting room*]: Baron?

KEITH: Would you care to help serve at my friend's garden party?

SASHA: That would be a real pleasure, Baron. [*Goes off.*]

KEITH: May I introduce you today to my oldest boyhood friend, Count Trautenau?

ANNA: I've never had much luck with counts.

KEITH: That doesn't matter. All I ask is that you don't discuss my domestic relations with him. The fact is he's a moralist, by nature and by conviction. He's already catechized me today regarding my domestic arrangements.

ANNA: Good Lord, the one who's training to become a sensualist?

KEITH: Oh, it's a total contradiction! Ever since I've known him, he's lived a life of sacrifice, without realizing that there are, in fact, two souls inside him.

ANNA: Mercy! I have trouble with just one! But I thought his name was Scholz.

KEITH: One of his souls is Ernst Scholz, the other Count Trautenau.

ANNA: Thank you, but no thank you. I want nothing to do with people who can't make up their minds.

KEITH: But he's a paragon of decision. The world has no more pleasures to offer him unless he starts in again from the bottom.

ANNA: Then let him start his climb, step by step.

KEITH: Why are you so upset?

ANNA: Because you're trying to pair me off with this frightful monster!

KEITH: He's gentle as a lamb.

ANNA: Thank you very much, but I don't invite incarnations of disaster into my boudoir!

KEITH: You're not understanding me. Just now I can't do without his confidence, and therefore I don't want to expose myself at this time to his disapproval. If he fails to get to know you, all the better for me: I won't have his reproaches to look forward to.

ANNA: One never knows where your calculations are going to lead.

KEITH: What did you have in mind?

ANNA: I thought you wanted me to play his little whore.

KEITH: How could you think such a thing!

ANNA: You said a moment ago you use every mortal according to his talents. By that standard, haven't I the talent of a whore?

KEITH [*taking her in his arms*]: Anna—I'm going to Paris tomorrow, not to look into the stock market or to buy fireworks, but because I need a breath of fresh air, because I need to stretch my arms, if I'm not to lose the image of myself that I have so carefully constructed here in Munich. Anna, would I be taking you with me to Paris if you didn't mean everything to me?— Do you know something, Anna? Not a night goes by but I dream of you with a diadem in your hair. If ever you asked me to pull down a star for you from the firmament, I wouldn't be afraid, I'd find the way and means to do it.

ANNA: Go on! Use me as a whore!—You'll see soon enough the kind of profit I yield!

KEITH: All I can think of at this moment is the concert dress I'll have made for you at St. Hilaire's. . . .

SASHA [*enters from the hall*]: A Herr Sommersberg would like to see you.

KEITH: Show him in. [*To* ANNA, *describing the dress.*] A silvery torrent of mauve silk and paillettes from shoulder to ankle, so tightly laced and cut so deep, front and back, that the dress will appear a glittering jewel on your slender body!

[SOMMERSBERG *has entered. In his late thirties, deeply lined face, hair and beard streaked with gray and unkempt. A heavy winter overcoat covers his shabby clothes; torn kid gloves.*]

SOMMERSBERG: I am the author of *Songs of a Happy Man*. I don't look it.

KEITH: I looked like that once myself.

SOMMERSBERG: I would never have found the courage to come to you, except that I have had almost nothing to eat for two days.

KEITH: I've been there myself hundreds of times. How can I help you?

SOMMERSBERG: A little something—for lunch. . . .

KEITH: Is that all the use you think I can be to you?

SOMMERSBERG: I'm an invalid.

KEITH: But you still have half a life ahead of you!

SOMMERSBERG: I've wasted my life living up to the expectations people had set for me.

KEITH: Perhaps you'll find a current to take you out to open sea again. Or are you afraid?

SOMMERSBERG: I can't swim; and here in Munich resignation isn't so hard to bear.

KEITH: Come to our founders' party in Brienner Strasse two weeks from today. You'll make some very necessary contacts there. [*Gives him some money.*] Here are a hundred marks. Keep enough of it to rent a dress suit for the evening.

SOMMERSBERG [*hesitantly taking the money*]: I feel as if I'm deceiving you. . . .

KEITH: Just don't deceive yourself! And in doing so you will be doing a good turn for the next poor devil who comes to me.

SOMMERSBERG: Thank you, Baron [*Goes off.*]

KEITH: Don't mention it. [*He closes the door and puts his arms around* ANNA.] And now, my queen, we're off to Paris!

Act 3

[*A room overlooking a garden is lighted with electric lamps; a wide glass door in the right side wall leads into the garden. The middle door in the back wall leads into the dining room where dinner is being served. When the door is opened one sees the upper end of the table. In the left wall is a curtained door into the game room. Near the door is an upright piano. Downstage right, a lady's writing table; downstage left, a settee, chairs and table, etc. In the upstage right corner there is a door which leads into the hallway. A toast is being drunk in the dining room. As the glasses clink,* SOMMERSBERG, *in shabbily elegant evening dress, and* KEITH, *in a full-dress suit, enter the salon through the center door.*]

KEITH [*closing the door behind him*]: You've drawn up the telegram?

SOMMERSBERG [*paper in hand, reading*]: "The founding of the Munich Fairyland Palace Company brought together yesterday evening a gathering of notable citizens of the convivial city on the Isar for a highly spirited garden party at the villa of the Marquis of Keith on Brienner Strasse. A magnificent fireworks display, lasting till after midnight, delighted the residents of the neighborhood. We wish to extend to this enterprise begun under such favorable auspices . . . ."

KEITH: Excellent!—Whom can I send to the telegraph office . . . ?

[SOMMERSBERG *goes off into the hallway; at the same time* ERNST SCHOLZ *enters; he is in full-dress suit and overcoat.*]

KEITH: You've certainly kept us waiting long enough!

SCHOLZ: And I've merely come to tell you I can't stay.

KEITH: They're making a laughing stock of me! Old Casimir has already left me in the lurch; but at least he sent a congratulatory telegram.

SCHOLZ: I don't belong with people! You complain about being outside of society; I'm outside of humanity!

KEITH: Haven't you every pleasure now that a man can dream of?

SCHOLZ: Pleasure? What pleasure? This frenzied whirl of sensations I'm wallowing in makes me no different from a barbarian. True, I *have* learned to go into raptures over Rubens and Wagner. The disaster that once aroused pity in me has become almost insupportable in its ugliness. And I've become an aficionado regarding the artistic achievements of dancers and acrobats.—But after all this, I haven't made even one step of progress! It's because of my money that I'm treated like a human being. But no sooner do I want to *be* one than I find myself ramming into invisible walls!

KEITH: There are humans that are like weeds, they take root anywhere, and are uprooted just as easily. If they're the ones you envy, don't look to me for pity! The world's a damned sly beast, and a bitch to conquer. But succeed once and you're proof against any misfortune.

SCHOLZ: If such phrases satisfy you, then there's nothing from you I can hope for. [*About to leave.*]

KEITH [*detaining him*]: Phrases? No! I'm beyond misfortune. We're too well acquainted, misfortune and I. Misfortune for me is an opportunity like any other. Any stupid ass can suffer misfortune; the trick is to exploit it to one's advantage.

SCHOLZ: You cling to the world like a whore to her pimp. You don't understand that a man who exists only for himself can become as loathsome to himself as carrion.

KEITH: Goddamn it, then, be satisfied with this "piety" of yours! With this purgatory of earthly vice and joy behind you, you'll look down on this miserable sinner that I am like a Father of the Church!

SCHOLZ: If only I had my human birthright! Better to crawl into the wilderness like a beast than to apologize every step of the way for my very existence!—I can't stay here!—I met Countess Werdenfels yesterday!—How I offended her, I can only guess. Unintentionally I assumed the tone I use with our Simba.

KEITH: I've had more slaps from women than I have hairs on my head! But not one has ever laughed at me behind my back because of it!

SCHOLZ: I'm a man without breeding—and with a woman for whom I have the highest regard!

KEITH: The man whose every step from youth on has led to a spiritual conflict, can rule the world long after the rest of us have become food for worms! And that's *you!*

SCHOLZ: And then there's our Simba—playing the waitress here tonight! The world's most experienced diplomat never handled such a situation!

SCHOLZ: Simba doesn't know you!

SCHOLZ: I'm not afraid she'll be too friendly with me; what frightens me is she'll be insulted if I ignore her for no good reason.

KEITH: How would *that* insult her? She knows a hell of a lot more about class distinction than you.

SCHOLZ: Oh, don't worry, I know about class distinction! They're the chains that teach us how utterly weak we are!

KEITH: And you suppose that *I* don't battle weakness? My conduct can be as correct as the course of the planets, my dress as elegant as a lord—it doesn't matter. There is nothing, nothing, that can change this plebeian hand into what it is not. You could as easily turn an imbecile into a paragon of intellect. With my intellectual gifts, I could long ago have enjoyed a better social position except for these hands.—Come, you'd do best to put your overcoat in the next room.

SCHOLZ: Leave me alone! I couldn't talk calmly with the Countess today if I wanted to.

KEITH: Then talk with the two divorcées; they're both experiencing conflicts similar to yours.

SCHOLZ: Both at once?!

KEITH: Neither one over twenty-five, absolute beauties, ancient Nordic aristocracy, and so ultramodern in their way of life that they make me feel like an old flintlock beside them.

SCHOLZ: I feel I'm not far from being a modern myself.

[SCHOLZ *goes off into the game room;* KEITH *is about to follow him when* SARANIEFF *enters from the hallway.*]

SARANIEFF: Is there anything left to eat?
KEITH: Would you kindly leave your coat outside!—I haven't eaten all day long.
SARANIEFF: They're not so particular here. But first I must ask you something rather important.

[SARANIEFF *hangs his hat and coat in the hallway; meanwhile* SASHA *in frock coat and satin breeches enters from the game room with a filled champagne cooler on his way into the dining room.*]

KEITH: When you set off the fireworks, Sasha, be careful with the big mortar. There's all hellfire in it.
SASHA: Oh, I'm not scared, Baron! [*He goes off into the dining room, closing the door behind him.*]
SARANIEFF [*returns from the hallway*]: Do you have any money?
KEITH: But you've just sold a picture! Why do you think I sent my friend to see you?
SARANIEFF: What can I get out of a squeezed lemon? You've already robbed him of all he has. It'll be three days before he can pay me a penny.
KEITH [*gives him a note*]: Here are a thousand marks.

[SIMBA, *a typical Munich girl, ruddy complexion, with nimble movements, luxuriant red hair, in a tasteful black dress with white pinafore, enters from the dining room with a serving tray of half-empty wine glasses.*]

SIMBA: The Councilor wants to toast the Baron another round.

[KEITH *takes one of the glasses from the tray and goes to the table through the open door.* SIMBA *goes off into the game room.*]

KEITH: Ladies and gentlemen! This evening signifies the beginning of an era for Munich that will eclipse all that has proceeded it. We are creating a center in which all the arts of the world will be welcome. If our enterprise has caused general astonishment, then you must be mindful that only the truly astounding wins the greatest success. I empty my glass in honor of the principle which has ordained Munich a city of the arts, in honor of Munich's citizens and its lovely women.

[*While the glasses are still clinking,* SASHA *enters from the dining room and goes into the game room.* SIMBA *enters from the game room with a platter of cheese under a glass cover on her way into the dining room.*]

SARANIEFF: Simba! Are you blind?! Your sensualist is about to escape your snare only to be reeled in again by the Countess from Perusa Strasse! Why?

SIMBA: What are you doing out here? Go inside! Sit at the table!

SARANIEFF: I? With the caryatids!—Simba! Think of all the marvelous money your sensualist has in his pockets! Do you want to have it devoured by the insane Marquis of Keith?!

SIMBA: Leave me alone, you hear? I'm workin'!

SARANIEFF: The caryatids have had enough cheese! Let them wipe their mouths and be done with it! [*He places the cheese platter on the table and takes* SIMBA *on his knee.*] Simba! Don't you care for me anymore? Must I continue begging twenty marks from the Marquis of Keith amid wailing and the gnashing of teeth, while you have access to thousand mark notes fresh from their source?

SIMBA: Oh, thanks a lot! I never been plagued by *any*one like this sensualist with his stupid compassion! He tells me I'm a martyr to civilization! You ever heard anything so crazy? A martyr to civilization! I tell *him,* I say: "Tell your *society* ladies that! They'll *love* it," I says, "you calling 'em martyrs to civilization, 'cause what're they otherwise? Nothin'!" Martyr to civilization he calls me, when I drink champagne and have all the fun I want!

SARANIEFF: If I were a woman, Simba, a woman of your qualities, this sensualist would have to pay for every mug glance with an ancestral castle!

SIMBA: That's how he talks, all right! Askin' me why he's a man. Like there ain't enough ghosts in the world! Ever hear *me* ask why I'm a *girl?*

SARANIEFF: Nor do you ask us to throw away fifty million marks on some confounded idea of yours!

SIMBA: Oh, all those sad millions! You know, I only seen him laugh once since I met him. I told him, I told this sensualist, he had to learn to ride a bicycle. So he learned. We ride out to Schleissheim and while we're in the woods lookin' around a thunderstorm breaks out like the world was gonna end. Then, for the first time since I met him, he started in laughing. Oh, God, how he laughed! "There," I said, "there, *now* you're a sensualist! A *real* one!" Every stroke of lightning, he laughed! The more it lightninged and thundered the crazier he laughed!—"Don't go standin' there under the trees," I says, "that's where the lightning hits!"—"No lightning'll hit me," he says, and laughs and laughs!

SARANIEFF: Simba! Simba! You could have become an imperial countess on the spot!

SIMBA: Thanks a lot! A Social Democrat is what I could've become. Improve the world, humanitarianism, those are his specialties. No thanks, I ain't made for the Social Democrats. Too moralistic for me. They get into power once and goodbye champagne suppers.—You seen my lovey?

SARANIEFF: Seen your lovey? I thought *I* was your lovey!

SIMBA: That could be almost anybody!—I gotta watch out for him, he don't get tipsy, or the Marquis of Keith won't hire him for his new Fairyland Palace.

[SOMMERSBERG *enters from the hallway.*]

SIMBA: Here he is! Where you *been* all this time?

SOMMERSBERG: Sending a telegram to the newspapers.

SARANIEFF: Good God! Have graves begun to open? Sommersberg! Shame on you rising from the dead to be secretary of the Fairyland Palace!

SOMMERSBERG [*indicating* SIMBA]: This angel has restored me to the world.

SIMBA: Oh, go on, lovey!—He comes and asks me where he can get money.—"The Marquis of Keith," I says to him. "If he's all out, there ain't another penny in all Munich."

[RASPE, *dressed in the most elegant evening clothes, a small chain with an Order on his chest, enters from the game room.*]

RASPE: Simba, this is simply scandalous, making the Fairyland Palace Company wait for its cheese!

SIMBA [*catches up the cheese platter*]: Holy Mother of God!—I'm comin'! Right now!

SARANIEFF: Why not just stay with the old crones you were hired to see to?

SIMBA [*taking* RASPE's *arm*]: You leave this bubby of mine alone, you hear?—You'd be pleased as punch if you was as handsome as him! Both of you!

SARANIEFF: Simba—you're a born whore!

SIMBA: I'm what?

SARANIEFF: You're a born whore!

SIMBA: One more time?

SARANIEFF: You're a born whore!

SIMBA: No, I ain't no born whore. I'm a born cheese toaster. [*Goes off into the dining room with* RASPE.]

SOMMERSBERG: I personally dictate her love letters for her.

SARANIEFF: Then it's you I have to thank for destroying my castles in the air!

[SASHA *enters from the game room with a lighted lantern.*]

SARANIEFF: Jesus, what are you all got up for! You expecting to find a rich countess to marry?

SASHA: I'm going to the garden to set off the fireworks. Wait'll you see the big mortar. That'll be an eye-opener! The Marquis says it's the fires of hell! [*Goes off into the garden.*]

SARANIEFF: His master's afraid of blowing himself up if he sets them off himself.—No wonder Dame Fortune never hoists him into the saddle! He'd ride the poor beast into the ground till it was a bag of bones.

[*The center door opens and the guests leave the dining room.*]

SARANIEFF: Come along, Sommersberg! Let's have our Simba dish us up a real Lucullan feast!

[*The guests stream into the salon; at their head,* RASPE *between* FRAU COUNCILOR OSTERMEIER *and* FRAU KRENTZL; *then* KEITH *with* OSTERMEIER, KRENTZL, *and* GRANDAUER; *then* ZAMRI-AKI *with* BARONESS VON TOTLEBEN; *and finally* SCHOLZ *and*

ANNA.—SARANIEFF *and* SOMMERSBERG *sit down at the table in the dining room.*]

RASPE: Will their royal highnesses join me in a cup of exquisite coffee?

FRAU OSTERMEIER: My! There's no more gracious cavalier in all southern Germany!

FRAU KRENTZL: The gentlemen of our nobility could certainly take lessons from you!

RASPE: On my word of honor, ladies, this is the most glorious moment of my life.

[*Goes off with both ladies into the game room.*]

OSTERMEIER [*to* KEITH]: It was quite nice, you know, of old Casimir to send us a congratulatory telegram. But then, you see, my dear friend, old Casimir is a most cautious man.

KEITH: No matter! No matter! Old Casimir will have joined us by the time of our first general meeting. Won't you gentlemen have some coffee?

[OSTERMEIER, KRENTZL *and* GRANDAUER *go off into the game room.*]

BARONESS VON ROSENKRON [*to* KEITH, *who is about to follow the gentlemen*]: Promise me now, Marquis, that you will allow me to study to be a dancer for the Fairyland Palace.

BARONESS VON TOTLEBEN: And me to be a trick rider!

KEITH: You have my word, divine ladies, the Fairyland Palace will not open without you! What is it, Zamriaki? You're as pale as a corpse . . .

ZAMRIAKI [*a slender, short conservatory musician, with long, black wavy hair parted down the middle, speaks with a Polish accent*]: On my symphony I am working day and night. [*Takes* KEITH *to one side.*] You permit, Marquis, I like ask advance twenty mark on conductor salary for Fairyland Palace Orchestra.

KEITH: With the greatest pleasure. [*Gives him the money.*] Do you think, perhaps, you might give us a sampling of your new symphony soon in an up-coming concert?

ZAMRIAKI: I play Scherzo. Scherzo will be great success.

BARONESS VON ROSENKRON [*at the glass door into the garden*]: My, just look at this sea of light! Look, Martha, look! Come, Zamriaki, take us into the garden!

ZAMRIAKI: I come, ladies! I come! [*He goes into the garden with* BARONESS VON ROSENKRON *and* BARONESS VON TOTLEBEN.]

KEITH [*following them*]: Good God, people, stay away from the big mortar! It's loaded with my most splendid rockets! [*Goes off into the garden.*]

[SIMBA *closes the door from inside the dining room.* ANNA *and* SCHOLZ *stay behind alone in the salon.*]

ANNA: I can't imagine what in the world I could have taken amiss. This tactlessness you speak of, could it have been in your relations with some other woman?

SCHOLZ: Quite impossible. Please understand, I'm as happy as a person imprisoned since earliest childhood breathing free air for the first time. It's why I'm so uncertain of every step; afraid of losing my happiness.

ANNA: It must be fascinating to live in darkness without ever opening your eyes!

SCHOLZ: Countess, if I could exchange my life for one that strives for the common good, I'd never be able to thank my Creator enough.

ANNA: I thought you came to Munich to learn to be a sensualist?

SCHOLZ: Learning to be a sensualist is only a means to an end. You have my most sacred assurance of that. But don't think me a hypocrite because of it.—There's still so much good to fight for in this world! And I *will* find a place for myself in it. The more blows Fortune rains down on my head, the more precious this bag of bones will become, though it's been such a burden up to now. And there's one thing I am absolutely certain of: If ever I succeed in serving my fellow men, I will never, never once, take any credit for it! My path may lead me up or lead me down, no matter, I will always obey the terrible and ruthless instinct of self-preservation!

ANNA: Maybe the famous became famous because they couldn't endure living with us run-of-the-mill mortals.

SCHOLZ: You still don't understand me, Countess.—As soon as I've found my proper sphere of activity, I'll be the most modest and gracious company. I've already begun. I've been riding a bicycle here in Munich. It was as if I hadn't looked at the world since the days of my earliest childhood. Every tree, every body of water, the mountains, the heavens, they were all one great revelation that I seemed to have had a presentiment of in a former life.—May I invite you to a cycling party sometime?

ANNA: Say, tomorrow morning at seven? Or aren't you one for getting up early?

SCHOLZ: Tomorrow morning at seven! My life has suddenly become an endless spring landscape!

ANNA: Just don't keep me waiting!

[ZAMRIAKI, BARONESS VON ROSENKRON *and* BARONESS VON TOTLEBEN *return from the garden.* SIMBA *enters from the game room.*]

BARONESS VON ROSENKRON: Oh, but it's cold!—Martha, we'll have to take our shawls when we go out next. Play us a cancan, Zamriaki! [*To* SCHOLZ.] Do you dance the cancan?

SCHOLZ: I regret that I do not, madam.

BARONESS VON ROSENKRON [*to* BARONESS VON TOTLEBEN]: Then we'll dance together!

[ZAMRIAKI *has seated himself at the piano and begun playing a waltz.*]

BARONESS VON ROSENKRON: Do you call that a cancan, maestro?

ANNA [*to* SIMBA]: But you *do* dance the waltz?

SIMBA: If madam wishes . . .

ANNA: Come!

[BARONESS VON ROSENKRON, BARONESS VON TOTLEBEN, ANNA *and* SIMBA *dance the waltz.*]

BARONESS VON ROSENKRON: More tempo, please!

[KEITH *returns from the garden and turns off all the electric lights but one, so that the salon is only dimly lighted.*]

ZAMRIAKI [*breaks off playing with annoyance*]: I come with each beat closer to my symphony!

BARONESS VON TOTLEBEN: But why is it suddenly so dark?

KEITH: To show off my rockets better! [*He opens the door to the dining room.*] If you please, ladies and gentlemen. . . .

[RASPE, HERR *and* FRAU OSTERMEIER *and* HERR *and* FRAU KRENTZL *enter the salon.* SIMBA *goes off.*]

KEITH: It pleases me to announce that in the next few weeks the first of our grand Fairyland Palace concerts will take place, concerts that will publicize our Munich enterprise. Countess Werdenfels will introduce us to some songs of very recent composition, while our conductor Herr Zamriaki will personally direct excerpts from his symphonic poem *The Wisdom of the Brahmans.*

[*General applause. In the garden a rocket rises into the air, casting a reddish shimmer into the salon.* KEITH *turns off all the electric lights and opens the glass door.*]

KEITH: Into the garden, ladies and gentlemen! Into the garden if you want to see!

[*A second rocket rises into the air as the guests leave the salon.* KEITH, *who is about to follow them, is held back by* ANNA. *The stage remains dark.*]

ANNA: What do you mean announcing I'm to take part in your Fairyland Palace concert?

KEITH: If you wait till your teacher proclaims you ready, you'll be old and gray without ever having sung a note. [*Throws himself into a chair.*] At last, at last this perilous tightrope act of mine is coming to an end! For ten years I've used every ounce of energy just to keep my balance.—From here on out the way is upwards!

ANNA: And just where do I get the cheek to appear in front of a Munich audience with my so-called singing?!

KEITH: But you were going to be the best Wagnerian soprano in Germany in two years.

ANNA: I was joking.

KEITH: How was I to know that!

ANNA: Concerts are prepared for months in advance!

KEITH: I haven't denied myself thousands of times, only to do what people *usually* do. If they happen not to like your so-called singing, they'll be left breathless by your brilliant Parisian gown.

ANNA: If only others saw me as you do!

KEITH: I'll make certain they use the right glasses!

ANNA: Every time I appear you see and hear the most fantastic things. You overrate my appearance as much as you overrate my art.

KEITH [*jumping up*]: I've never been suspected of overrating women, but I knew you inside out at first glance. Is it any wonder I spent ten years looking for you on two continents? We had met on numerous occasions, but you were always either in the clutches of a bandit like myself, or I was so down and out that there was no practical advantage in my entering your luminous social circle.

ANNA: If your love for me is making you lose your mind, what reason is that for me to heap the scorn of Munich on my back?

KEITH: Other women have heaped quite different things on themselves for my sake!

ANNA: I am not infatuated with you!

KEITH: It's what they all say! Surrender to your inevitable good fortune, why don't you? I'll inspire you with all the confidence you'll need for your debut—even if I have to drive you out there with a loaded revolver!

ANNA: Keep treating me like an animal and soon it'll all be over between us!

KEITH: You can be confident of one thing, that I'm a man who takes life damned seriously! Although I like to bathe in champagne, I can also, like few others, deny myself all of life's pleasures. Three whole days without having made at least one step of progress toward my goal are unbearable!

ANNA: It's about time, don't you think, that you reached that goal?

KEITH: Can you really suppose, Anna, that I'd arrange this concert if I weren't absolutely certain you'd turn it into a brilliant triumph? Let me tell you something: I'm a man of *faith*. . . .

[*In the garden a rocket rises hissingly into the air.*]

KEITH: I believe in nothing so firmly as that our efforts and sacrifices are rewarded in this world!

ANNA: You'd *have* to, to overwork yourself as you do!

KEITH: And if we aren't the ones rewarded, then our children will be.

ANNA: But you haven't any!

KEITH: You'll give them to me, Anna—children with my intelligence, with robust, healthy bodies and aristocratic hands. And for that I'll build you a home fit for a queen, one that a woman of your stamp deserves! And I'll place a husband at your side with the power to fulfill every desire mirrored in your great, black eyes. [*He kisses her passionately.*]

[*In the garden some fireworks are set off which for the moment bathe the couple in a dark red glow.*]

KEITH: Go into the garden. The caryatids are dying to kneel to their goddess!

ANNA: Aren't you coming, too?

KEITH [*turns on two of the electric lights so that the salon is dimly lighted*]: I need to dash off a newspaper article about our concert. It must appear in tomorrow morning's paper. In it I'll congratulate you in advance for your triumph.

[ANNA *goes into the garden.* KEITH *sits at the table and notes down a few words.* MOLLY GREISINGER, *a colored shawl over her head, enters from the hallway excited and disturbed.*]

MOLLY: I have to speak to you for a moment.

KEITH: As long as you like, my dear; you aren't disturbing me. Although I did tell you that you wouldn't be able to stand it at home alone.

MOLLY: Dear God, let some dreadful disaster overtake us! Nothing else can save us now!

KEITH: Then why don't you come with me when I ask you?

MOLLY [*shuddering*]: To your friends?

KEITH: The people in these rooms are the *business* that keeps us *alive!* But you can't bear to know I'm here with my thoughts and not with you!

MOLLY: And that surprises you?!—You know, when you're around these people, you're not at all the same person; you're someone I've never known, never loved, someone I'd never have followed even a step, to say nothing of sacrificing home, family, happiness, everything.—You're so good, so wonderful, so dear!—But around these people—to me you're worse than—than dead!

KEITH: Go home and dress up a little. Sasha will go with you. You *mustn't* be alone tonight.

MOLLY: Yes, I'm just in the mood for getting all dolled up. You frighten me the way you carry on. It's as if the world would end tomorrow. I feel like I have to *do* something, *any*thing, to keep these horrors away from us.

KEITH: As of yesterday I began drawing an annual salary of one hundred thousand marks. You needn't fear dying of hunger any longer.

MOLLY: Don't joke! It's *me* you're sinning against. I almost can't bring myself to say what frightens me!

KEITH: Then how can I calm you? Tell me. I'll do it at once.

MOLLY: Come with me! Come with me out of this murderer's den where all they want is to destroy you. It's true; I've complained to others about you; but I did it because I couldn't go on watching your childish delusions. You're so stupid, stupid as stupid can be! You *are!* You let yourself be taken in by the lowest, commonest swindlers, and you patiently let them cut your throat.

KEITH: It's better to *suffer* injustice, my dear, than to *do* injustice.

MOLLY: Yes, but you need to know when it's *happening!*—But they make very certain your eyes stay tight closed. They flatter you, these people, saying what a marvel of cleverness and diplomacy you are! Only because your vanity strives for nothing higher! And all the while they're quietly and cold-bloodedly placing the rope around your neck!

KEITH: What is this terrible thing you're so afraid of?

MOLLY [*whimpering*]: I can't tell you. I can't make myself say it!

KEITH: Please say it; you *must;* then you'll be able to laugh about it.

MOLLY: I'm afraid . . . I'm afraid that. . . .

[*A muffled report sounds from the garden;* MOLLY *screams and falls to her knees.*]

KEITH [*helping her up*]: That was the big mortar.—Calm yourself now!—Come, have a couple glasses of champagne, then we'll go out and watch the fireworks together. . . .

MOLLY: I've had *enough* fireworks in my head these last two weeks!—You were in Paris!—Who was with you in Paris!—I swear by everything that's holy, I'll forget that I ever trembled because of you, forget that I ever suffered for you, if only you will come with me now!

KEITH [*kisses her*]: Poor creature!

MOLLY: —A penny to the poor.—Yes, yes, I'm going. . . .

KEITH: You're staying here; what are you thinking of! Dry your tears! Someone's coming up from the garden. . . .

MOLLY [*throws her arms passionately around his neck and covers him with kisses*]: You're so dear!—so wonderful!—so good!— [*She lets loose of him, smiling.*] All I wanted was to see you, just once, just today, with your friends. There are times, you know, when I'm a little . . . [*She rotates her fist in front of her forehead.*]

KEITH [*wanting to hold her back*]: You're staying here, my . . . !

[MOLLY *rushes out through the hall door.* SCHOLZ, *limping and holding his knee, enters from the garden through the glass door.*]

SCHOLZ [*very pleased*]: Please don't be alarmed!—Put out the light so they can't see me from out there. No one noticed anything. [*He drags himself to the chair into which he lets himself down.*]

KEITH: What is it?

SCHOLZ: Turn the lights out first.—It's nothing. The big mortar exploded! A piece of it struck me in the kneecap!

[KEITH *has put the light out; the stage is dark.*]

KEITH: That could only happen to you.

SCHOLZ [*in a blissful voice*]: The pain's already beginning to subside.—Believe me, there's no happier creature under the sun! I won't be going cycling tomorrow with Countess Werdenfels, in any case. But so what! [*Jubilantly.*] I've triumphed over the evil spirits; happiness lies before me; I belong to life! From today on I am another man. . . .

[*A rocket rises from the garden and bathes* SCHOLZ's *features in a lurid glow.*]

KEITH: Good God—I almost didn't recognize you there for a moment!

SCHOLZ [*jumps up from the chair and hops about the room triumphantly on one foot, while holding onto his injured knee with his hands.*] For ten long years I regarded myself as an outcast!

Outlawed by society! But it was all just imagination! Imagination! All of it—imagination!

Act 4

[*In the garden room of Countess Werdenfels a number of enormous laurel wreaths are lying about on armchairs; a splendid bouquet of flowers is placed on the table.* ANNA, COUNTESS WERDENFELS, *dressed in an attractive morning costume, is found in conversation with* POLICE INSPECTOR RASPE *and* HERMANN CASIMIR. *It is late morning.*]

ANNA [*a piece of colored paper in her hand, to* HERMANN]: Thank you, my young friend, for the lovely verses you composed for me yesterday after our first Fairyland Palace concert.—[*To* RASPE.] But I find it most odd, sir, that on this morning in particular you should come to me with such serious rumors concerning your friend and benefactor.

RASPE: The Marquis of Keith is neither my friend nor my benefactor. Two years ago I asked him, as a psychiatric expert, to bear witness at my trial. He might have saved me a year and a half in prison. Instead, he dashed off to America with a fifteen-year-old girl!

[SIMBA, *in a tasteful maid's uniform, enters from the hallway and hands* ANNA *a card.*]

SIMBA: The gentleman would like to see you.

ANNA [*to* HERMANN]: Good Lord, your father!

HERMANN [*frightened, looking at* RASPE]: How could my father suspect I've come here!

RASPE: He didn't hear it from me.

ANNA [*lifts the curtain to the game room*]: Go in there. I'll send him on his way.

[HERMANN *goes into the game room.*]

RASPE: It's best, then, if I pay my respects and be on my way, too.

ANNA: Yes, that would be best.

RASPE [*bowing*]: Madam! [*Goes off.*]

ANNA [*to* SIMBA]: You may show the gentleman in.

[SIMBA *shows* CONSUL CASIMIR *in; he is followed by a lackey from whom he has taken a bouquet of flowers;* SIMBA *goes off.*]

CONSUL CASIMIR [*handing her the flowers*]: You will permit me, madam, to extend to you my sincere congratulations on your triumph of yesterday evening. Your debut has taken all Munich by storm; you could not, however, have made a more lasting impression on any of your audience than you did on me.

ANNA: Even if that were true, I'm overwhelmed that you've come personally to tell me so.

CASIMIR: Do you have a moment?—It has to do with a purely practical matter.

ANNA [*invites him to be seated*]: I'm certain you'll find yourself on the wrong track.

CASIMIR [*after both have been seated*]: We shall see presently.—I wanted to ask you if you would be my wife.

ANNA: But I don't understand . . .

CASIMER: That's why I've come, to reach an understanding about it. Allow me to make it clear from the start; you will, of course, be required to give up the enticing career you embarked on yesterday evening.

ANNA: Surely you can't have considered this step thoroughly.

CASIMIR: A man of my age, madam, takes no ill-considered step. Later, yes—or earlier. Would you care to tell me what other scruples come to mind?

ANNA: Surely you must know that I can't answer such a proposal.

CASIMIR: I'm quite aware of that. I am, however, thinking of a time in the not too distant future, when you will be utterly free to make your own decisions concerning yourself and your prospects.

ANNA: At the moment I really can't imagine such a possibility.

CASIMIR: Today, you see, I'm the most respected man in Munich; tomorrow, however, I could find myself behind bars. I would find no fault with my best friend if he questioned whether to stand by me in such a reversal of fortune.

ANNA: Would you also not find fault with your wife if she considered the same question?

CASIMIR: My wife, certainly; my mistress, never. I'm not looking for an answer now. I refer to a time when you may find yourself with nowhere to turn or when the situation alters and frees you from all obligations; in short, then, for the time when you need someone to turn to.

ANNA: And that's when you'd make me your wife?

CASIMIR: All this must seem quite insane to you; and yet it does honor to your modesty. But as it happens, I am accountable only to myself. As you may know, I have two small children at home, girls of three and six. Then, as you might well imagine, there are other considerations. . . . As for you, I take full responsibility that you will not disappoint my expectations—even in spite of yourself.

ANNA: I admire your self-confidence.

CASIMIR: You may have absolute confidence in me.

ANNA: But after a success like yesterday evening!—It was as if a new spirit had come over the people of Munich.

CASIMIR: Believe me, I sincerely envy the founder of the Fairyland Palace for his subtle shrewdness. I must also compliment you in particular on your choice of a dress for yesterday evening. You exhibited such confidence in how it showed off your figure to best advantage that I must confess I found it quite impossible to devote proper attention to your recital.

ANNA: Please don't think the applause inflated my opinion of my artistic capabilities.

CASIMIR: And if it did, I wouldn't blame you; but your teacher tells me that a success such as yours yesterday evening has brought misfortune to many. But there is one thing that you mustn't forget: Where would the most celebrated singer today be if rich men did not consider it their moral duty to listen to her without hope of return? No matter how splendid the salary may be in individual cases, the fact remains that these people almost always live on charity.

ANNA: I was amazed at the favorable reception given every number.

CASIMIR [*rising*]: Except for that unfortunate symphony of this Herr Zamriaki. I have no doubt whatever that with time we will come to venerate the noise occasioned by this Herr Zamriaki as a divine artistic revelation. Let us therefore allow the world its ways, hope for the best, and expect the worst. You will permit me, madam, to bid you good day. [*Goes off.*]

[ANNA *clasps her temples in both hands, goes to the game room, lifts the curtain and steps back.*]

ANNA: You didn't even close the door!

[HERMANN CASIMIR *enters from the game room.*]

HERMANN: Who would ever have dreamed of such an experience!

ANNA: Go on now, so that your father will find you at home.

HERMANN [*notices the second bouquet*]: The flowers are from him?—I seem to have inherited the proclivity from him.—Except that to *him* the expense means *nothing*.

ANNA: Where do you get money for such insane expenses?

HERMANN: The Marquis of Keith.

ANNA: Please, go now! You look worn. I hope your carouse didn't go on too long last night!

HERMANN: I helped save Zamriaki's life.

ANNA: Do you count that among your worthy accomplishments?

HERMANN: What better have I to do?

ANNA: It's all very well for you to feel for the unfortunate; but you needn't sit at the same table with them. Misfortune is contagious.

HERMANN [*significantly*]: The Marquis of Keith says the same thing.

ANNA: Go now! Please!

[SIMBA *enters from the hallway and hands* ANNA *a card.*]

SIMBA: The gentleman would like to see you.

ANNA [*reading the card*]: "Representative of the South German Concert Agency."—Tell him to come back in two weeks.

[SIMBA *goes off.*]

HERMANN: What answer will you give my father?

ANNA: I think it's time you leave! You're becoming impertinent!

HERMANN: I'm going to London—even if I have to steal the money. Then my father will have no reason to complain about me.

ANNA: That's more to your benefit than to his.

HERMANN [*uneasily*]: I owe that much to my little sisters. [*Goes off.*]

ANNA [*reflects a moment, then calls*]: Kathi!

[SIMBA *enters from the dining room.*]

SIMBA: Madam?
ANNA: I want to get dressed.

[*A bell rings in the corridor.*]

SIMBA: At once, madam. [*Goes to open the door.*]

[ANNA *goes off into the dining room. Immediately following,* SIMBA *shows in* ERNST SCHOLZ, *who walks supported by an elegant crutch, limping on his stiff knee, and carrying a large bouquet of flowers.*]

ERNST SCHOLZ: I've had no opportunity, dear child, to thank you for your tactful, sensitive conduct recently at the garden party.
SIMBA [*formally*]: Does the Baron wish to be announced to madam?

[KEITH *enters from the hallway in a light-colored overcoat, with a bundle of newspapers in his hand.*]

KEITH [*removing his overcoat*]: Finding you here is a real act of Providence, I must say! [*To* SIMBA.] Why are you still here?
SIMBA: Madam has took me on as a housemaid.
KEITH: You see, I brought you luck.—Announce us!
SIMBA: Very well, Baron. [*Goes off into the game room.*]
KEITH: The reviews in the morning papers are quite enthusiastic! [*Sits at the table downstage, left, and pages through the newspapers.*]
SCHOLZ: Any word yet where your wife is staying?
KEITH: With her parents in Bückeburg. You disappeared suddenly during the banquet yesterday.
SCHOLZ: I had the most pressing need to be alone. How *is* your wife?
KEITH: Thanks; her father's on the verge of bankruptcy.
SCHOLZ: Surely you have enough left over to spare her family that!
KEITH: Have you any idea what yesterday's concert cost me?
SCHOLZ: You really do take things too lightly!
KEITH: What would you have me do, help you hatch the eggs of eternity?

SCHOLZ: If only I could transfer some of my excess sense of duty to you.

KEITH: God save me from that! I need all the flexibility possible to make the most of this success.

SCHOLZ: Thanks to you, today I can face life calmly and with confidence. And so I feel it my duty to speak as frankly to you as you spoke to me two weeks ago.

KEITH: The only difference is I haven't asked for your advice.

SCHOLZ: One *more* reason, then, for complete and open frankness. My exaggerated zeal for duty caused the death of twenty people; but *you* act as though one had *no* duty what*ever* to his fellow men. What's more, you *enjoy* playing with people's lives!

KEITH: In my case all they come away with is a black eye.

SCHOLZ [*with growing self-confidence*]: Then you're lucky! What you fail to realize is that others have the same claims to life's pleasures as you. And as for morality, that sphere of man's highest achievement, you haven't the meagerest understanding of it.

KEITH: You do remain true to yourself, don't you!—You come to Munich with the express purpose of training to be a sensualist, but by some oversight you train to be a moralist.

SCHOLZ: Because of the variegated life here in Munich, I've reached a modest yet all the more reliable evaluation of myself. During these last two weeks I've gone through such enormous inner transformations that if you care to listen I actually *can* speak as a moralist.

KEITH [*irritated*]: The fact is my good fortune galls you.

SCHOLZ: I don't believe in your good fortune! I'm so unspeakably happy that I could embrace the entire world, and quite honestly and sincerely I wish you the same. But as long as you jeer in your puerile way at life's highest values, you'll never have it. Before coming to Munich I appreciated only the *spiritual* significance of the relationship between men and women, because sensual gratification seemed vulgar to me. I've learned that it's the other way around. But you have never in your entire life valued a woman for anything higher than the sensual gratification she brings. As long as you refuse to make concessions to the moral order, as I have had to, you'll find that your good fortune is founded on quicksand!

KEITH [*to the point*]: I'm afraid you have it all wrong. I can thank these last two weeks for my *material* freedom, and as a result I am finally able to *enjoy* my life. And you can thank these last two weeks for your *spiritual* freedom, and as a result *you* are finally able to enjoy *your* life.

SCHOLZ: With one difference: all *my* pleasures are concerned with becoming a useful member of human society.

KEITH [*jumping up*]: Why should anyone even *want* to become a useful member of human society?!

SCHOLZ: Because otherwise one's existence has no justification!

KEITH: My existence *needs* no justification! I *asked* no one for my existence and *from* that I deduce I am justified in existing *any way I choose!*

SCHOLZ: And so with utter peace of mind you resign your wife to a life of misery, the woman who shared with you every danger and hardship these last three years!

KEITH: What am I to do! My expenses are so monumental I haven't a penny left over for my own use. I paid up my share of the founding capital with the first installment of my salary. I considered for a moment appropriating the money given me to defray the costs of the preliminary work. But I can't do that.— Or would you advise me otherwise?

SCHOLZ: Possibly I can let you have ten or twenty thousand marks if you can't help yourself in any other way. Just by chance I received a draft today from my steward in excess of ten thousand marks. [*Takes the draft from the portfolio and hands it to* KEITH.]

KEITH [*tears the paper from his hand*]: Just don't come to me tomorrow saying you want the money back!

SCHOLZ: I don't need it just now. The remaining ten thousand marks I'll need to send through my banker in Breslau.

[ANNA, *dressed in elegant street clothes, enters from the game room.*]

ANNA: Forgive me, gentlemen, for keeping you waiting.

SCHOLZ [*hands her the flowers*]: I could not deny myself the pleasure, madam, of wishing you luck with all my heart on the first morning of your very promising artistic career.

ANNA [*places the flowers in a vase*]: Thank you. In last night's excitement, I completely forgot to ask how your injuries are doing.

SCHOLZ: God knows, they're not worth talking about. My doctor says if I wanted to I could be climbing mountains inside of a week. What pained me yesterday were the peals of scornful laughter that Zamriaki's symphony received.

KEITH [*has seated himself at the writing table*]: I cannot do more than give people the opportunity to show what they are capable of. Whoever doesn't make the grade, falls by the wayside. Conductors are not hard to come by in Munich.

SCHOLZ: Wasn't it you who said he was the greatest musical genius since Richard Wagner?

KEITH: Just because I *own* a nag doesn't mean I *call* it one. I have to be answerable at any moment for the accuracy of my accounts. [*Rising.*] I and the caryatids have just been to the city council. They were asked to consider whether the Fairyland Palace is something Munich really needs. The answers were unanimously in the affirmative. A city like Munich can't even begin to dream of all it needs!

SCHOLZ [*to* ANNA]: I presume madam has world-embracing plans to discuss with her fortunate impresario.

ANNA: Thank you, no, not really. Leaving us already, are you?

SCHOLZ: May I have the honor of calling on you again in the next few days?

ANNA: My pleasure, you're always welcome.

[SCHOLZ *has shaken* KEITH's *hand; goes off.*]

KEITH: The morning reviews of your performance are quite enthusiastic.

ANNA: Any news about Molly?

KEITH: She's with her parents in Bückeburg; wallowing in an ocean of petit-bourgeois sentimentality.

ANNA: Next time we won't be so frightened for her! She also needed to prove how completely unnecessary she is to you!

KEITH: Thank God that violent passion for you is a book with seven seals. If a woman isn't capable of making a man happy, the least she wants is to set fire to the roof over his head.

ANNA: Nonetheless, you need to inspire a bit more confidence in
your business enterprises! Sitting on a volcano day and night
isn't a particularly pleasant experience.

KEITH: Why is everything I hear today a moral lecture?

ANNA: Because you act as though you were in constant need of
being drugged. You don't know what rest is. I've discovered that
when one is in doubt between one thing and another, the best
thing is to do *nothing at all*. It's *doing* things that makes one
susceptible to all kinds of unpleasantries. I do as little as possible
and I've always been happy. How can you blame someone for
distrusting you, when all you do is chase after luck day and
night like a ravenous wolf?

KEITH: It's not my fault I'm insatiable.

ANNA: And yet at times people sit in sleighs with loaded rifles, and
then they go bang-bang.

KEITH: I'm bulletproof. I still carry around in my body two Spanish bullets from the fighting in Cuba. Besides, I have an inviolable
guarantee of my good fortune.

ANNA: This is too much!

KEITH: Too much, at least, for the mentality of the herd!—It must
be twenty years now since that young Trautenau and I stood in
short pants at the altar of the whitewashed village church. My
father was playing the organ. The village priest handed each of
us a picture with a Bible verse on it. Since that time I've scarcely
seen the inside of a church, but my confirmation verse has been
fulfilled in ways that have often amazed me. Even today if some
adversity arises I smile scornfully in recollection of that saying:
"We know that all things work together for the good of them
that love God."

ANNA: "Them that love God"?!—And you want to be capable of
this love?

KEITH: As to whether I love God, I've looked into all existing
religions and in no religion have I found a difference between
love of God and love of one's own well-being. Love of God is
everywhere only a summary and symbolic way of expressing
love of oneself.

[SIMBA *enters from the hallway.*]

SIMBA: Would the Marquis kindly come out for a moment. Sasha's here.

KEITH: Why doesn't the boy come in?

[SASHA *enters with a telegram.*]

SASHA: I didn't know whether to or not; the Baron always says not to deliver telegrams in company.

KEITH [*opens the telegram, wads it into a ball and throws it down*]: —Damn!—My coat!

ANNA: From Molly?

KEITH: No!—I just hope to God nobody finds out about it!

ANNA: Then she isn't with her parents in Bückeburg?

KEITH [*while* SASHA *helps him into his coat*]: No!

ANNA: But you just said. . . .

KEITH: Is it *my* fault she's not in Bückeburg? You no sooner have a bit of luck than you find a noose around your neck!

[KEITH *and* SASHA *go off.*]

SIMBA [*picks up the telegram and hands it to* ANNA]: The Marquis forgot his telegram.

ANNA: Where is Sasha from?

SIMBA: The country. His mother's a housekeeper.

ANNA: Then surely his name can't be Sasha?

SIMBA: At first his name was Sepperl, but the Marquis christened him Sasha.

ANNA: Bring me my hat.

[*The bell rings in the corridor.*]

SIMBA: Right away, madam. [*Goes to open the door.*]

ANNA [*reads the telegram*]: ". . . Molly not here. Please answer by return wire if you have any word. In anxious fear. . . ."

[SIMBA *returns.*]

SIMBA: The Baron forgot his gloves.

ANNA: Which baron?

SIMBA: Oh, I meant the sensualist.

ANNA [*searches hastily*]: Merciful heaven, where could the gloves be . . . !

there are only two possibilities: either he achieves his goal or he loses his mind.

ANNA: Yes, I'm inclined to agree.

SCHOLZ: I'll take the chance! It all depends on which is more resistant, your lack of feeling or my mind. I expect the worst and will not look back till I've reached my goal; because if I'm unable to fashion a happy life out of the bliss that fills me now, then there's no hope for me. The opportunity will never offer itself again!

ANNA: I thank you from the bottom of my heart for reminding me of that! [*She sits down at the writing table.*]

SCHOLZ: This is the last time the world will lie before me in all its glory!

ANNA [*writing a note*]: That applies to me, too! [*Calls.*] Kathi— [*To herself.*] The opportunity will never offer itself to me again either.

SCHOLZ [*suddenly coming to himself*]: Why are you so mistrustful, madam?!—Why are you so mistrustful? You're mistaken, Countess!—You're harboring a terrible suspicion. . . .

ANNA: Are you still unaware of the fact that you are detaining me? [*Calls.*] Kathi!

SCHOLZ: I couldn't possibly leave you like this! Give me your assurance that you do not doubt my sanity!

[SIMBA *enters with* ANNA's *hat.*]

ANNA: Where were you so long?

SIMBA: I was afraid to come in.

SCHOLZ: Simba, you know better than anyone that I'm in possession of my five senses.

SIMBA [*pushing him back*]: Go on, don't talk so dumb!

ANNA: You will leave my maid alone. [*To* SIMBA.] Do you know the address of Consul Casimir?

SCHOLZ [*suddenly petrified*]:—The mark of Cain on my brow. . . .

Act 5

[*All the doors in the Marquis of Keith's study are wide open. As* HERMANN CASIMIR *leans against the center table,* KEITH *calls into the living room.*]

KEITH: Sasha! [*Receiving no answer he goes into the waiting room; to* HERMANN.] Excuse me. [*Calls into the waiting room.*] Sasha! [*Comes downstage; to* HERMANN.] So you're going to London with your father's consent. I can give you the best of recommendations to take with you to London. [*Throws himself onto the divan.*] In the first place I recommend you leave your German sentimentality at home. Social Democracy and anarchism are passé in London these days. But let me tell you one thing more: the only way to properly exploit one's fellow man is to appeal to the good in him. Therein resides the art of being liked, the art of getting what one wants. The more fully you take advantage of your fellow man, the more careful you have to be that you have right on your side. Never seek your own gain to the detriment of a virtuous man, but only to the detriment of scoundrels and blockheads. And now let me transmit to you the philosopher's stone: the most splendid business in the world is *morality.* I'm not yet at the point of having made it my business, but I wouldn't be the Marquis of Keith if I let the opportunity slip through my fingers entirely.

[*The bell rings in the corridor.*]

KEITH [*calls*]: Sasha! [*Rising.*] I'll slap that rascal's ears! [*He goes into the hallway and returns with* COUNCILOR OSTERMEIER.]

KEITH: You couldn't have come at a more opportune moment, my dear Herr Ostermeier. . . .

OSTERMEIER: My colleagues on the Board of Directors, my dear friend, have commissioned me to . . .

KEITH: I have a plan to discuss with you that will increase our intake many times over.

OSTERMEIER: Do you want me to report at the general meeting that I failed again today to inspect your account books?

KEITH: You're raving, my dear Herr Ostermeier! Why don't you explain to me calmly and impartially what this is all about?

OSTERMEIER: What it is about is your account books, dear friend.

KEITH [*irritably*]: To think I slave away for these bleary-eyed numskulls. . . .

OSTERMEIER: So he's right, then! [*Turning to leave.*] Your servant, sir!

KEITH [*tears open the drawer of the writing table*]: Here, you may reveal all you like in the account books! [*Turning to face* OSTERMEIER.] Who's right?

OSTERMEIER: A certain Herr Raspe, police inspector, who bet five bottles of Pommery last night at the American Bar that you *don't keep* account books.

KEITH [*bridling*]: Quite right, I *don't* keep account books.

OSTERMEIER: Then show me your notebook.

KEITH: I have established a company, sir, I have *not* had time to set up an office!

OSTERMEIER: Then show me your notebook.

KEITH [*bridling again*]: I *have no notebook.*

OSTERMEIER: Then show me the deposit receipts from the bank.

KEITH: Can you actually think I took your money to let it out on interest?!

OSTERMEIER: Don't excite yourself, dear friend. Even if you don't keep books, at least you note down your expenditures elsewhere. An errand boy does that much.

KEITH [*tosses his memorandum book onto the table*]: There you have my memorandum book.

OSTERMEIER [*opens it and reads*]: "A silvery torrent of mauve silk and pailettes from shoulder to ankle."—That's all!

KEITH: Sir, I have served up one success to you after another. If, however, you choose to place obstacles in my path, then you may rest assured of one thing: you will never again see as much as one penny of your money, in this world or the next!

OSTERMEIER: Our shares in the Fairyland Palace aren't so bad off, my friend. We'll see our money again. Your servant! [*About to leave.*]

KEITH [*holding him back*]: Your snooping about is undermining the enterprise, sir! I beg your pardon; I'm excited; my feeling for the Fairyland Palace is that of a father toward his child.

OSTERMEIER: Then your worries about your child are over. The Fairyland Palace is secured and will be built.

KEITH: Without *me?*

OSTERMEIER: If need be, then without you, dear friend.

KEITH: But you can't do that!

OSTERMEIER: In any case you would be the last one to hinder us!

KEITH: That would be a low and rotten trick!

OSTERMEIER: Oh, that's good! It really is! Just because we refuse to be cheated by *you* any longer, you call *us* the cheats!

KEITH: If you're so sure you're being cheated, then sue me!

OSTERMEIER: What a marvelous idea, my friend! If only we weren't on the Board of Directors!

KEITH: What are you talking about! You're on the Board of Directors to support me in my work.

OSTERMEIER: And that's why I've come; but you don't seem to have anything to work at.

KEITH: My dear Herr Ostermeier, I am a man of honor. You have no right to subject me to such abominable treatment. You take over the business side of the operation, and I'll manage the artistic. I admit to certain managerial shortcomings, but I was able to overlook them, knowing they would never occur again; and that once my position was secure, I would never be found guilty of even the slightest infraction.

OSTERMEIER: We could have talked of this yesterday when I was here with the other gentlemen; but you were more determined to talk our ears off. I might say to you even today: Let's make another stab at it—if only you had shown yourself to be sincere. But when all we hear are lies, well. . . .

KEITH [*bridling.*]: Then you may tell the gentlemen: I will build the Fairyland Palace just as surely as the idea burst full-grown from my brain. If, however, *you* build it—and you may tell the gentlemen this, too!—then I will blow the Fairyland Palace, together with its Board of Directors *and* its stockholders—sky high!

OSTERMEIER: I will give an exact accounting, neighbor! You know, I really don't like insulting people to their faces, not to mention throwing them out on their. . . . Your servant, sir! [*Goes off.*]

KEITH [*staring after him*]: . . . on their asses! I thought as much. [*To* HERMANN.] Don't leave me now; I may go to pieces and wither away to nothing.—How is this possible? [*Tears in his eyes.*] After all those fireworks!—Am I to be driven like an outcast again from country to country? No! No! I mustn't allow myself to be pushed against a wall!—This is the last time the world will lie before me in all its glory! [*Pulling himself up straight.*] No!—Not only am I not tottering *yet,* I'll take a leap that will astonish all of Munich. And while the city is still trembling with astonishment, I'll fall on its prostrate body, to the accompaniment of trumpets and drums, and tear it limb from limb. We'll see *then* who'll be the first to get to his feet!

[COUNTESS WERDENFELS *enters.*]

KEITH [*rushing toward her*]: My queen. . . .

ANNA [*to* HERMANN]: Would you excuse us for a moment?

[KEITH *shows* HERMANN *into the living room.*]

KEITH [*closing the door behind him*]: You look terribly self-confident today.

ANNA: That's quite possible. Every day since our Fairyland Palace concert, I've had a good half-dozen proposals of marriage.

KEITH: That means damned little to me!

ANNA: But not to me!

KEITH [*scornfully*]: Have you fallen in love with him?

ANNA: Whom do you mean?

KEITH: The sensualist!

ANNA: Are you making fun of me?

KEITH: Then whom *do* you mean?

ANNA [*indicating the living room*]: His father.

KEITH: And you want to talk with me about this?

ANNA: No, I just wanted to ask if there's been any sign of Molly.

KEITH: No, but what's this with Casimir?

ANNA: What's this with Molly?—Are you keeping her disappearance a secret?

KEITH [*uneasily*]: Frankly, I'm less afraid that she's had an accident than that her disappearance will pull the ground out from under my feet. Should that seem inhuman, I've at least paid for it by sitting out the last three nights in the telegraph office.— My crime against her is that in all the time we've known each other she's never once heard an angry word from me. She allows herself to be consumed with longing for her petit-bourgeois world where, packed in like sardines, they drudge and humiliate and love one another! No free view, no free breath! As much as possible and of the commonest sort!

ANNA: Suppose they don't find Molly, what then?

KEITH: I can be consoled with the prospect that once my house has collapsed about me, she will come back, penitent and smiling, and say: "I'll never do it again!"—Her goal has been reached; I can start packing.

ANNA: And what's to become of *me?*

KEITH: Up to this point you've gained the most from our enterprise and I hope you will continue to gain by it. You can't lose anything because you haven't invested anything.

ANNA: Are you so sure?!

KEITH: —I see . . .!

ANNA: I'm glad!

KEITH: —What did you answer him?

ANNA: I wrote saying I couldn't answer him just yet.

KEITH: That's what you wrote him?

ANNA: I wanted to discuss it first with you.

KEITH [*takes her by the wrist and pushes her from him*]: If all you had in mind was to discuss it with me—then marry him!

ANNA: Anyone as contemptuous of feelings as you ought surely to be able to discuss a purely practical matter calmly!

KEITH: My feelings have nothing to do with this! What infuriates me is that you have so little family pride as to sell your birthright for a mess of pottage!

ANNA: Yes, well, anything *you* have no part in has no *choice* but to be a mess of *pottage!*

KEITH: I'm well aware of my weaknesses; but these "men" are domesticated animals! One of them weak in the head, the other in the spine! Do you want to bring creatures into the world that can't see for the first week?!—If it's all over with me, I'll gladly give you whatever glowing spirit I've breathed into you for use in your career. But take refuge from the hard lot of the artist behind a sack of money and you are worth no more today than the grass that will one day grow on your grave!

ANNA: —If only you had the faintest idea where Molly could be!

KEITH: Don't insult me as well! [*Calls.*] Sasha!

ANNA: If you absolutely insist that we should part. . . .

KEITH: Of course I insist.

ANNA: Then give me back my letters!

KEITH [*scornfully*]: Planning to write your memoirs?

ANNA: No, but they just *might* fall into the wrong hands.

KEITH [*jumping up*]: Sasha!

ANNA: What do you want Sasha for?—I sent him on an errand.

KEITH: How did you come to do that?!

ANNA: Because he came to me. I've done so a number of times. When worse comes to worst the boy always knows where he can earn a little something.

KEITH [*sinks into the chair by the writing table*]: My Sasha! [*Wipes a tear from his eye.*] You didn't forget him either!—If you leave the room now, Anna, I'll collapse like an ox in a slaughter-house.—Give me a reprieve!

ANNA: I have no time to lose.

KEITH: Only till I'm accustomed to doing without you, Anna!—I need mental clarity now more than ever. . .

ANNA: Are you going to give me back my letters?

KEITH: You're dreadful!—But of course you're doing it out of pity! I should at least be able to curse you now that you're no longer my mistress.

ANNA: You'll never understand women even on your deathbed!

KEITH [*straightening up proudly*]: Not even on the rack will I renounced my faith! You're on your way to good fortune; that's human enough. To me you will always be what you once were.

ANNA: Then give me back my letters.

KEITH: No, my dear! Your letters I keep for myself. Otherwise one day on my deathbed I'll wonder if perhaps you weren't a phantom after all. [*Kissing her hand.*] Good luck!

ANNA: Even without you! [*Goes off.*]

KEITH [*alone, wrenched by heart spasms*]: —Ah!—Ah!—I'm dying!—[*He lunges for the writing table, removes a handful of letters from the drawer and hurries toward the door.*] Anna! Anna!

[*In the open doorway he is met by* ERNST SCHOLZ *who walks without even a trace of his injury.*]

KEITH [*starting back*]: . . . I was just going to your hotel.

SCHOLZ: No sense in that. I'm leaving.

KEITH: Then at least give me the twenty thousand marks you promised me yesterday!

SCHOLZ: There'll be no more money from me.

KEITH: The caryatids are crushing me! They want to strip me of my directorship!

SCHOLZ: Then that confirms me in my resolution.

KEITH: It's a momentary crisis, is all! I can handle it!

SCHOLZ: My wealth is more important to me than you! My wealth secures for the members of my family a free and lofty position of power for all time! You, on the other hand, will never be of use to *any*one!

KEITH: Parasite! How *dare* accuse you me of being useless?

SCHOLZ: Let's not argue!—I'm finally making that great renunciation that many a man must agree to in this life.

KEITH: And what's that?

SCHOLZ: I've torn free of all my illusions.

KEITH [*scornfully*]: Wallowing in the love of another lower-class girl?

SCHOLZ: I've torn free of everything.—I'm entering a private sanatorium.

KEITH [*screaming*]: There is nothing more shameful than being a traitor to your own self!

SCHOLZ: I can well understand your anger. These last three days I've fought the most terrible battle that a mere mortal can endure.

KEITH: To crawl away a coward at the end?—As victor to renounce your worth as a human being?

SCHOLZ [*flaring into a rage*]: I am *not* renouncing my worth as a human being! You have no cause to insult me, to jeer at me!— If a man forces himself, *against his will*, to accept the restraints I put upon myself now, *then* he may very *well* lose his worth as a human being. And yet, because of that, he remains relatively happy; he protects his illusions.—A man who comes to terms with reality dispassionately, as I am, resigns neither the respect nor the sympathy of his fellow men.

KEITH [*shrugs his shoulders*]: I'd take a little more time to think it over.

SCHOLZ: I've given it mature consideration. It's the last duty my destiny requires me to fulfill.

KEITH: Once you're in, getting out won't be so easy.

SCHOLZ: If I had even the slightest hope of getting out again, I'd never go in. The renunciation that I've burdened myself with, the self-conquest and joyful hope that I've wrested from my soul, I undertook in order to change my fate. I bewail God that there is no longer any doubt that I am different from other men.

KEITH [*very proudly*]: And I *praise* God that I have never *doubted* that I was different from other men!

SCHOLZ [*very calmly*]: Bewail God or praise God—until this very moment I have thought of you as the most cunning of scoundrels!—But I've given up even this illusion. A scoundrel counts on luck just as surely as an honorable man counts on good conscience not deserting him even in irrevocable misfortune. Your luck is as threadbare as mine, except that you don't know it. That's the horrible danger hanging over you!

KEITH: The only danger hanging over me is that tomorrow I'm out of money!

SCHOLZ: None of your tomorrows will have money, no matter how long you live!—I wish I knew you were safe from the hopeless consequences of your delusion. It's why I've come to see you this last time. I'm profoundly convinced that the best thing for you is to come with me.

KEITH [*cunningly*]: Where?

SCHOLZ: To the sanitorium.

KEITH: Give me the thirty thousand marks and I'll be right there with you.

SCHOLZ: Come with me and there will be no more need of money—ever. You'll find a more comfortable life than you may ever have known. We'll keep a carriage and horses, we'll play billiards. . . .

KEITH [*embracing him*]: Give me the thirty thousand marks!! Shall I humiliate myself here at your feet? I could be arrested on the spot!

SCHOLZ: So it's gone that far, has it? [*Pushing him back.*] I don't give sums like that to madmen!

KEITH [*shouts*]: *You're* the madman!

SCHOLZ [*calmly*]: I'm the one come to his senses.

KEITH [*scornfully*]: If a lunatic asylum lures you because you've come to your senses—go right ahead!

SCHOLZ: You're one they have to bring there by force!

KEITH: —I suppose you'll reassume your title once you're there?

SCHOLZ: You've gone bankrupt on two continents in every conceivable way that bourgeois life permits!

KEITH [*venomously*]: If it is your moral duty to free the world of your superfluous existence, I'm sure there are more radical means than going for drives and playing billiards!

SCHOLZ: I tried that long ago.

KEITH [*shouts at him*]: Then what are you still doing here?!

SCHOLZ [*gloomily*]: I failed at that as I have at everything else.

KEITH: May I suppose you shot someone else—by mistake?

SCHOLZ: They cut the bullets from between my shoulders; near the spinal column.—This is the last time anyone will ever offer you a helping hand. You already know the sort of experiences that are in store for you.

KEITH [*throws himself on his knees and clasps* SCHOLZ's *hands*]: —Give me the forty thousand marks and I'm saved!

SCHOLZ: That won't save you from the penitentiary!

KEITH [*starts up in terror*]: Shut up!

SCHOLZ [*pleading*]: Come with me and you'll be safe. We grew up together; why shouldn't we wait for the end together, too? To bourgeois society you're a criminal and subject to all kinds of inhuman medieval tortures. . . .

KEITH [*moaning*]: If you won't help me, then go, please, I beg of you!

SCHOLZ [*tears in his eyes*]: You mustn't turn your back on your only refuge! You didn't choose your pitiable fate anymore than I chose mine.

KEITH: Go! Go!

SCHOLZ: Come. Come.—As a companion I'll be gentle as a lamb. It would be a dim ray in the dark night of my life to rescue my boyhood friend from his terrible fate.

KEITH: Go! Please!

SCHOLZ: —I want you to entrust yourself to my guidance as of this moment—as I once wanted to entrust myself to you . . .

KEITH [*cries out in despair*]: Sasha! Sasha!

SCHOLZ: —At least, then, don't forget that . . . that you have a friend who will welcome you at any time. [*Goes off.*]

KEITH [*crawling around on all fours, searching*]: Molly!—Molly!—This is the first time I've ever whimpered on my knees in front of a woman! [*Suddenly hears a sound from the direction of the living room.*] Oh, it's you?

[HERMANN CASIMIR *enters from the living room.*]

KEITH: I can't ask you to stay here any longer. I'm not—I'm not quite well. I—I have to—to sleep on it first—to master the situation again.—Have a good . . . a good. . . .

[*Heavy footsteps and many voices are heard from the front stairs.*]

KEITH: Listen . . . The noise! The uproar!—That's bad. . . .
HERMANN: Close the door, then.
KEITH: I can't!—I can't!—It's her . . . !

[*A number of patrons from the neighboring Hofbräuhaus drag in a lifeless* MOLLY. *Water drips from her body, her clothes hang from her in shreds. Her undone hair covers her face.*]

BUTCHER'S HELPER: Here's the crook we're after!—[*To the others behind him.*] Is it him?—You bet! [*To* KEITH.] Look here what we fished up! Look here what we're bringin' you! Look here—if you got the guts!
PORTER: Pulled her out of the sewer! From under the iron grate! Must've been in the water a whole week!
BAKERY WOMAN: An' all the time the dirty tramp runs around with his shameless pack! Ain't paid for his bread in six weeks! Lets his poor wife beg at all the shops for something to eat! Would've made a stone cry the way she looked at the end!
KEITH [*retreats backwards to the writing table, while the crowd presses around him with the body*]: I beg of you, please, calm down!
BUTCHER'S HELPER: Shut your mouth, you bastard! I'll clout you one!—Over there! Look!—Is it her or not? Look at her, I said!
KEITH [*has grabbed from the writing table* HERMANN's *revolver left there earlier by Countess Werdenfels*]: Touch me just once and I'll use this!
BUTCHER'S HELPER: What's the bastard say?—What's he say?—You goin' to give me the revolver?—Ain't you done enough to her, you shit? Give it here, I said!

[*The* BUTCHER'S HELPER *grapples with* KEITH *who has succeeded in getting close to the doorway through which at that moment* CONSUL CASIMIR *enters.* HERMANN CASIMIR *in the meanwhile has gone to the body; he and the* BAKERY WOMAN *carry the body to the divan.*]

KEITH [*defending himself like a desperate man, calls*]: Police!—Police! [*Notices* CASIMIR *and clings to him.*] For God's sake, save me! They'll hang me!

CONSUL CASIMIR [*to the crowd*]: All right! That's enough! I refuse to see any more of this!—Leave that woman on the divan!—Get out, I say! Now! There's the door! [*Pulling downstage his son who is about to leave with the crowd.*] Hold on there, sonny! You'll be taking a nice lesson with you on your trip to London!

[*The people from the Hofbräuhaus have left the room.*]

CONSUL CASIMIR [*to* KEITH]: I was about to invite you to leave Munich within twenty-four hours. But now I think it's best you leave by the next train.

KEITH [*still holding the revolver in his left hand*]: —I'm not responsible—for this—for this disaster. . . .

CASIMIR: Settle that with yourself! But you *are* responsible for forging my signature on a congratulatory telegram delivered to your founders' party on Brienner Strasse.

KEITH: I can't leave. . . .

CASIMIR [*hands him a paper*]: You will sign this receipt. In it you certify that the sum of ten thousand marks owed you by Countess Werdenfels has been received from me.

[KEITH *goes to the writing table and signs.*]

CASIMIR [*counting the money out of his wallet*]: As your successor in the directorship of the Fairyland Palace Company, I request that in the interest of our enterprise's successful development you do not show yourself again in Munich for some time!

[KEITH, *standing at the writing table, hands the paper to* CASIMIR *and mechanically receives the money.*]

CASIMIR [*pocketing the paper*]: Pleasant journey! [*To* HERMANN.] And you come with me!

[HERMANN *slips out shyly.* CASIMIR *follows him.*]

KEITH [*the revolver in his left hand, the money in his right, takes a few steps toward the divan, but recoils in horror. He then looks irresolutely from the revolver to the money in turn. As he lays down the revolver behind him on the center table, with a grin on his face*]. Life is a slippery bitch. . . .

Translated by Carl R. Mueller

Ödön von Horváth

Tales from the Vienna Woods

A Folk Play in Three Parts

Characters

ALFRED	ZAUBERKÖNIG
HIS MOTHER	TWO AUNTS
HIS GRANDMOTHER	ERICH
FERDINAND VON HIERLINGER	EMMA
VALERIE	HELENE
OSKAR	THE SERVANT
IDA	THE BARONESS
HAVLITSCHEK	THE CONFESSOR
CAPTAIN	THE AMERICAN
A LADY	THE MASTER OF
MARIANNE	CEREMONIES

TIME AND PLACE

The play takes place in our own time, in Vienna, in fact, the Vienna Woods and out in the Wachau.

PART 1

Nothing gives so
profound a sense of infinity
as stupidity.

1

Out in the Wachau

[*In front of a cottage at the foot of a castle ruin.* ALFRED *sits devouring bread, butter and curds. His* MOTHER *is busy bringing him a sharper knife. Hovering in the air we hear a silvery shimmer—as if somewhere, eternally repeated, Johann Strauss's waltz* Tales from the Vienna Woods *were being played. And somewhere in the neighborhood flows the beautiful blue Danube.* MOTHER *watches* ALFRED. *Suddenly she grasps the hand holding the knife and looks deeply into his eyes.* ALFRED *freezes and stares suspiciously at her, his mouth full of food. Silence.* MOTHER *slowly strokes his hair.*]

MOTHER: It's very sweet of you, Alfred, dear—not to forget your poor old mother altogether, dear Alfred—

ALFRED: Forget you altogether? I'd have come out a long time ago if I could have managed it—but who can get anything done these days, what with the Depression and all the confusion. If my friend Ferdinand von Hierlinger hadn't driven me out in his convertible, God knows when we'd have seen each other.

MOTHER: That was very thoughtful of your friend Herr von Hierlinger.

ALFRED: He's quite charming. He's picking me up in half an hour.

MOTHER: So soon?

ALFRED: Unfortunately.

MOTHER: Then don't eat all the curds, I'll have nothing to offer him—

ALFRED: Oh, he's not allowed curds, he has chronic nicotine poisoning. He's a very upstanding merchant. I see a lot of him.

MOTHER: Business?
ALFRED: That, too.

[*Silence.*]

MOTHER: Are you still with the bank?
ALFRED: No.
MOTHER: Why not?

[*Silence.*]

ALFRED: I don't belong in that kind of work, no chance of making anything of myself. Work in the old sense just isn't worth it anymore. If you want to get ahead in today's world you have to build on *other* people's work. I've gone independent. Managing money, things like that—[*He chokes and coughs violently.*]
MOTHER [*hitting him on the back*]: Taste good?
ALFRED: Except that I almost choked.
MOTHER: I'm glad you like it.

[*Silence.*]

ALFRED: Speaking of choking, where's dear old granny?
MOTHER: In the kitchen, I think, praying.
ALFRED: Praying?
MOTHER: She worries a lot.
ALFRED: Worries?

[*Silence.*]

MOTHER: Just don't forget her birthday—she'll be eighty next month—because if you do, there will be hell to pay. You were always her favorite.
ALFRED: I'll make a note of it. [*He rises, having had enough to eat.*] A biblical age, no less. [*He looks at his watch.*] I think it's time. Hierlinger will be here any moment. There's a lady with him.
MOTHER: Lady? What sort of lady?
ALFRED: Over the hill.

[*Silence.*]

MOTHER: How old?
ALFRED: Middle age.

MOTHER: Money?

ALFRED: I really don't know her.

[*Silence.*]

MOTHER: Never turn your nose up at money. You just haven't found the right girl yet.

ALFRED: Who knows. At times I think I'd like a couple of kids running around, but then again I think maybe not—

GRANDMOTHER [*enters from the cottage with her bowl of curds*]: —Frieda! Frieda!

MOTHER: Where's the fire?

GRANDMOTHER: Somebody's been stealing my curds!

MOTHER: I did. Our poor Alfred was still hungry.

[*Silence.*]

GRANDMOTHER: Oh, is that so? Is that so?—But nobody bothers to ask *me!* I might as well be dead. [*To* MOTHER.] *Would you like that?*

[ALFRED *sticks his tongue out at her as he bleats like a goat. Silence.* GRANDMOTHER *also sticks her tongue out at him and bleats like a goat. Silence.*]

GRANDMOTHER [*screaming*]: I don't want the old curds anyway! So there! [*Shaking the bowl empty.*]

[FERDINAND VON HIERLINGER *enters with* VALERIE, *a well made-up woman in her fifties wearing a motoring outfit.*]

ALFRED: May I do the honors? My mother, my friend Ferdinand von Hierlinger—and Frau Valerie—and over there my dear old granny—

MOTHER: How nice of you, Herr von Hierlinger, to bring my Alfred out here to see me—thank you, thank you so much—

HIERLINGER: Oh, not at all, not at all. Alfred knows I'd bring him out anytime. All he has to do is say so.

MOTHER: Oh?

HIERLINGER: As I said, I—[*He breaks off, noticing he's said more than he ought. Embarrassed silence.*]

VALERIE: It's really quite lovely out here—

MOTHER: Would you like to look around the tower?

HIERLINGER: What sort of tower?

MOTHER: Our tower. Yes, over there—

HIERLINGER: Am I to assume those lovely romantic ruins belong to *you?*

MOTHER: No, to the state. We just look after them. If you like, I can show you around—at the top you'll be rewarded with a magnificent view and quite an instructive panorama.

HIERLINGER: Oh, but I'd love to, love to. How very charming of you.

MOTHER [*smiles, embarrassed*]: No, please! [*To* VALERIE.] would you like—?

VALERIE: Oh, thank you, thank you, no—I really can't climb that high, my lungs, you know—

MOTHER: Then we'll see you later. [*She goes off with* FERDINAND VON HIERLINGER.]

VALERIE [*to* ALFRED]: Would you care to enlighten me on a certain point?

ALFRED: Shoot.

[GRANDMOTHER *sits at the table trying unsuccessfully to overhear their conversation.*]

VALERIE: You've been cheating me again.

ALFRED: Anything else?

VALERIE: Hierlinger tells me that the payoff at the last race at Saint-Cloud wasn't one-hundred and sixty-eight shillings but two-hundred and twenty shillings—

ALFRED: Hierling's lying.

VALERIE: And I suppose the paper's lying, too? [*She sticks a racing paper under his nose.*]

[*Silence.*]

VALERIE [*triumphantly*]: Well?

ALFRED: You're just not being fair, that's all. You're driving us apart—with this sort of thing—

VALERIE: Now, if you don't mind, I'll have the twenty-seven shillings you owe me. *S'il vous plait.*

ALFRED [*handing her the money*]: *Voilá!*

VALERIE: *Merci.* [*She counts the money.*]

ALFRED: You're a very petty individual.

VALERIE: I am not an individual! And from now on I insist on a written receipt whenever you—

ALFRED [*interrupting*]: Oh, don't give yourself such airs!

[*Silence.*]

VALERIE: You really shouldn't cheat me all the time, Alfred.

ALFRED: And you really shouldn't be so suspicious all the time— it undermines our relationship. You should understand that any young man's character has its light and dark sides, it's only natural. And just between us: a personal relationship is only workable when there's something in it for both parties. Anything else you can forget. So I agree with you, there's no reason to break off a friendly business relationship just because one party isn't on the up-and-up—

VALERIE [*interrupting him*]: No! Shame on you! Shame on you—

ALFRED: There you go, changing horses in midstream again. You're not only frivolous, you're arrogant. Here I take a civil service widow's pension, and with my knowledge of horses turn it into the salary of a major government official!—What's wrong now?

VALERIE: I just thought about the grave.

ALFRED: What grave?

VALERIE: *His* grave. Whenever I hear the term civil service I automatically think of his grave. [*Silence.*] I don't take enough trouble over it. Goodness, it must be all grown over by now—

ALFRED: Listen, Valerie, if I win at Maisons-Laffitte tomorrow we'll have his grave completely redone. We'll go halvsies. [VALERIE *suddenly kisses his hand.*] No, stop that—

HIERLINGER [*from the tower*]: Alfred! Alfred! It's beautiful up here! I'll be down in a moment.

ALFRED [*calls up to him*]: Anytime you're ready. [*Staring at* VALERIE.] What's this? Crying?

VALERIE [*tearfully*]: I don't know what you're talking about—[*She looks at herself in the mirror.*] God, I'm a sight—time I shaved again—[*She puts on more lipstick as she hums Chopin's* Funeral March.]

GRANDMOTHER: Alfred! [ALFRED *goes to her.*] When are you coming back? Soon?

ALFRED: Of course.

GRANDMOTHER: I don't like saying good-bye. Just so you're all right, I always worry about you—

ALFRED: What could happen to me?

[*Silence.*]

GRANDMOTHER: When do I get my money back?

ALFRED: As soon as I have it.

GRANDMOTHER: I need it now.

ALFRED: What do you need money for?

GRANDMOTHER: Next month I'll be eighty—and I want to be buried with my own money, no charity, you know how I am—

ALFRED: Don't worry about it, Granny.

2

Quiet Street in Vienna 8

[*From left to right: Oskar's superior quality butcher's shop, with sides of beef, veal, sausages, hams and pigs' heads in the window. Beside it, under a sign reading* ZUM ZAUBERKONIG, *is a dolls' hospital with practical joke articles, death's heads, dolls, toys, rackets, tin soldiers and a skeleton in the window. Finally a small tobacco shop with newspapers, journals and picture postcards at the door. Above the dolls' hospital there is a balcony with flowers that is part of* ZAUBERKÖNIG's *apartment.* OSKAR, *wearing a white apron, stands in the doorway of his shop cleaning his nails with a penknife. Off and on he stops to listen, for out of the second floor come the sounds of someone playing Johann Strauss's* Tales from the Vienna Woods *on a worn out piano.* IDA, *a gentle, thin, short-sighted eleven-year-old leaves the butcher's shop with her basket and is about to go off, right, when she stops in front of the dolls' hospital and looks in.* HAVLITSCHEK, *Oskar's assistant, a giant of a man with bloody hands and an equally bloody apron, appears in the doorway to the butcher's shop eagerly eating a small sausage and very angry.*]

HAVLITSCHEK: Stupid bitch, stupid—

CAPTAIN [*smiling*]: Who?

HAVLITSCHEK [*points at* IDA *with his long knife*]: That one! said my blood-sausage wasn't right! Stupid bitch! I'd like to stick her with this once, like the pig yesterday, running around with the knife in its throat. Some laugh that'd be.

OSKAR [*smiling*]: Think so?

[IDA *senses* OSKAR's *glance and it makes her uncomfortable. Suddenly she runs off, right.* OSKAR *laughs. The* CAPTAIN *enters from the left. He has been on pension since the end of the war and is dressed in civilian clothes. He nods to* OSKAR *in greeting.* OSKAR *and* HAVLITSCHEK *bow—and the waltz comes to an end.*]

CAPTAIN: I really must say, that blood-sausage yesterday was— first class. My compliments.

OSKAR: Not to say tender? Hm?

CAPTAIN: A poem.

OSKAR: Hear that, Havlitschek?

CAPTAIN: Is that the one?

HAVLITSCHEK: At your service, Captain, sir!

CAPTAIN: My respects.

HAVLITSCHEK: I can see the captain's a real connoisseur. A goumand. A man of the world.

CAPTAIN [*to* OSKAR]: In my time I've been transferred to just about every part of this old monarchy, but it always comes down to one thing: Standards! Standards!

OSKAR: A matter of tradition, Captain.

CAPTAIN: If your poor old mother were still among us she'd be mighty proud of her son.

OSKAR [*smiles, flattered*]: It just wasn't meant to be, Captain.

CAPTAIN: The way of the world.

OSKAR: Been gone a year today.

CAPTAIN: Who?

OSKAR: My mama. After lunch about half past two, the Good Lord relieved her of her mortal coil.

[*Silence.*]

CAPTAIN: Has it been a year, then?

[*Silence.*]

OSKAR: Excuse me, please, Captain. I must get dressed—for the requiem mass.

[*He goes off.*]
[*The* CAPTAIN *doesn't react; he's off on some thought. Silence.*]

CAPTAIN: Another year gone—pace till twenty, trot till forty, then gallop on home—

[*Silence.*]

HAVLITSCHEK [*eating again*]: They gave that nice old lady a real good funeral.

CAPTAIN: Yes, it was quite a success—[*He leaves him standing there and walks over to the tobacco shop, stopping for a moment to look at the skeleton in the dolls' hospital.*]

[*From the second floor we again hear the sound of the piano, this time* Over the Waves. HAVLITSCHEK *follows the* CAPTAIN *with his eyes, spits out the sausage-skin and goes back into the butcher's shop.* VALERIE *appears in the doorway of her tobacco shop. The* CAPTAIN *nods to her in greeting.* VALERIE *acknowledges him.*]

CAPTAIN: Might I have a look at the lottery results? [VALERIE *hands them to him from the rack by the door.*] You're too kind. [*He buries himself in the results.*]

[*The waltz breaks off suddenly in mid-phrase.*]

VALERIE [*maliciously*]: So, Captain, what have we won? The big prize?

CAPTAIN [*handing her back the list*]: Sorry to say, I've never won anything, Frau Valerie. God knows why I play. The most I've ever won back is my stake.

VALERIE: Lucky in love, as they say.

CAPTAIN: Not any more—unfortunately.

VALERIE: Oh, come now, Captain, with your profile?

CAPTAIN: That has very little to do with it if one is at all choosy in his tastes. It can also be expensive. If only the war had lasted another two weeks I'd be drawing a major's pension.

VALERIE: If the war had lasted another two weeks we'd have won.

CAPTAIN: That's certainly possible—

VALERIE: "Certainly" nothing. [*She goes off into her tobacco shop.*]

[MARIANNE *accompanies a* LADY *out of the dolls' hospital. Every time the shop door is opened the sound of bells is heard. The* CAPTAIN *leafs his way through a newspaper and eavesdrops.*]

LADY: Well then, I can leave it in your hands.

MARIANNE: Absolutely, madam. Our shop is not only the first but the oldest in the district. Punctuality is our motto. You'll have your tin soldiers on time.

LADY: Let me go over it once more, may I, to avoid any misunderstanding? That's three boxes of seriously wounded soldiers and two boxes of dead—but not just infantry, cavalry as well—and be sure they're delivered as early as possibly the day after tomorrow, or there will be torrents of tears. Friday's the little one's birthday, you know, and he's wanted to play doctor for such a long time—

MARIANNE: We guarantee the little gentleman will have his soldiers, and on time, madam. Thank you, madam.

LADY: Well, goodbye. [*She goes off left.*]

ZAUBERKÖNIG [*appears on his balcony in a dressing-gown and with his mustaches taped*]: Marianne. Are you there?

MARIANNE: Papa?

ZAUBERKÖNIG: Who's hidden my suspenders?

MARIANNE: The pink or the beige ones?

ZAUBERKÖNIG: There's only the pink.

MARIANNE: Chest-of-drawers, top left, right hand side, rear.

ZAUBERKÖNIG: Top left, right hand side, rear. *Difficle est, satiram non scribere.* [*He goes off.*]

CAPTAIN [*to* MARIANNE]: Never idle, Fräulein Marie, never idle.

MARIANNE: No shame in work, Captain.

CAPTAIN: On the contrary. Apropos: when will congratulations be in order?

MARIANNE: For what?

CAPTAIN: Your engagement, of course.

ZAUBERKÖNIG [*reappears on the balcony*]: Marianne!

CAPTAIN: Good morning, Herr Zauberkönig.

ZAUBERKÖNIG: Good morning, Captain. Marianne, for the last time, where are my suspenders?

MARIANNE: Where they always are.

ZAUBERKÖNIG: What kind of an answer's that? Is that anyway to talk to your poor old father? And wherever it is they always are, they aren't.

MARIANNE: Then they're in the cupboard.

ZAUBERKÖNIG: No.

MARIANNE: In the night table, then.

ZAUBERKÖNIG: No.

MARIANNE: Then with your underpants.

ZAUBERKÖNIG: No.

MARIANNE: Then I don't know.

ZAUBERKÖNIG: I'm asking you for the last time. Where are my suspenders?

MARIANNE: I'm not a magician! I can't just make them appear.

ZAUBERKÖNIG [*yelling at her*]: How can I go to the requiem mass with my socks around my ankles! You're supposed to take care of my clothes! Now come up here and do something! *Avanti, avanti!*

[MARIANNE *goes off into the dolls' hospital—and the waltz* Over the Waves *starts up again.* ZAUBERKÖNIG *listens.*]

CAPTAIN: Who's playing?

ZAUBERKÖNIG: A schoolgirl on the second floor—very talented.

CAPTAIN: Musical, too.

ZAUBERKÖNIG: Precocious—[*He hums along, smells the flowers, enjoying their fragrance.*]

CAPTAIN: Spring's on its way, Herr Zauberkönig.

ZAUBERKÖNIG: About time, too. Even the weather's gone crazy.

CAPTAIN: Haven't we all.

ZAUBERKÖNIG: Not me. [*Pause.*] Times are terrible, Captain, terrible. Can't even afford to keep a servant any more. If it weren't for my daughter—

[OSKAR *enters from the butcher's shop, dressed in black and wearing a top hat and pulling on a pair of kid gloves.*]

ZAUBERKÖNIG: Be right there, Oskar! Marianne's put a hex on my suspenders again.

CAPTAIN: Herr Zauberkönig, do me the honor of accepting my suspenders, won't you? I've also begun wearing garters these days—

ZAUBERKÖNIG: Too kind of you. Thank you. but we must have order. Dear Marianne will just have to conjure them up.

CAPTAIN: May I congratulate the prospective bridegroom?

[OSKAR *raises his top hat and bows slightly.*]

ZAUBERKÖNIG: God willing.

CAPTAIN: Good day, gentlemen. [*He goes off—and the waltz is finished.*]

MARIANNE [*appears on the balcony with the pink suspenders*]: Here are your suspenders.

ZAUBERKÖNIG: About time.

MARIANNE: You threw them in with the dirty wash by mistake— and I've just had to rummage through the whole pile.

ZAUBERKÖNIG: Fancy that! [*He smiles paternally and pinches her on the cheek.*] That's a good girl. Oskar's down there. [*He goes off.*]

OSKAR: Marianne! Marianne!

MARIANNE: Yes?

OSKAR: Why don't you come down?

MARIANNE: I have to anyway. [*She goes off.*]

HAVLITSCHEK [*appears in the doorway of the butcher's shop, eating again*]: Herr Oskar. What I wanted to ask you—say an Our Father for me, please, would you?—for your poor old mother.

OSKAR: Glad to, Havlitschek.

HAVLITSCHEK: Thank you, Herr Oskar. [*He goes off.*]

[MARIANNE *enters from the dolls' hospital.*]

OSKAR: I'm so happy, Marianne. My year of mourning will be over soon, and tomorrow I'll be able to take off my crepe. And on Sunday the engagement will be announced, and at Christmas we'll be married.—How about a kiss, Marianne, a little good-morning kiss—

MARIANNE [*kisses him, then pulls suddenly away*]: Ow! Why do you always bite?

OSKAR: Did I?

MARIANNE: How could you not know?

OSKAR: I could have sworn—
MARIANNE: Why must you always hurt me?

[*Silence.*]

OSKAR: Angry? [*Silence.*] Well?
MARIANNE: Sometimes I believe you actually want me to behave badly—
OSKAR: Marianne! You know how religious I am and how seriously I take my Christian principles.
MARIANNE: And I suppose you think I *don't* believe in God? Oh!
OSKAR: I didn't mean to insult you. I know how you hate me.
MARIANNE: What are you saying? You idiot!

[*Silence.*]

OSKAR: Then you don't love me?
MARIANNE: What's love?

[*Silence.*]

OSKAR: What are you thinking?
MARIANNE: Oskar, if anyone can make us split up, it's you. Just stop pestering me all the time about what I'm thinking—
OSKAR: I want to see inside your head, I want to crawl into your skull to know what you're thinking—
MARIANNE: Well, you can't.
OSKAR: Each man is an island. [*Silence. He takes a bag of candy from his pocket*]. Would you like a candy? I forgot I had them—those in gold wrappers are liqueur—

[MARIANNE *mechanically sticks a large bonbon into her mouth, as* ZAUBERKÖNIG *rushes out of his shop, also dressed in black and wearing a top hat.*]

ZAUBERKÖNIG: Well, here we are. What have you got there? Bonbons again? How thoughtful of you, yes, indeed. [*He tastes one.*] Pineapple! Wonderful! Well, what do you say to your fiancé? Happy?

[MARIANNE *rushes off into the dolls' hospital.*]

ZAUBERKÖNIG [*nonplused*]: What's the matter with *her?*
OSKAR: Bad mood.

ZAUBERKÖNIG: Insolence is what it is. Doesn't know when she's got it good!

OSKAR: Come on, Papa, we don't have time—the mass—

ZAUBERKÖNIG: Behaving like that! Just be sure you don't spoil her, Oscar. Whatever you do, don't do that. You'll pay for it in the end. You can't imagine what I had to put up with in my marriage. And why? Not because my dear wife was a virago, God save her soul, but because I was too much of a gentleman. Never resign authority. Keep your distance. It's a patriarchy we live in, not a matriarchy. Chin up, thumbs down! *Ave Caesar, morituri te salutant!* [*He and* OSKAR *go off.*]

[*The schoolgirl on the second floor starts playing Ziehrer's* In Lauschiger Nacht. MARIANNE *appears in the display window rearranging its contents—taking special trouble with the skeleton.* ALFRED *enters, left, catches sight of* MARIANNE *from the rear, stops and watches her.* MARIANNE *turns—sees* ALFRED *and regards him with fascination.* ALFRED *smiles.* MARIANNE *smiles back.* ALFRED *bows charmingly.* MARIANNE *acknowledges him.* ALFRED *approaches the display window.* VALERIE *is standing in the doorway of her tobacco shop watching* ALFRED. ALFRED *drums with his fingers on the window.* MARIANNE *looks at him in a sudden fright, quickly lowers the blind—and again the waltz breaks off in midphrase.* ALFRED *sees* VALERIE. *Silence.*]

VALERIE: And where are we off to?

ALFRED: To see you, my sweet.

VALERIE: Lost something in the window?

ALFRED: I was going to buy you a dolly-wolly.

VALERIE: A dolly-wolly, hm? How can I have pinned all my hopes on a beast like you!

ALFRED: Well, excuse me. [*Silence.* ALFRED *tickles* VALERIE *under the chin.* VALERIE *slaps his hand away. Silence.*] Who's the young lady?

VALERIE: That's none of your damned business.

ALFRED: Very pretty.

VALERIE: Haha!

ALFRED: Beautiful, in fact. How can I have not noticed her before? One of those whims of fortune, I suppose.

VALERIE: And what if it is?

ALFRED: Look, I've had about enough of your hysterical jealousy. I will not be tyrannized by anyone! I just don't need it!
VALERIE: Really?
ALFRED: And don't think I give two hoots about your money!

[*Silence.*]

VALERIE: Yes, that would be best, I think—
ALFRED: What would?
VALERIE: It would be best for both of us if we simply parted.
ALFRED: And about time, too, if you ask me! Good riddance!— Here. That's what I still owe you. With your receipt. Nothing lost at Saint-Cloud and we won at Le Tremblay. Outsiders. I suggest you count it. [*He goes off.*]
VALERIE [*alone, counts the money mechanically—then looks lingeringly after* ALFRED; *softly*]. Bastard. Shit. Pimp. Pig—

3

Next Sunday in the Vienna Woods

[*A clearing on the bank of the beautiful blue Danube.* ZAUBER-KÖNIG *and* MARIANNE, OSKAR, VALERIE, ALFRED, *several distant relatives, among whom is* ERICH *from Kassel in Prussia, and some ugly little children dressed in white are having a picnic. At the moment they are forming an artistic grouping that* OSKAR, *fiddling with his tripod, is getting ready to photograph. Finished,* OSKAR *joins the group, standing beside* MARIANNE, *and triggers the automatic release. The operation carried out flawlessly, the group dissolves into movement.*]

ZAUBERKÖNIG: Wait! Stop! *Da capo!* I think I twitched!
OSKAR: Oh, Papa!
ZAUBERKÖNIG: Better safe than sorry.
FIRST AUNT: Absolutely.
SECOND AUNT: What a pity it would be.
ZAUBERKÖNIG: Let's go! *Da capo, da capo!*
OSKAR: Oh, all right. [*He once again prepares his equipment and the automatic release works flawlessly as before.*]
ZAUBERKÖNIG: Many thanks!

[*The group gradually disperses.*]

FIRST AUNT: Dear Herr Oskar, would you do me a very great favor? Would you photograph the children by themselves, they're so awfully sweet today.

OSKAR: It would be my pleasure. [*He arranges the children into a group and kisses the littlest one.*]

SECOND AUNT [*to* MARIANNE]: Isn't he just wonderful with children. What a good father he'd make. Wild about children, just wild about them. Knock on wood, eh? [*She embraces* MARIANNE *and gives her a kiss.*]

VALERIE [*to* ALFRED]: Well, this is just the limit!

ALFRED: What's the limit?

VALERIE: Your coming out here with these people when you knew I'd be here—after all that's happened between us.

ALFRED: Like what? Just because we've split up doesn't mean we're not good friends.

VALERIE: You're obviously not a woman—or you'd have some respect for my feelings.

ALFRED: What feelings? Still?

VALERIE: A woman doesn't forget so easily. There's something inside that's always the same. Even if you *are* just a big swindler.

ALFRED: Could you just be reasonable for once?

VALERIE [*suddenly hateful*]: That'd just suit you, wouldn't it!

ALFRED: Might the swindler take his leave, madam?

VALERIE: Who invited you in the first place?

ALFRED: Who knows?

VALERIE: Not that it's any big secret. [ALFRED *lights a cigarette.*] Where did we get to know each other? In the toy shop?

ALFRED: Shut up.

ZAUBERKÖNIG [*approaches* ALFRED *with* ERICH]: What's this? You haven't met? Then let me introduce you. This is my nephew Erich, my wife's brother-in-law's son by his second marriage—and this is Herr Zentner. Right?

ALFRED: Yes.

ZAUBERKÖNIG: Herr von Zentner.

ERICH [*a haversack and canteen at his belt*]: Very pleased to meet you.

ZAUBERKÖNIG: Erich's a student. From Dessau.

ERICH: From Kassel, Uncle.

ZAUBERKÖNIG: Kassel, Dessau—I'm always mixing them up. [*He moves on.*]

ALFRED [*to* VALERIE]: You know each other?

VALERIE: For ages.

ERICH: I had the pleasure only recently. We discussed the Burgtheater and the alleged triumph of the sound film.

ALFRED [*to* VALERIE]: Interesting. [*He bows formally and withdraws.*]

[ONE OF THE AUNTS *puts on a recording of* "Che gelida manina" *sung in German.*]

ERICH [*listening*]: *Bohéme.* Divine Puccini.

MARIANNE [*now beside* ALFRED; *listens*]: Your tiny hand is frozen—

ALFRED: It's *Bohéme.*

MARIANNE: Puccini.

VALERIE [*to* ERICH]: What operettas do you know?

ERICH: Operettas can scarcely be called art.

VALERIE: Oh! How can you say such a thing!

ERICH: Do you know *The Brothers Karamazov?*

VALERIE: No.

ERICH: That's art.

MARIANNE [*to* ALFRED]: I once wanted to study eurythmics, and then I dreamed of having an institute of my own, but my relatives aren't interested in that sort of thing. Papa always says that when women become financially independent of men we're knee-deep in Bolshevism.

ALFRED: I'm no politician, but I can tell you this: a man's being financially dependent on a woman is no bed of roses either. Kind of a law of nature.

MARIANNE: I don't believe that.

[OSKAR *is busy taking pictures of* ZAUBERKÖNIG *in a number of positions. The phonograph record has ended.*]

ALFRED: He does love photography, doesn't he, your fiancé.

MARIANNE: He's passionate about it. We've known each other for eight years.

ALFRED: How old were you? I beg your pardon, that just came automatically.

MARIANNE: I was fourteen at the time.

ALFRED: That's very young.

MARIANNE: You might say we were childhood friends. We lived next door.

ALFRED: And what if you hadn't lived next door?

MARIANNE: I don't understand.

ALFRED: Well, I mean, it's all kind of a law of nature. And fate.

[*Silence.*]

MARIANNE: Fate, yes. I suppose it's not really what you could call love—well, maybe as far as he's concerned, but—well, as for me, I—[*She suddenly looks at* ALFRED.] Goodness, what am I saying, I hardly know you—God, you sure know how to drag things out of a person—

ALFRED: I don't want to drag anything out of you. On the contrary.

MARIANNE: Are you a hypnotist?

OSKAR [*to* ALFRED]: Excuse me. [*To* MARIANNE.] May I? [OSKAR *gives her his arm and leads her over to a beautiful group of old trees under which the entire assembly has settled down to a picnic.*]

[ALFRED *follows* OSKAR *and* MARIANNE *and sits down as well.*]

ZAUBERKÖNIG: Now what were we talking about?

FIRST AUNT: The transmigration of souls.

SECOND AUNT: The what?

ERICH: It's the religious philosophy of the Buddhists. Buddhists believe that the soul of a dead person passes over into an animal—an elephant, for example—

ZAUBERKÖNIG: Crazy!

ERICH: Or into a snake.

FIRST AUNT: Pfui!

ERICH: What's pfui about it? Just another of our petty human prejudices. Why can't we simply admit to the secret beauty of the spider, the beetle and the centipede—

SECOND AUNT [*interrupting him*]: Please, not when we're eating.

FIRST AUNT: I already feel sick—

ZAUBERKÖNIG: Nothing can spoil *my* appetite today. Not even a caterpillar.

VALERIE: Enough!

ZAUBERKÖNIG [*rises and taps his glass with a knife*]: Dear friends! It has recently become an open secret that my dear daughter Marianne has cast a favoring eye on my dear Oskar—

VALERIE: Bravo!

ZAUBERKÖNIG: Quiet, please, I'll be done soon, and now that we've all gathered here, or rather, now that I've invited you all here, to celebrate an important moment in the lives of these two young people in the flower of their youth, celebrate, I say, simply but with dignity, in a small but select circle. It saddens me, however, that Almighty God has not seen fit to allow my dear and unforgettable wife the pleasure of sharing this joyous day with her only daughter. But I know one thing for sure—she is up there somewhere in eternity, looking down on us here from behind a star, raising her glass—[*raising his glass*]—in a heartfelt toast to the happy and herewith officially engaged pair, Oskar and Marianne. Hip, hip—

ALL: Hooray!

ZAUBERKÖNIG: Hip, hip—

ALL: Hooray!

ZAUBERKÖNIG: Hip, hip—Hooray!

[IDA, *the skinny, sweet, short-sighted little girl who complained about Havlitschek's blood-sausage, steps forward in a white dress and carrying a bouquet and recites a poem to the engaged couple. She has a speech defect.*]

IDA:

> Love, sweet love's a precious flame,
> That burns forever and e'er the same
> And cannot fade away.
> It burns as long as heaven's light
> Shines ever in our eyes so bright,
> Transfiguring the day.

ALL: Bravo! Hip, hip, hooray! Oh, how sweet! Etc.

[IDA *hands* MARIANNE *the bouquet with a curtsey. Then everyone caresses* IDA *and congratulates the engaged couple in the highest of spirits. The portable phonograph now plays the* Wedding March, *and* ZAUBERKÖNIG *kisses* MARIANNE *on the forehead and* OSKAR *on the mouth. He then wipes away his tears and lies down in his hammock.* ERICH *and* OSKAR *have meanwhile drunk a toast of friendship from* ERICH's *canteen.*]

ERICH: Ladies and gentlemen, excuse me, please! Oskar and Marianne! I take the liberty of drinking a very special toast to you from my canteen. Health and happiness to you always and to a lot of honest German children! Cheers!

VALERIE [*a bit wobbly*]: Just no niggers! Cheers!

ERICH: Excuse me, madam, but this is a matter on which I permit no frivolous remarks. The matter is sacred to me. I believe you know my attitude regarding our racial problems.

VALERIE: Ah, a man with problems! No! Wait! Don't run off, you complicated man, you—

ERICH: Complicated. What do you mean by that?

VALERIE: Interesting—

ERICH: How so?

VALERIE: What do you think, I like Jews? Big baby—[*She attaches herself to the big baby and drags him off.*]

[*Everyone now settles down in the forest and the little children play and disturb them.*]

OSKAR [*sings while playing the lute*]:

> *Blessed be that heavenly night*
> *When two young hearts as one took flight.*
> *Red roses on the altar fair*
> *The next year saw them kneeling there.*
> *And the white-plumed stork soon left his nest*
> *And dropped at their house a bundle blest.*
> *And even though May is no longer around,*
> *When you are young great joys abound.*

[*He plays the song again, humming this time instead of singing, as all the others, except for* MARIANNE, *join in.* ALFRED *approaches* MARIANNE.]

ALFRED: May I congratulate you again?

[MARIANNE *closes her eyes.* ALFRED *gives her hand a long kiss.* OSKAR, *who has been watching, hands the lute to the* SECOND AUNT, *slips over to them and now stands beside* MARIANNE.]

ALFRED [*formally*]: Congratulations.
OSKAR: Thank you. [ALFRED *bows formally and goes off.* OSKAR *watches him go.*] He's jealous of me. What a tactless man. Who is he, anyway?
MARIANNE: A customer.
OSKAR: For how long?
MARIANNE: He came in yesterday and we got to talking—not for long, and I invited him. He bought a game.
VALERIE [*shrilly*]: I have a forfeit! What is it?
ERICH: To moo three times.
VALERIE: Aunt Henriette, Aunt Henriette's it!
FIRST AUNT [*strikes a pose and bellows*]: Moo! Moo! Moo!

[*Loud laughter.*]

VALERIE: And I have a forfeit! What is it?
ERICH: To baa three times.
VALERIE: You're it!
ZAUBERKÖNIG: Baa! Baa! Baa!

[*Roars of laughter.*]

VALERIE: And I have a forfeit! What is it?
SECOND AUNT: To give a demonstration!
ERICH: Of what?
SECOND AUNT: Whatever you can.
VALERIE: Oskar! Did you hear, Oskar? You have to give a demonstration!
ERICH: Whatever you want.
ZAUBERKÖNIG: Whatever you want.

[*Silence.*]

OSKAR: Ladies and gentlemen, I will now demonstrate for you something particularly useful. I have recently been studying the Japanese art of self-defense. Otherwise known as jujitsu. Pay attention now—this is the simplest method of disarming your opponent. [*He suddenly lunges at* MARIANNE *to demonstrate his method, and pulls her to the ground.*]

MARIANNE: Ow! Ow! Ow!

FIRST AUNT: Oh! What's he doing!

ZAUBERKÖNIG: Bravo! Bravissimo!

OSKAR [*to the* FIRST AUNT]: I was only pretending, otherwise I'd have broken her spine.

FIRST AUNT: Oh, goodness!

ZAUBERKÖNIG [*claps* OSKAR *on the back*]: Very clever! Very illuminating!

SECOND AUNT [*helps* MARIANNE *to her feet*]: Poor little dear!— So, do you have another forfeit?

VALERIE: Alas, no! No more! All played out!

ZAUBERKÖNIG: In that case, I have an idea. Let's all go for a swim. A dip in the cool river. I'm hot as a pig on a spit.

ERICH: Great idea!

VALERIE: But where are the ladies to change?

ZAUBERKÖNIG: Couldn't be simpler. Ladies to the right, gents to the left. And we'll all meet again in the beautiful blue Danube.

[*The portable phonograph is now playing* The Beautiful Blue Danube *as the ladies disappear to the right and the gentlemen to the left.—*VALERIE *and* ALFRED *remain.*]

VALERIE: Alfred.

ALFRED: Yes? [VALERIE *hums the waltz melody and takes off her blouse.*] What? [VALERIE *throws him a kiss.*] Good-bye.

VALERIE: No, just a moment. What does his lordship think of the bride-to-be?

ALFRED [*fixes her with his gaze, then goes quickly up to her and stops just in front of her*]: Let me smell your breath.

VALERIE: Why should I?

ALFRED: Let me smell you breath. [VALERIE *breathes on him.*] You sure know how to lap it up.

VALERIE: A healthy little glow, is all. What are you, a vegetarian? Man proposes, God disposes. Don't celebrate an engagement every day, do we—or is it a disengagement, you swine?

ALFRED: I suggest you try adopting a different tone.

VALERIE: Don't you touch me, just don't you touch me!

ALFRED: When the hell did I ever touch you?

VALERIE: Seventeenth of March!

[*Silence.*]

ALFRED: Some memory you've got.

VALERIE: I remember everything. The good and the bad. [*She suddenly holds her blouse in front of her.*] Go away. I want to undress.

ALFRED: It would hardly be a first, dear heart.

VALERIE [*shrieking*]: Stop looking at me like that! Go away! Go away!

ALFRED: Hysterical cow. [*He goes off left.*]

VALERIE [*alone, watches him leave.*]: Bastard. Shit. Pig. Beast. [*She undresses.*]

[ZAUBERKÖNIG *in swimming gear appears from among the bushes and watches her.* VALERIE, *now dressed only in slip, underwear and stockings, notices him.*]

VALERIE: Oh, Jesus! You dreadful creature! You're, you're a voyeur, that's what you are!

ZAUBERKÖNIG: Don't be silly, I'm not a pervert. Just go on undressing.

VALERIE: No, I do have some modesty.

ZAUBERKÖNIG: Nobody worries about that these days.

VALERIE: I know—I have a wild imagination. [*She trips along till she is behind a bush.*]

ZAUBERKÖNIG [*sits in front of the bush, discovers* VALERIE's *corset, picks it up and smells it*]: Imagination or no imagination—today's world is an upside-down mess. No loyalty, no faith, no moral principles. Everything's falling apart, nothing holds. Time for the second deluge. [*He puts the corset aside since it obviously doesn't get him off.*] I'm just glad I got Marianne settled. Butcher's shops are always sound investments—

VALERIE [*from behind the bush*]: So what's wrong with tobacco shops?

ZAUBERKÖNIG: Tobacco, too! Sure! Smoke and eat! People will do that no matter what. But magic? When I consider the future I get terribly pessimistic. I haven't exactly had an easy time of it in my life, just think of my poor wife, all that endless fuss over the specialists—

VALERIE [*appears in a knitted bathing outfit, busying herself with the buttons on the shoulder straps*]: What was it she died of exactly?

ZAUBERKÖNIG [*staring at her bosom*]: Breasts.

VALERIE: Not of cancer?

ZAUBERKÖNIG: Yes. Cancer.

VALERIE: Poor thing.

ZAUBERKÖNIG: I didn't get a bang out of it either. They had to remove her left breast. She was never really healthy, but, of course, her parents didn't tell me that. But when I look at you by comparison: stately—regal, actually. A regal figure.

VALERIE [*does a few bends to touch her toes*]: What do you men know about the tragedy of women? If we didn't spend half our time fixing ourselves up and taking care of our appearance—

ZAUBERKÖNIG [*interrupting her*]: You think I don't have to take care of my appearance?

VALERIE: Yes, of course. But with men you look for inner qualities first. [*She does a set of eurythmics.* ZAUBERKÖNIG *watches her and begins doing knee bends.*] Oh, God, I'm exhausted. [*She throws herself down next to him.*]

ZAUBERKÖNIG: The dying swan. [*He sits down beside her.*]

[*Silence.*]

VALERIE: Mind if I lay my head in your lap?

ZAUBERKÖNIG: There are no sins in Eden.

VALERIE [*does so*]: The earth's still hard—it was a long winter. [*Silence. Then softly.*] When the sun shines on me like this, I just get—oh, I don't know—

ZAUBERKÖNIG: Get what?

[*Silence.*]

VALERIE: You were playing with my corset awhile ago—I saw you.

[*Silence.*]

ZAUBERKÖNIG: So?

VALERIE: So? [ZAUBERKÖNIG *suddenly throws himself on top of her and kisses her.*] My God, what are you doing—I never expected such a thing of you—you terrible man, you—

ZAUBERKÖNIG: *Am* I terrible? *Am* I terrible?

VALERIE: Yes—no, you! Stop, someone's coming! [*They roll apart.*]

ERICH [*enters dressed in a swim suit and carrying an air gun*]: Excuse me, Uncle. You don't mind if I do some shooting, do you?

ZAUBERKÖNIG: Do what?

ERICH: Shooting.

ZAUBERKÖNIG: Shooting? Here?

ERICH: At the target on that beech tree over there. The monthly shooting match of our student cadet corps is the day after tomorrow, and I thought I'd get in a little practice. All right?

VALERIE: Of course.

ZAUBERKÖNIG: Of course? [*To* VALERIE.] Of course! [*He gets up.*] The cadet corps! Of course! You certainly mustn't forget how to shoot!—I'm going to cool off now. In our beautiful blue Danube. [*To himself.*] Hang yourselves, for all I care! [*He goes off.*]

[ERICH *loads his gun, aims and shoots.*]

VALERIE [*watches him, then, after the third shot*]: Excuse me, I don't mean to molest you—but what are you studying exactly?

ERICH: Law. Third semester. [*He aims.*] Industrial law. [*He shoots.*]

VALERIE: Industrial law. Isn't it boring?

ERICH [*loads*]: I'm planning on becoming a—[*aiming*]—corporation lawyer.

[*He shoots.*]

VALERIE: What do you think of our Vienna?

ERICH: I love the Baroque.

VALERIE: And our Viennese sweet young things?

ERICH: As a matter of fact, I don't get on too well with young girls. I was engaged once and became bitterly disillusioned, because Kathy was too young to bring any understanding to the problems relating to my ego. You're barking up the wrong tree when you get involved with young girls. I like the more mature woman who can bring something to a relationship. [*He shoots.*]

VALERIE: Where do you live?

ERICH: I think I'll be moving soon.

VALERIE: I have a furnished room.

ERICH: Cheap?

VALERIE: Depends—[*He shoots.*] So, Mr. Corporation Lawyer—how about giving me a shot?

ERICH: My pleasure.

VALERIE: Mine, I assure you. [*Taking the gun from him.*] Were you in the war?

ERICH: Unfortunately, no. I was born in 1911.

VALERIE: 1911—[*She takes a long time aiming.*]

ERICH [*giving the commands*]: Ready! Aim! Fire! [VALERIE *doesn't shoot—but lets the gun sink slowly and looks intensely at him.*] What is it?

VALERIE [*suddenly doubles over, whimpering*]: I have these pains.—My poor kidneys—

[*Silence.*]

ERICH: Can I help you?

VALERIE: Thank you.—It's over now. It happens when I get excited—we must pay for our little pleasures. But now I can't see where I'm aiming—

ERICH [*confused*]: Where you're aiming?

VALERIE: It's gotten so dark—[*She embraces him, and he doesn't fight it. They kiss.*]

VALERIE: Getting what you aim for is always worth the effort. A person with no aim in life isn't human.—Oh, you—you—you—Mr. Nineteen-hundred-and eleven—

4

By the Beautiful Blue Danube

[*The sun has now gone down, it's already growing dark, and in the distance the portable phonograph is playing Johann Strauss's waltz* The Voices of Spring. ALFRED *is in a bathrobe and straw hat—he is looking dreamily toward the other bank.* MARIANNE *climbs out of the beautiful blue Danube and notices* ALFRED. *Silence.* ALFRED *lifts his hat.*]

ALFRED: I knew you'd come out of the water here.

MARIANNE: How did you know?

ALFRED: I knew.

[*Silence.*]

MARIANNE: The Danube's soft as velvet.
ALFRED: Velvet.
MARIANNE: Today I'd like to be somewhere far away.—You could even sleep out in the open tonight.
ALFRED: Easily.
MARIANNE: I feel sorry for us—we're so civilized. What's happened to our real nature?
ALFRED: We've turned our real nature into a straitjacket. No one's allowed to do what they want to do.
MARIANNE: And no one wants to do what they're allowed to do.

[*Silence.*]

ALFRED: And no one's allowed to do what they're able to do.
MARIANNE: And no one's able to do what they ought to do—
[ALFRED *embraces her elaborately and she offers no resistance. A long kiss. She catches her breath.*] I knew it, I knew it—
ALFRED: Me, too.
MARIANNE: Do you love me like you should—?
ALFRED: I feel like I do. Come, let's sit down.

[*They sit. Silence.*]

MARIANNE: I'm just glad you're not stupid—I'm surrounded by them—everywhere—stupid people. Even papa's nothing to write home about—sometimes I think he uses me to get even with my poor mother. She was very strong willed.
ALFRED: You think too much.
MARIANNE: I feel good now. I feel like singing. I always want to sing when I'm sad. [*She hums, then stops.*] Why don't you say something?

[*Silence.*]

ALFRED: Do you love me?
MARIANNE: Very much.
ALFRED: Like you should? I mean, do you love me sensibly?
MARIANNE: Sensibly?

ALFRED: I mean, you won't do anything rash—because I couldn't take the responsibility.

MARIANNE: You worry too much—stop worrying, look at the stars—they'll still be up there when we're deep under the earth.

ALFRED: I'm going to be cremated.

MARIANNE: Me, too.—Oh, you—you—you—[*Silence.*]—you— you entered my life like a bolt of lightning and split me in two. I know now for certain.

ALFRED: What?

MARIANNE: That I won't marry him.

ALFRED: Marianne!

MARIANNE: What's the matter?

[*Silence.*]

ALFRED: I don't have any money.

MARIANNE: Why must you talk about that now!

ALFRED: Because I don't have a choice. I've never, never in my life destroyed someone else's engagement. On principle. Falling in love, yes, but making two people split up because of it—No, I don't have the moral right for that. It's a matter of principle.

[*Silence.*]

MARIANNE: I was right, you *are* a sensitive person. I feel doubly close to you now. I'm just not right for Oskar and that's that.

[*It has meanwhile grown dark, and fireworks are being set off nearby.*]

ALFRED: Fireworks. For your engagement.

MARIANNE: For *our* engagement.

ALFRED: And Bengal lights.

MARIANNE: Blue, green, yellow, red—

ALFRED: They'll be looking for you.

MARIANNE: Let them find us—just stay with me, you're an angel from heaven—my guardian angel.

[*Bengal lights—blue, green, yellow, red—illuminate* ALFRED *and* MARIANNE *and* ZAUBERKÖNIG *who stands close in front of them with his hand on his heart.* MARIANNE *stifles a scream. Silence.* ALFRED *goes to* ZAUBERKÖNIG.]

ALFRED: Herr Zauberkönig—

ZAUBERKÖNIG [*interrupting him*]: Be quiet! No need to explain, I heard it all.—So, some scandal we've got here! And on your engagement day—! Laying around naked! Nice kettle of fish, this! Marianne! Get dressed! What if Oskar comes! Jesus, Mary and Joseph help us!

ALFRED: I'll naturally take the consequences, if need be.

ZAUBERKÖNIG: There will be no consequences! All you have to do, my man, is raise a cloud of dust in your wake. This engagement will not be broken, even for *moral* reasons. Just make sure nobody gets wind of it, you—you good-for-nothing! On your word of honor!

ALFRED: My word of honor.

MARIANNE: No!

ZAUBERKÖNIG [*stifling his anger*]: Stop howling! Are you ready? Get dressed! On the double! Slut!

OSKAR [*appears and surveys the situation*]: Marianne! Marianne!

ZAUBERKÖNIG: Holy Mother of God!

[*Silence.*]

ALFRED: Your fiancée's just come out from swimming.

MARIANNE: Don't lie! Just don't lie! No, I *wasn't* swimming, and I don't *want* to swim! I won't be tyrannized by you any longer. The slave is breaking her chains—there! [*She throws the engagement ring in* OSKAR's *face.*] I'm not going to let my life be ruined! It's *my* life! God sent this man to me at the last moment.—No, I won't marry you, I won't marry you, I won't marry you! And for all I care, the toy shop can go up in smoke, and the sooner the better!

ZAUBERKÖNIG: My only child! I'll remember that!

[*Silence. During* MARIANNE's *tantrum the other picnickeres have appeared and are listening with malicious interest.* OSKAR *walks up to* MARIANNE.]

OSKAR: Marianne, I hope you never have to go through what I'm going through now. And I'm going to continue loving you, you're not escaping me—and thank you for everything. [*He goes off.*]

[*Silence.*]

ZAUBERKÖNIG [*to* ALFRED]: Who do you think you are anyway?

ALFRED: Me?

VALERIE: Nothing. He's a nothing.

ZAUBERKÖNIG: A nothing. On top of everything else. And I don't have a daughter any more. [*He goes off with the picnickers.*]

[ALFRED *and* MARIANNE *remain behind alone. The moon is shining.*]

ALFRED: Please forgive me. [MARIANNE *gives him her hand.*] I mean, for not wanting you just now. It was because I felt responsible. I don't deserve your love, I can't offer you any sort of existence, I'm not even a man—

MARIANNE: Nothing can shake me now. Let me make a man of you. You make me feel so big and important—

ALFRED: And you lift me up. Spiritually I feel like nothing compared to you.

MARIANNE: And you, you lift me out of myself. I see myself fade away. Don't you see, I'm so far away now—so far from myself—way over there—I can hardly see myself any more.—I want to have your child—

THE END OF THE FIRST PART

PART 2

1

[*Back again in the quiet street of Vienna 8, in front of* OSKAR'*s butcher's shop, the dolls' hospital and* VALERIE'*s tobacco shop. The sun is shining as before and even the schoolgirl on the second floor is still playing Johann Strauss's* Tales from the Vienna Woods. HAVLITSCHEK *stands in the doorway of the butcher's shop demolishing a sausage.* EMMA, *a girl poised for any eventuality, stands beside him; she holds a shopping bag and listens to the music.*]

EMMA: Herr Havlitschek—

HAVLITSCHEK: Can I help you?

EMMA: Music's such a nice thing, don't you think?

HAVLITSCHEK: Oh, I can think of something even nicer, Fräulein Emma. [EMMA *hums along softly with the waltz tune.*] But that would take a little doing on your part, Fräulein Emma.

EMMA: Looks to me like you're some kind of Casanova, Herr Havlitschek.

HAVLITSCHEK: You can call me Ladislaus if you want.

[*Pause.*]

EMMA: Last night I had a dream about your Herr Oskar.

HAVLITSCHEK: That the best you can do?

EMMA: Herr Oskar always has such big melancholy eyes—it almost hurts when he looks at a person—

HAVLITSCHEK: Blame it on love.

EMMA: How do you mean?

HAVLITSCHEK: What I mean is, he fell in love with some cheap little bag of goods who dumped him about a year ago, and then she runs off with another cheap bag of goods.

EMMA: And he still loves her? That's nice.

HAVLITSCHEK: Nice? That's stupid.

EMMA: But a grand passion is so romantic—

HAVLITSCHEK: It's sick, if you ask me. Look at him—torturing himself. Can't even look at another woman, and he's worth a bundle—he could have any woman he wants. But no. He sets his mind on the little bitch, and, by God, nothing else'll do. How the hell does he handle it?

EMMA: How do you mean, Herr Havlitschek?

HAVLITSCHEK: What I mean is, what does he do for exercise?

EMMA: Oh, you awful man.

[*Pause.*]

HAVLITSCHEK: Fräulein Emma. I got a day off tomorrow. I'll be at the number 68 bus terminal.

EMMA: I can't make it before three.

HAVLITSCHEK: No problem.

[*Pause.*]

EMMA: Half past three, then—and don't forget your promise to be a good little boy—nothing naughty—Ladislaus—[*She goes off.*]

HAVLITSCHEK [*follows her with his eyes and spits out the sausage skin*]: Stupid bitch, stupid—

OSKAR [*steps out of the butcher's shop*]: Remember we still have to stick the pig today. You do it, I'm not in the mood.

[*Pause.*]

HAVLITSCHEK: Excuse me, Herr Oskar—but do you mind if I tell you what I think?

OSKAR: About the pig?

HAVLITSCHEK: More or less.—Look, Herr Oskar, don't take it so much to heart, I mean your former fiancée. Women are cheap as dirt. Even a cripple can get a woman—a guy with the clap even. And where it really counts, women are all the same, believe me! I'm only trying to help. Women got no souls, it's all meat. And don't treat them like they're made out of china—big mistake. Best thing's a good right to the jaw now and then.

[*Pause.*]

OSKAR: Women are a riddle, Havlitschek. Like the Sphinx. I've taken Marianne's handwriting around to a number of graphologists. The first one said it was the handwriting of a vampire, the second that she'd make a good friend, and the third that she's the housewife personified. An angel.

2

Furnished Room in Vienna 8

[*The cheapest possible. Around seven o'clock in the morning. AL-FRED is still in bed, smoking cigarettes. MARIANNE is brushing her teeth. An old baby carriage stands in the corner; diapers on a clothes line. It's a gray day and the light is dim.*]

MARIANNE [*gargling*]: You once said I was an angel and I told you I wasn't—just an ordinary person with no ambitions. But you're so calculating.

ALFRED: You know perfectly well I'm not calculating.

MARIANNE: You are. [*She fixes her hair.*] I need to get my hair cut.

ALFRED: Me, too. [*Silence.*] Why are you getting up so early?

MARIANNE: I can't sleep.

[*Silence.*]

ALFRED: Aren't you happy?

MARIANNE: Are you?

[*They stare at each other.*]

ALFRED: Who was it who ruined racing for me? For one whole year I haven't spoken to a bookie, not to mention a tipster—I might as well throw in the towel. New seasons, new favorites—two-year-olds, three-year-olds—a whole new generation I don't even know. And why? Because I work my butt off trying to sell a skin cream that nobody buys because it stinks.

MARIANNE: People haven't got the money.

ALFRED: That's right, find excuses.

MARIANNE: I'm not blaming you, you can't help it.

ALFRED: That's big of you.

MARIANNE: I mean, there isn't much I can do about the economic crisis.

ALFRED: You're so egocentric.—Who was it put the idea in my head to run around selling cosmetics? You! [*He rises.*] Where are my suspenders?

MARIANNE [*points at a chair*]: There.

ALFRED: No.

MARIANNE: On the night table, then.

ALFRED: No.

MARIANNE: Then I don't know.

ALFRED: But you're *supposed* to know.

MARIANNE: You're just like papa.

ALFRED: Don't compare me with that old idiot!

MARIANNE: Not so loud! If you wake the baby, I'll go out of my mind.

[*Silence.*]

ALFRED: And that's another thing—something's got to be done about that baby. The three of us can't just sit here in this hole rotting away. The baby will have to go.

MARIANNE: The baby stays here.

ALFRED: The baby has to go.

MARIANNE: No. Never!

[*Silence.*]

ALFRED: Where are my suspenders?
MARIANNE [*looking at him wide-eyed*]: Do you know what the date is today?
ALFRED: No.
MARIANNE: It's the twelfth.

[*Silence.*]

ALFRED: What are you trying to say?
MARIANNE: It's an anniversary. A year ago today, I saw you for the first time. In our display window.
ALFRED: Will you please not always talk in hieroglyphics. We're not Egyptians. What display window?
MARIANNE: I was just arranging the skeleton and you knocked on the window. And I let down the blind because I was suddenly scared.
ALFRED: Right.
MARIANNE: I was alone a lot—[*She weeps softly.*]
ALFRED: Are you going to start blubbering again?—Look, Marianne, I understand you a hundred percent, your motherly feelings, and all that, but it's for our child's sake that we get him out of this gray, damp, dismal hole-in-the-wall. I mean, out at my mother's in the Wachau it's bright and sunny.
MARIANNE: That's true.
ALFRED: All right, then.

[*Silence.*]

MARIANNE: Our lives are a matter of fate—[*She suddenly stares hard at* ALFRED.] What did you just say?
ALFRED: What?
MARIANNE: You said, stupid cow.
ALFRED: What!
MARIANNE: Don't lie! [ALFRED *brushes his teeth and gargles.*] Why are you always insulting me?

[*Silence.*]

ALFRED [*soaps up his face in preparation for shaving*]: My dear child—there is one thing that I hate from the depths of my soul, and that is stupidity. And there are times when you are penetratingly stupid. I just don't understand why you're so stupid. There's no need for you to be so stupid.

[*Silence.*]

MARIANNE: Once you said that I lifted you up—spiritually.
ALFRED: I never said that. I could never have said that. And if I did, I was wrong.
MARIANNE: Alfred!
ALFRED: Not so loud! The baby.
MARIANNE: I'm so afraid, Alfred.
ALFRED: It's all in your imagination.
MARIANNE: Have you really forgotten everything, then—
ALFRED: Shit!

3

Small Cafe in Vienna 2

[FERDINAND VON HIERLINGER *is playing billiards against himself.* ALFRED *enters.*]

HIERLINGER: Alfred! Hello! Nice to see you again.—Why the long face?
ALFRED: Oh—nerves—
HIERLINGER: So, relax. Come on, how about a game—get your mind off things. [*He hands him a cue.*] Fifty, your break.
ALFRED: Good. [*He has a bad shot.*] Shit!
HIERLINGER [*takes his shot*]: I hear you're working in a bank again.
ALFRED: It's all I could get.
HIERLINGER: *Cherchez la femme!* When love begins to stir, your brains are at the other end of your anatomy.
ALFRED: My dear Ferdinand—it's not keeping a level head that's at stake, the organ concerned is otherwise located. [*He places his hand on his heart.*] There's a fairy tale by Andersen where a

wicked boy shoots a poor old poet right in the heart. Cupid, Ferdinand, the god Cupid.

HIERLINGER [*concentrates on his break*]: Why didn't he pull it out—

ALFRED: My problem is I'm a very softhearted person, and she appealed to my youthful idealism. At first there was a certain normal passion, of course, but then once the initial attraction faded, I began to feel sorry for her. She's the kind of girl a man could really get into mothering, though there are times she can be a regular little bitch. God, sometimes I think I'm infatuated with her.

HIERLINGER: Infatuation is in the blood. Something to do with the blood's heat.

ALFRED: Really?

HIERLINGER: No doubt about it. Your turn. Eleven. [ALFRED *takes his turn.*] Alfred—do you know what really knocked me for a loop? Having a baby in the middle of the Depression.

ALFRED: God knows, I never wanted a baby, that was all her doing—then all of a sudden there it was. I wanted to dump it, she throws a fit, so I force her into it. What a barrel of laughs that was, not to mention a waste, and it still cost a fortune. Life's a crock when you've got no choice. [MARIANNE *appears.* ALFRED *sees her and calls to her.*] Sit over there—I'm finishing my game.

[MARIANNE *sits at a table and thumbs through some fashion magazines. Silence.*]

HIERLINGER: That your lady?

ALFRED: Yes.

[*Silence.*]

HIERLINGER: So that's your lady. Funny. Here my good friend Alfred lives with a girl like that for over a year and I'm seeing her now for the first time.—I thought only the envious Turks kept their lovers locked away from their friends.

ALFRED: It's the other way around—she's kept *me* locked away from *my* friends—

HIERLINGER [*interrupting him*]: What's her name?

ALFRED: Marianne. [*Silence.*] So, what do you think?

HIERLINGER: I had another image of her.

ALFRED: What?

HIERLINGER: Maybe a little more—well endowed—

ALFRED: Well endowed?

HIERLINGER: Well, I mean—you get a picture of somebody in your head, who knows why—

[*Silence.*]

ALFRED: She's well endowed. More than you think.

[*Silence.*]

HIERLINGER: Shit, you really blew it when you broke up with that crazy tobacco-shop owner. You'd really be sitting pretty right now—not a worry in the world.

ALFRED: Fuck the past! Just get me out of the scrape I'm in now.

HIERLINGER: That won't be easy. I mean, you're not exactly lying in a bed of roses—financially speaking.

ALFRED: It's more like a bed of thorns, Ferdinand. A bed of thorns and nettles, just like poor old Job.

HIERLINGER: Where's the baby?

ALFRED: At my mother's. Out in the Wachau. Finally!

HIERLINGER: At least that's a start. The next thing is to get your Marianne set up so she's financially independent—some kind of profession. It's a well known fact that once a woman's entered a profession, any love relationship she's involved in will be gradually undermined, even marriage. That's the Church's main argument against women taking jobs, it destroys the family. Those cardinals aren't exactly stupid, you know, they're the *créme de la créme*, they've got heads on their shoulders.

ALFRED: I know, I know. But Marianne wasn't trained for a profession. Her only interest is eurythmics.

HIERLINGER: Eurythmics! Great!

ALFRED: Really?

HIERLINGER: You bet!

ALFRED: I don't know, I just can't think any more.

HIERLINGER: Well, I mean, eurythmics is a kind of dancing, and that could be just what we're looking for. I know a baroness with international connections who puts together ballets and such things for elegant establishments—who knows? She also owes me a few favors.

ALFRED: I'd be eternally grateful—

HIERLINGER: Just being friends will do. Look, if I leave right now, I can catch the baroness at her bridge party. In which case, I'll see you, Alfred, just be so good as to settle the bill, keep your chin up, and you'll hear from me. It'll turn out. [*He goes off.*]

[ALFRED, *the cue still in his hand, slowly approaches* MARIANNE *and sits at her table.*]

MARIANNE: Who won?

ALFRED: I lost—because I'm lucky in love—[*He smiles, then suddenly stares at her neck.*] What's that?

MARIANNE: This? An amulet—for luck.

ALFRED: What kind?

MARIANNE: Saint Anthony.

ALFRED: Saint Anthony? Since when?

[*Silence.*]

MARIANNE: Since I was little—whenever I lost anything, I'd always say: Saint Anthony, help me!—And I'd find it again.

[*Silence.*]

ALFRED: Is it supposed to be symbolic?

MARIANNE: It was just—

[*Silence.*]

ALFRED: Personally I don't believe in an afterlife, but I do believe in a Higher Being, otherwise we wouldn't be here.—So—Saint Anthony—how about I bend your ear a minute with a few important facts.—

4

The Home of the Baroness with International Connections

[HELENE, *the blind sister of the baroness, sits in the salon improvising on the spinet.* FERDINAND VON HIERLINGER *and* MARIANNE *are led in by the* SERVANT. HELENE *interrupts her improvisation.*]

HELENE: Anna! Who's that?

SERVANT: Herr von Hierlinger and a young lady, ma'am. [*Goes off.*]

HIERLINGER: I'm delighted, Countess.

HELENE [*rises and gropes toward him*]: Oh, good afternoon, Herr von Hierlinger. I'm so happy to see you again—

HIERLINGER: The pleasure is mine, Countess. Is the baroness in?

HELENE: Yes, my sister's home, but just now she's busy with the plumber. The other day I stuffed something down the drain that I shouldn't have, and now everything's stopped up. Who've you brought with you, Herr von Hierlinger?

HIERLINGER: A young lady with a strong interest in eurythmics— I mentioned her to the baroness. May I introduce you—

HELENE [*interrupting him*]: Oh, very pleased to meet you, I'm sure! Unfortunately I can't see you, but you have a most sympathetic hand. So please leave me your hand for a moment, dear lady of the hand—

HIERLINGER: Countess Helene has an enormous talent for reading palms.

[*Silence.*]

MARIANNE: What sort of hand do I have?

HELENE [*still holding her hand tightly*]: It's not all that simple, my dear child, we blind must use our sense of touch to orient ourselves.—You have very little experience behind you, and much still ahead of you—

MARIANNE: Such as?

[*The* BARONESS, *wearing a cosmetic face mask, enters unnoticed and listens.*]

HELENE: I might almost say that this is the hand of a sensualist.— You also have a child, don't you?

MARIANNE: Yes.

HIERLINGER: Fantastic! Fantastic!

HELENE: Boy or girl?

MARIANNE: Boy.

[*Silence.*]

HELENE: Yes, that boy's going to bring you a lot of joy—he'll turn out quite all right—

MARIANNE [*smiles*]: Really?

BARONESS: Helene! What is this nonsense! You're not a gypsy! Try not stopping up the lavatory instead. My God, the mess you've caused! Imagine you reading palms! A bit of a paradox, I'd say! [*She removes her face-mask.*]

HELENE: Oh, I have my premonitions.

BARONESS: Unfortunately you had no premonitions about the lavatory! This mess you've made is costing me another five shillings! Just remember, you're living off of me, not me off of you! [*Silence.*] Well—my dear Hierlinger.—I assume this is the young lady you telephoned me about the day before yesterday.

HIERLINGER: Right. [*Softly.*] And just remember—one good turn deserves another.

BARONESS [*threatens him playfully with her forefinger*]: Do I smell blackmail?

HIERLINGER: None of your pointing at me now, it's rude to point.

BARONESS: Ah, a man of honor! [*She leaves him with a poisonous look and walks over to* MARIANNE, *regarding her from all sides.*] Hm. So, Fräulein, I hear you have a strong interest in eurythmics?

MARIANNE: Yes.

BARONESS: And would like to find some practical use for it?

MARIANNE: Yes.

BARONESS: Do you sing?

MARIANNE: Sing?

BARONESS: I operate on the principle that there's no such thing as can't. Anything's possible as long as there's determination. The dance groups I assemble are international attractions for first-class establishments. So you can't sing?

MARIANNE: Unfortunately—

BARONESS: Didn't you learn to sing in school?

MARIANNE: Oh, yes.

BARONESS: Well, then! All I want to hear is your voice. You must know some Viennese songs—you are from Vienna, I take it— some folk song or other—

MARIANNE: "The Song of the Wachau"?

BARONESS: Yes, of course. Let's hear it. "The Song of the Wachau."

MARIANNE [*sings while* HELENE *accompanies her at the spinet*].

There once was a young man who strolled down the lane
As the shadows of evening lengthened the plain.
He was met by a smile and a pair of bright eyes
That he'll not forget till the day that he dies.
Her cheeks were like cherries, her eyes like the sun,
Her head was all golden, this radiant one.
The maid that he saw there he never forgot,
And along as he wandered he sang of his lot:
Out in the lovely Wachau
Where the Danube flows so blue,
From a window covered with vines
The face of my true love shines.
Her lips are red as blood,
Her kisses are so good,
Her eyes are violet-blue,
The girl out in the Wachau.

5

Out in the Wachau

[*The sun is shining here as before—only now a baby carriage stands in front of the house.*]

MOTHER [*to* ALFRED]: Little Leopold looks a lot like you—and doesn't cry much either. You were a nice baby, too.

ALFRED: I'm just glad he's not in Vienna right now. He'll do a lot better out here in the good air than in that hole-in-the-wall we live in.

MOTHER: Is Marianne with the ballet yet?

ALFRED: No, she starts next Saturday.

[*Silence.*]

MOTHER [*troubled*]: I remember you said if you had a child you'd get married. Do you still feel that way?

ALFRED: I remember you said I could make a good marriage.

[*Silence.*]

MOTHER: Naturally the relationship you're in now isn't a bed of roses.

ALFRED: Do you mind if I talk to Granny now?

MOTHER: I'll go tell her—I have to go down to the cellar again anyway. [*She goes off into the cottage.*]

[ALFRED *is alone: he bends over the baby carriage and looks at his child.*]

GRANDMOTHER [*enters from the cottage*]: Can I help the young gentleman?

ALFRED: Have you thought it over?

GRANDMOTHER: I don't have any money. As long as you live with that person, I don't have any money. You live with your whore like dogs in a kennel, bring bastards into the world and pawn them off to others to suffer with, and you haven't an ounce of shame coming to ask your old granny to lend you money. Not a penny! Not a penny!

ALFRED: And that's your last word?

GRANDMOTHER: Dogs in a kennel! Dogs in a kennel!

ALFRED: You old witch.

[*Silence.*]

GRANDMOTHER: What did you say? [ALFRED *is silent.*] I dare you to say it again.

ALFRED: I will.

GRANDMOTHER: Then say it.

ALFRED: Witch. Old witch.

[GRANDMOTHER *slowly approaches him and pinches him on the arm.*]

ALFRED [*smiling*]: And what was that supposed to be?

GRANDMOTHER [*pinching him*]: Just you wait, you'll feel it soon enough. There. There. There.

ALFRED [*shakes her off as he begins to feel something*]: People can hurt me all they want, just not frogs.

GRANDMOTHER [*weeping in a rage*]: Give me back my money, you lout! I want my money! Thief! Criminal! [ALFRED *laughs. Shrieking.*] Don't laugh! [*She gives him a knock with her walking stick.*]

ALFRED: Ow!

[*Silence.*]

GRANDMOTHER [*grins with satisfaction*]: Felt that, did you? You felt that?

ALFRED: Witch! You old witch! [GRANDMOTHER *raises her walking stick in triumph.*] Don't you dare!

GRANDMOTHER: You just watch out, you stupid boy, I can do anything I want to you—I can do anything I want to anybody.— Ayayay, there's another button hanging off there. How can you live with such a sloppy pig?

ALFRED [*interrupting her*]: She's not sloppy!

[*Silence.*]

GRANDMOTHER: Her mouth's too big.

ALFRED: It's a matter of taste.

GRANDMOTHER: Wait, I'll sew on your button. [*She sews it on.*] What do you need a wife for anyway, when your old granny'll sew your buttons on for you—not that you're worth it—running off with some beggar-woman, and then a child on top of it, a child!

ALFRED: It happens.

GRANDMOTHER: Try using your brains sometime.

ALFRED: I did. I almost wore them out, for God's sake. But it didn't work.

[*Silence.*]

GRANDMOTHER: You're stupid, Alfred, stupid.

ALFRED: Why?

GRANDMOTHER: Because you're always getting mixed up with women like that. [*Silence.*] Listen, Alfred—if you could manage to leave your sweet little Marianne, I could manage to lend you some money—

[*Silence.*]

ALFRED: How's that?

GRANDMOTHER: Didn't you understand me?

[*Silence.*]

ALFRED: How much?

GRANDMOTHER: You're still young and handsome—

ALFRED [*points at the baby carriage*]: And that there?

GRANDMOTHER: Don't think about that now. Just go away—

[*Silence.*]

ALFRED: Where?

GRANDMOTHER: To France. I read in the paper where things are going really well there.—If I were young, I'd take off for France without a thought—

6

And Back in the Quiet Street in Vienna 8

[*It is already late afternoon and the schoolgirl on the second floor is playing Johann Strauss's waltz* Voices of Spring. OSKAR *stands in the doorway of his butcher's shop, manicuring his nails with his pocket knife. The* CAPTAIN *enters from the left and nods to* OSKAR, *who bows.*]

CAPTAIN: I really must say, that blood-sausage yesterday was— first class. My compliments.

OSKAR: Not to say tender? Hm?

CAPTAIN: A poem. [*He approaches the tobacco shop.*]

[VALERIE *appears in the door of the shop. The* CAPTAIN *nods to her in greeting.* VALERIE *responds.*]

CAPTAIN: Might I have a look at the lottery results? [VALERIE *hands them to him from the rack by the door.*] You're too kind. [*He buries himself in the results and the waltz comes to a close.*]

[ZAUBERKÖNIG *accompanies the* LADY *out of the dolls' hospital.*]

LADY: I've bought tin soldiers here before. Last year, in fact. At the time, however, I was served by a very polite young woman.

ZAUBERKÖNIG [*surly*]: Possible.

LADY: Was she your daughter?

ZAUBERKÖNIG: Daughter? I have no daughter. I *never* had a daughter!

LADY: Pity. Then you won't order the box of tin soldiers for me?

ZAUBERKÖNIG: I thought I explained it inside. Too much paperwork. All for a box of tin soldiers! Buy the little tyke something similar. Like a nice trumpet!

LADY: I'm sorry. No. Good-bye. [*She leaves him in a huff and goes off.*]

ZAUBERKÖNIG: *Enchanté!* Drop dead! [*He goes off into the dolls' hospital.*]

VALERIE [*spitefully*]: Well, Captain, what have we won this time? [ERICH *enters from the tobacco shop.*] Stop right there! What have you got?

ERICH: Five Memphis.

VALERIE: What, again? He smokes like an adult!

[*The* CAPTAIN *and* OSKAR *are listening.*]

ERICH [*under his breath*]: If I don't smoke, I don't work. If I don't work, I'll never be a lawyer. And if I don't become a lawyer, I'll never be able to pay off my debts.

VALERIE: What debts?

ERICH: You know perfectly well. I'm very particular about these things, madam.

VALERIE: Particular? Are you trying to upset me again?

ERICH: Upset you? It's a point of honor. I pay off my debts to the last penny. If it takes me a hundred years! We do not allow ourselves to be compromised. It's a point of honor. And now I have to get to the college! [*He goes off.*]

VALERIE [*staring after him*]: Point of honor. Brute—

[*The* CAPTAIN *and* OSKAR *grin to themselves.*]

CAPTAIN [*spitefully, taking his revenge*]: And how are things otherwise, Frau Valerie?

ERICH [*suddenly reappears; to the* CAPTAIN]: Did I see you leering just now? Sir!

VALERIE [*nervously*]: Are you gentlemen acquainted?

CAPTAIN: By sight—

ERICH: You're Austrian, I believe. All bark and no bite.

VALERIE: Erich!

CAPTAIN: What did he say?

ERICH: I *said:* the Austrians were a spineless bunch of bastards in the war, and except for us Prussians—

CAPTAIN [*finishing his sentence*].—there'd have been no war!

ERICH: Aha! And what about Sarajevo? What about Bosnia-Herzegovina?

CAPTAIN: What do you know about the war, you young whippersnapper? What you were taught in school? Ha!

ERICH: Better than teaching old Jewish women to play bridge!

VALERIE: Erich!

CAPTAIN: Better than sucking the blood from old tobacco shop owners!

VALERIE: Captain!

CAPTAIN: I beg your pardon. That was a *faux pas*. A *lapsus linguae*—[*He kisses her hand.*]

CAPTAIN: Deplorable, simply deplorable. But this neophyte hasn't earned a penny in his whole life!

ERICH: Sir!

VALERIE: Oh, no, not a duel, for God's sake!

ERICH: I presume you're prepared to give satisfaction.

CAPTAIN: Go to court?

VALERIE: Jesus, Mary and Joseph!

ERICH: I *will not* be insulted!

CAPTAIN: No one insults me and gets away with it! Certainly not you!

VALERIE: Stop this! Please! This is a scandal—[*Goes off, sobbing, into her tobacco shop.*]

CAPTAIN: I *will not* be spoken of in this way by this *Prussian*! Where were your Hohenzollerns when our Habsburgs were already Holy Roman Emperors? Out there swinging in some tree!

ERICH: This has gone too far. [*He goes off.*]

CAPTAIN [*calling after him*]: Here's twenty groschen. Get a haircut, you cockatoo! [*Turning to go off left, he stops again in front of the butcher's shop; to* OSKAR.] By the way, I just remembered: You're slaughtering the pig today, aren't you?

OSKAR: Absolutely, Captain.

CAPTAIN: Save me a nice piece of kidney, hear?

OSKAR: Don't worry.

CAPTAIN: *Enchanté!*

[He goes off left, and from the second floor we again hear the schoolgirl begin to play, nothing less that the waltz Over the Waves. ALFRED strolls on from the left. OSKAR is about to return to his shop when he catches sight of ALFRED, who doesn't see him, and secretly observes him. ALFRED stops in front of the dolls' hospital, lost in reminiscence, then moves to the open door of the tobacco shop and stands looking in. Pause. ALFRED nods in greeting. Pause. VALERIE gradually appears in the doorway—and again the waltz breaks off suddenly in mid-phrase. Silence.]

ALFRED: Could I have five Memphis?
VALERIE: No.

[Silence.]

ALFRED: This is a tobacco shop, isn't it?
VALERIE: No.
ALFRED: I was just passing, by chance—
VALERIE: I see.
ALFRED: Yes—

[Silence.]

VALERIE: And how is the young gentleman today?
ALFRED: Oh, so-so.
VALERIE: And your young bride?
ALFRED: So-so, too.
VALERIE: I see.

[Silence.]

ALFRED: And you?
VALERIE: I have what I need.
ALFRED: Everything?
VALERIE: Everything. He's a law student.
ALFRED: The things they take for lawyers these days.
VALERIE: I beg your pardon?
ALFRED: Congratulations.

[Silence.]

VALERIE: Where's Marianne keeping herself?
ALFRED: I suspect I'm losing sight of her—

[*Silence.*]

VALERIE: You're really quite a bastard, aren't you? Not even your worst enemy would deny you that.

ALFRED: Valerie, he that is without sin, let him cast the first stone at me.

VALERIE: Are you sick?

ALFRED: No. Just tired. A bit overwhelmed. Not as young as I used to be.

VALERIE: Since when?

ALFRED: I'm off to France this evening. Nancy. I just might find something better suited to me, in forwarding perhaps. Staying here I'd have to sink too far below my standard.

VALERIE: And what about the horsies?

ALFRED: No idea! Besides, I don't have the capital—

[*Silence.*]

VALERIE: If I ever find the time, I'll feel sorry for you.

ALFRED: Would you like it if I were really down on my luck?

VALERIE: What are you saying, things are going rosy?

ALFRED: Is that what you'd like to hear? [*Silence.*] I was just— just passing by, by chance—melancholy nostalgia, I guess—for the old stamping grounds—[*He goes off and the waltz* Over the Waves *starts up once more.*]

VALERIE [*sees* OSKAR]: Herr Oskar! Guess who I've just been talking to.

OSKAR: I saw him.

VALERIE: Ah. They're in a bad way.

OSKAR: I heard.

[*Pause.*]

VALERIE: He's still proud as a Spaniard—

OSKAR: Pride cometh before a fall. Poor Marianne—

VALERIE: Looks to me like you could marry her now she's unattached again—

OSKAR: If only it wasn't for the child—

VALERIE: If anyone had done that to me—

OSKAR: I still love her—Maybe the child'll die—

VALERIE: Herr Oskar!

OSKAR: Who knows! The mills of God grind slowly, yet they grind exceeding well. I'll never forget my Marianne. I'll take on all her sufferings, for whom God loveth, He putteth to the test.—He censureth. He chastiseth. With fiery tongs and molten lead—

VALERIE [*shouting at him*]: Stop it! Stop it, please!

[OSKAR *smiles.* HAVLITSCHEK *enters from the butcher's shop.*]

HAVLITSCHEK: So, what do you say? Do I stick the pig today or not?

OSKAR: No, Havlitschek. I'll stick it myself today—I'll stick the pig—

[*The peal of bells.*]

7

In St. Stephen's Cathedral

[*In front of St. Anthony's side altar.* MARIANNE *is at confession. The bells fall silent and all is at peace.*]

CONFESSOR: All right, then, to recapitulate. You have inflicted upon your poor old father, who loves you more than anything and who has never wanted less for you than the best, the most grievous suffering, grief and anxiety, you've been disobedient and ungrateful—driven on by lust, you have abandoned an honest, upright fiancé in order to attach yourself to a degenerate—silence! That much we know! And you have been living in union with this wretched individual outside of the sacrament of Holy Matrimony for over a year, and in this monstrous state of mortal sin you have conceived and given birth to a child—when was that?

MARIANNE: Eight weeks ago.

CONFESSOR: Nor have you seen fit to have this child of sin and shame baptized.—All right, now, you tell me: what good do you expect to come of all this? Nothing! Never! But even that wasn't enough. You didn't shrink even from wanting to kill the child in your womb—

MARIANNE: No, it was him! It was only for him that I agreed to go through with it!

CONFESSOR: Only for him?

MARIANNE: He didn't want children, because times are getting worse, and who knows what'll happen—but I—no—it tears my heart apart, every time it looks at me, knowing I wanted to get rid of it—

[*Silence.*]

CONFESSOR: Does the child live with you?

MARIANNE: No.

CONFESSOR: Where, then?

MARIANNE: With relatives. Out in the Wachau.

CONFESSOR: Are they Godfearing people?

MARIANNE: I'm sure.

[*Silence.*]

CONFESSOR: You repent, then, wanting to kill it?

MARIANNE: Yes.

CONFESSOR: And living with that brute in sin out of wedlock?

[*Silence.*]

MARIANNE: I thought I'd found the man who would fulfill my life—

CONFESSOR: Do you repent it?

[*Silence.*]

MARIANNE: Yes.

CONFESSOR: And for having conceived and borne your child in a state of mortal sin—do you repent that?

[*Silence.*]

MARIANNE: No. You can't—

CONFESSOR: What are you saying?

MARIANNE: He's still my child—

CONFESSOR: But you—

MARIANNE [*interrupting him*]: No, I won't do that.—No, it frightens me to think that I could repent that.—No, I'm happy to have him, very happy—

[*Silence.*]

CONFESSOR: If you can't repent, then what do you want from the Lord?

MARIANNE: I thought He might have something to tell me—

CONFESSOR: You come to Him only when things go badly for you?

MARIANNE: When things go well, I know He's with me—but, no, He can't ask a thing like that, to repent my—it would be so against nature—

CONFESSOR: Go on, then, go! And before you appear before the Lord again, I suggest you come to terms with yourself. [*He makes the sign of the cross.*]

MARIANNE: Then I'm sorry.—

[*She rises from the confessional already dissolving into darkness, and the murmur of a litany is heard. Gradually the voice of the priest can be distinguished from the voices of the congregation.* MARIANNE *listens. The litany ends with the Lord's Prayer.* MARIANNE'S *lips move. Silence.*]

MARIANNE: Amen. [*Silence.*] Dear God, if you are there—what's to become of me, God?—Dear God, I was born in Vienna 8 and I went to elementary school there, I'm not a bad person—can you hear me?—what's to become of me, dear God?—

[*Silence.*]

THE END OF THE SECOND PART

PART 3

1

The New Wine Festival

[*Tavern with music and falling blossoms. The atmosphere is one of boozy high spirits—and, in the middle of it all,* ZAUBERKÖNIG, VALERIE *and* ERICH. *Everyone is singing.*]

ALL

> *Out in the lovely Wachau*
> *The Danube flows so blue,*
> *From a window covered with vines*
> *The face of my true love shines.*
> *Her lips are red as blood,*
> *Her kisses are so good,*
> *Her eyes are violet-blue,*
> *The girl out in the Wachau.*
>
> *There will be wine so fine,*
> *But none of it will be mine.*
> *And lovely girls to love,*
> *But we'll be dead, my love.*

[*For a moment everything becomes still as death in the tavern—then everyone begins singing three times as loud.*]

> *So off we go to Nussdorf now*
> *For games and happy sights*
> *And dance away the night,*
> *And hear the snappy yodelers crow*
> *And then at morning light*
> *Go stumbling home, go stumbling home!*

[*Great enthusiasm; applause. People are dancing between the tables to the tune of the* Radetzky March.*—By this time everyone is fairly tipsy.*]

ZAUBERKÖNIG: Bravo, bravissimo! I'm my old self again today! *Da capo! Da capo!* [*He grabs at the breasts of a* GIRL *dancing past. Her* BOYFRIEND *slaps his hand.*]

BOYFRIEND: Hands off the tits!

GIRL: They're *my* tits!

ZAUBERKÖNIG: Here a tit, there a tit! We all have our troubles, but today I'm leaving all mine behind! The world can go fuck itself!

ERICH: Listen! Everybody! I propose a toast—no, an extravagant toast, to the famous Viennese New Wine Festival! [*He spills his wine.*]

VALERIE: Easy there, boy! Jesus, he splashed it all over me!

ERICH: Accidents happen. Point of honor.

ZAUBERKÖNIG: Got you wet, did he? Poor little thing!

VALERIE: Soaked to the skin.

ZAUBERKÖNIG: All the way to the skin—

VALERIE: You lost your mind?!

ERICH: Attention! [*He clicks his heels and stands at attention.*]

ZAUBERKÖNIG: What's the matter with him?

VALERIE: I'm used to it by now. Once he's soused, he orders himself around right and left.

ZAUBERKÖNIG: How can he stand still so long?—Stiff! Stiff as a rod! Good for him! We're on our way up again. [*He collapses under the table.*]

VALERIE: Jesus!

ZAUBERKÖNIG: The chair's broken—waiter, another chair!! [*Singing along with the music.*] "Oh, I kissed her white shoulder, was all that I did—Then I felt the light tap of her fan on my cheek—"

[*A* WAITER *brings a gigantic portion of salami.*]

VALERIE: Salami, Erich! Salami!

ERICH: Company! Dismissed! [*He reaches into the bowl and begins stuffing himself at an exorbitant pace.*]

ZAUBERKÖNIG: Look at him shovel it down!

VALERIE: *Bon appétit!*

ZAUBERKÖNIG: Don't be so greedy!

VALERIE: One thing's sure, he's not paying!

ZAUBERKÖNIG: He can't sing either!

[*Pause.*]

VALERIE [*to* ERICH]: Why won't you sing?

ERICH [*his mouth stuffed*]: Because I've got a chronic sore throat.

VALERIE: From smoking too much!

ERICH [*yelling at her*]: There you go again!

CAPTAIN [*appears, a little paper hat on his head; he is in high spirits*]: Enchanté, my dear Frau Valerie! Goodness, what a pleasant surprise! Greetings, Herr Zauberkönig!

ZAUBERKÖNIG: Prost, Captain! Prost, my dear Captain! [*He empties his glass and falls into a melancholy stupor.*]

VALERIE: May I offer you some of my salami, Captain?

[ERICH *freezes in mid-chew and fixes the* CAPTAIN *with a hateful glance.*]

CAPTAIN: Too kind, *enchanté!* Thank you, but, no, I couldn't eat another—[*He stuffs two thick slices of salami into his mouth.*] I've had two dinners already this evening, I have a visitor—sitting over there with him. A childhood friend of my brother who disappeared in Siberia—an American.

VALERIE: Ah, a Mister, then!

CAPTAIN: Vienna-born, however. Been in the States for twenty years now, and only now returned to the continent. Driving through the Hofburg this morning, tears came to his eyes.—He's a self-made man. Quite independent.

VALERIE: Oh, aren't you the terrible one!

CAPTAIN: Yes. And just now I'm showing him his own Vienna—it's our second day—I doubt that we'll ever be sober again—

VALERIE: Still waters run deep.

CAPTAIN: Not only in America.

ERICH [*sharply*]: Is that so?

[*Pause.*]

VALERIE [*approaches* ERICH]: You behave—and shut your mouth or I'll clout you one.—If you can stuff your face with my salami, you can at least show me some consideration.

ERICH: A remark like that, dear madam, is a testimonial to your meanmindedness.

VALERIE: Stop right there!

ERICH: Attention! Company—

VALERIE: Halt!

ERICH: Company—march! [*He goes off.*]

VALERIE [*calling after him*]: To the rear—march! To the rear—march!

[*Deathly silence.*]

CAPTAIN: Who is that, anyway?

VALERIE [*tonelessly*]: He fancies himself an entire army. I'll be leaving him soon, flat out—I can see it coming—and he's a distant relation of—[*pointing at* ZAUBERKÖNIG] that one over there.

[*Music starts up once more.*]

CAPTAIN: *Apropos* relations.—Tell me, Frau Valerie, do you find the way His Majesty Herr Zauberkönig has been treating Fraü-

lein Marianne justified? I just don't understand. If I were a grandfather—well, I mean, anyone can make a mistake. But to let
things come to such a pass—

VALERIE: Do you know any further details, Captain?

CAPTAIN: I had a colonel's wife once—what I mean is, the whole
regiment had her—what am I trying to say?! She was the wife
of our colonel—and the colonel had an illegitimate child by a
girl from the variety theater, but the wife took the child in as
though it were her own flesh and blood—she was barren, you
see.—But compare that with the way old Zauberkönig over there
has behaved—well, what more can I say!

VALERIE: I don't understand, Captain. What had the colonel's wife
to do with Marianne?

CAPTAIN: None of us understand each other anymore, dear Frau
Valerie. Often we fail to understand ourselves.

VALERIE: But where is Marianne?

CAPTAIN [*smiling as if he had a secret*]: Don't worry, an official
announcement will be made about that—at the right moment.

[*The* AMERICAN *appears; he is drunk.*]

AMERICAN: Dear old friend! What's this, what's this? Company?
Friends? Introduce me?—Good old friend!—[*He embraces the*
CAPTAIN.]

ZAUBERKÖNIG [*waking from his stupor*]: Who's that?

CAPTAIN: My friend from America!

AMERICAN: America! New York! Chicago and Sing Sing!—But
that's only on the outside. On the inside beats the same old
honest and true and eternal—Viennese heart of gold—and the
Wachau—and the castles on the blue Danube.—[*He hums along
to the music.*] "Danube so blue, so blue, so blue"—[*Everyone
joins in humming, swaying in their seats.*] Ladies and gentlemen!
A lot of things've changed in recent times, storms and whirl-
winds, earthquakes and tornadoes, and I had to start at the very
bottom, but here I'm at home, here I know my way around, here
I'm happy, it's here I want to die! O Thou my dear old Austrian
Lord God of Mariazell! [*He sings.*]

> *My mother was a Viennese,*
> *It's why I love it so.*

And life's first gift, from her
Was the love that 'gan to stir
For you, golden Vienna of mine!

ALL [*singing*]:

Vienna, Vienna, you alone,
Vienna, the city I call my own,
City of dreams that all come true,
Vienna, I love you!

AMERICAN: Long live Vienna! Home! And beautiful Viennese women! And memories of home! Long live the Viennese, all of us, each of us, every one!

ALL: Three cheers for Vienna! Hurray! Hurray! Hurray! [*They all drink like fishes.*]

ZAUBERKÖNIG [*to* VALERIE]: And beautiful Viennese women, you magnificent creature—you're the one I should've married, what a different child I'd've had with you—

VALERIE: Enough about Irene. I could never stand her.

AMERICAN: Who's Irene?

ZAUBERKÖNIG: Irene was my wife.

AMERICAN: Oh, pardon me.

ZAUBERKÖNIG: No harm done. Why shouldn't I make a stink about Irene? Because she's dead? She screwed up my whole life.

VALERIE: You devil.

ZAUBERKÖNIG [*sings*]:

Oh, my old lady's dead,
It's why my heart's so sore.
A good old soul like her
I never will find more.
I cry and cry,
I wouldn't lie,
For my old pal,
When I think of my old gal. Olé!

AMERICAN [*jumping up*]: Olé! Olé! Unless I'm sorely mistaken, it's just now beginning to rain. But no weather'll come between us and our fun. Tonight's a night we take it easy even if it rains cats and dogs. Who the hell cares! [*Shaking a threatening finger*

at the sky.] Shame on you, old rainman in the sky! You're all
my guests tonight, each of you, every one!

ALL: Hurray! Hurray!

AMERICAN: Come on! Let's go! Follow me!

VALERIE: Where?

AMERICAN: Wherever! Any place with a ceiling! So we won't be
sitting in the open. The Moulin Bleu!

[*Hefty applause.*]

CAPTAIN: No, wait! Friends! Not the Moulin Bleu! Let's rather go
to Maxim's!

[*Another moment of deathly silence.*]

ZAUBERKÖNIG: Why Maxim's?

CAPTAIN: Because there's a whole bundle of surprises waiting for
us there.

ZAUBERKÖNIG: Surprises? Such as?

CAPTAIN: Something spicy. Something very spicy—

ZAUBERKÖNIG: Maxim's it is, then!

ALL: To Maxim's!

[*They march off to Maxim's with umbrellas raised.*]

ALL [*singing*]:

> Vindobona, you glorious city,
> With all of your gardens and walkways so pretty,
> We'll never forget you, wherever we are,
> You'll draw us toward you, no matter how far.
> Wherever we wander, you'll live in our dreams,
> Well never forget you, Vienna, it seems.
> Old Austria's pearl you always will be,
> No other city can match your beauty.
>
> Now Mitzi and her Jean
> Go strolling arm in arm,
> We're not a nun and monk,
> We're young and full of spunk,
> And we're out to get laid.
> We're off to "Master Braid's"

Or maybe to "Maxim's"
Where life is like a dream!

Let's down another jug of wine,
Hollodero!
It needn't be the last in line,
Hollodero!
And if it is, then we won't mind,
Hollodero!

We'll sing it again just one more time, we'll sing it just one more time!

[*Gong. The stage is transformed into "Maxim's"—a bar and private booths; in the rear there is a cabaret stage with a wide ramp.— They all close their umbrellas and sit at the tables in the most effusive of moods.*]

MASTER OF CEREMONIES [*steps in front of the curtain*]: Honored guests! Ladies and gentlemen! Charming ladies and even more charming gentlemen!
VALERIE: Aha!

[*Laughter.*]

MASTER OF CEREMONIES: In the name of the management I bid you a most hearty welcome! As that prince of poets, Johann Wolfgang von Goethe, says in his masterpiece, the immortal *Faust:* "What you have inherited from your fathers, earn it for yourself to truly possess it!" Which means, ladies and gentlemen, that you are expected to join in the songs. It's house tradition, ladies and gentlemen. I invite you now to join us on a stroll down memory lane!—

[*The orchestra begins playing Johann Strauss's waltz* Wiener Blut, *the curtain parts, and a number of girls in Old Vienna costumes dance the waltz. The curtain then closes and there is tremendous enthusiasm from the audience while the orchestra plays the* Hoch- und Deutschmeister March.]

ZAUBERKÖNIG [*to the* CAPTAIN]: What are you talking about? It's a rock-solid fact that we humans are descended from animals!

CAPTAIN: That's open to question.

ZAUBERKÖNIG: Or do you still believe in Adam and Eve?

CAPTAIN: Who knows!

AMERICAN [to VALERIE]: Wildcat!

ZAUBERKÖNIG: Wildcat! Or maybe a leopard!

VALERIE: Prost Zauberkönig!

ZAUBERKÖNIG: The captain's some fabulous beast, you've got something of the kangaroo about you, and the American here's a Japanese pug.

AMERICAN [not disposed to laughter]: You're a barrel of laughs yourself, a barrel of laughs!

ZAUBERKÖNIG: And what about me?!

VALERIE: A stag! You're an old stag! Prost, old stag!

[Roars of laughter. The table telephone rings. Silence.]

ZAUBERKÖNIG [into the receiver]: Hello? Yes?—What? Who's talking? Mousey?—Never heard of Mousey. What?—Aha, yes, I see, that's what I am, all right, your uncle.—I should what? Oh, you little scamp, you little piggie, you!—Where? At the bar? The green dress?—What's that? You're still a virgin? And you expect your old uncle to swallow that? Well, I'll just have to check that out, won't I?—Buss, buss!—[He hangs up and empties the glass of champagne the AMERICAN has ordered.]

VALERIE: Don't drink so much, Leopold.

ZAUBERKÖNIG: You can go jump in a lake! [He rises.] When you're old as I am, alcohol's all you got left. Where's the bar?

VALERIE: What bar?

ZAUBERKÖNIG: The bar, for Chrissake!

CAPTAIN: I'll show you—

ZAUBERKÖNIG: I'll find my own way—you think I need a goddamn guide? OK then, show me the way! [He allows the CAPTAIN to lead him to the bar where two GIRLS are waiting for him. The one in green gives him a hearty welcome. The CAPTAIN remains at the bar as well.]

AMERICAN [to VALERIE]: Who is he, anyway?

VALERIE: He's the King of Magic, the Zauberkönig.

AMERICAN: Oh.

VALERIE: Yes. Besides that, he's a rare old bird, modest, respectable, cut from the old cloth. It's a dying breed.

AMERICAN: Too bad.

VALERIE: Today, unfortunately, he happens to be sloshed—

AMERICAN: The way you said that. With what charm. Back in the States it's all so much more brutal.

VALERIE: What do you weigh?

AMERICAN: Two hundred eighteen pounds.

VALERIE: Oh, God!

AMERICAN: May I be frank with you?

VALERIE: Be my guest.

AMERICAN: I'm complicated.

VALERIE: I'm afraid I don't—

AMERICAN: What I mean is, I'm dead, inside. The only women I can get it on with are prostitutes—because of all the disappointments in my past.

VALERIE: Imagine that! Such a sensitive soul in such a powerful body—

AMERICAN: I was born under Saturn.

VALERIE: Ah, those stars! We're stuck with them, I guess, and there's nothing to be done.

[*Gong.*]

MASTER OF CEREMONIES [*steps in front of the curtain*]: Ladies and gentlemen! We have for you now, once again, a marvelous number. Why waste words? Decide for yourselves. I give you now, designed for us especially by the most world-renowned artists, our sensational, highly artistic *tableaux vivants!*

[*The orchestra plays the waltz* On the Beautiful Blue Danube *and the scene blacks out. The curtains are then opened to reveal three half-naked girls with legs concealed in tail fins.—One of them holds a lyre, while all are picturesquely grouped in front of a black curtain lit by green spotlights.*]

ZAUBERKÖNIG'S VOICE [*from the bar*]: Naked women! About time!

[*The curtain is closed. Loud applause. Gong. The* MASTER OF CEREMONIES *appears in front of the curtain.*]

MASTER OF CEREMONIES: The second tableau: the Zeppelin!

[*The* Fridericus Rex *is now played and three naked girls are discovered standing on the stage. The first holds a propeller in her hands, the second a globe, and the third a model zeppelin. The audience goes wild, jumps from its seats and sings the first verse of* "Deutschland Über Alles," *after which things calm down.*]

MASTER OF CEREMONIES [*again appears in front of the curtain*]: And now, ladies and gentlemen, for the third tableau: "The Search for Happiness." [*Deathly silence.*] Maestro, if you please—

[*Schumann's* Träumerei *is taken up by the orchestra and the curtain opens for the third time—a group of naked girls are seen trampling each other in the attempt to run down a golden globe on which Happiness is seen standing on one foot.—Happiness is as naked as the rest and is named* MARIANNE. VALERIE *cries out shrilly in the dark auditorium.*]

VALERIE: Marianne! Jesus, Mary and Joseph! Marianne!

[MARIANNE *is startled and unable to maintain her balance on the globe, wobbles, steps down, and stares, blinded by the spotlights, into the dark auditorium.*]

AMERICAN: What's going on?!
VALERIE [*beside herself*]: Marianne, Marianne, Marianne!
AMERICAN [*growing furious*]: Will you stop screaming! Are you batty?!
VALERIE: Marianne!
AMERICAN: Shut up! I'll give you Marianne! [*He punches her in the breast.* VALERIE *screams. Pandemonium breaks loose.*]
VOICES [*shouting*]: Lights! Lights!
MASTER OF CEREMONIES [*rushes onto the stage*]: Curtain! What's going on here?! Lights! Curtain! Lights!

[*The curtain falls in front of* MARIANNE *who is still staring into the auditorium—the other girls have already departed the stage in alarm. The house lights come up now and once again, for only a moment, a deathly silence reigns. Everyone is staring at* VALERIE, *who, her head on the table, hysterical and drunk, is weeping and sobbing.* ZAUBERKÖNIG *stands at the bar, his hand on his heart.*]

VALERIE [*whimpering*]: Marianne—Marianne—dear little Marianne—oh, oh, oh—I've known her since she was five years old!

MASTER OF CEREMONIES: Who's she talking about?

AMERICAN: Got me.

MASTER OF CEREMONIES: Hysterical?

AMERICAN: Epileptic.

A FRIENDLY VOICE: Throw her out, the drunken sot!

VALERIE: I'm *not* drunk! That I certainly am not! I'm not, I'm not, I'm not! [*She jumps up with the intention of running out, but stumbles over her own feet, falls, and knocks over a table, cutting herself.*] No, I can't stand it, I'm not some piece of wood, I'm still full of life—I can't stand it, I can't stand it! [*She runs out bawling.*]

[*Everyone, except for* ZAUBERKÖNIG, *watches her go, perplexed. Silence, then a gong.*]

MASTER OF CEREMONIES [*jumps up onto a chair*]: Honored guests! Ladies and gentlemen! The official part of our program has just concluded—the unofficial part will now commence in the bar! [*Dance music strikes up in the bar.*] On behalf of the management, I thank you for turning out in such numbers and wish you a very pleasant evening!

[*The clientele gradually vacates the premises.*]

ZAUBERKÖNIG: Captain—

CAPTAIN: Yes?

ZAUBERKÖNIG: So this is why you wanted to come here and not the Moulin Bleu.—This was the spicy surprise you promised. I had a funny feeling when you said it—a suspicion nothing good would come of it—

CAPTAIN: I knew that Fräulein Marianne was appearing here— I've been here quite often—I was here yesterday—and I can't any longer be just a spectator! You and your heart of stone—

ZAUBERKÖNIG: Don't interfere in family affairs that you know nothing about, soldier!

CAPTAIN: I was doing what any human—

ZAUBERKÖNIG [*interrupting him*]: What's that?

CAPTAIN: You're not human!

ZAUBERKÖNIG: Well, isn't that just fine! Isn't that just—what am I then if I'm not human, *you?!* A cow?! That'd suit you just fine! But I'm *not* a cow and I also don't have a daughter!! Understand?!

CAPTAIN: Well, I guess there's nothing more I can do here. [*He bows stiffly and goes out.*]

ZAUBERKÖNIG: And what am I supposed to do here? Bastard! I think, Mr. American, I've come to the end of my rope. I think I'll write some picture postcards so everybody turns green with envy when they hear what a great time I'm having.

AMERICAN: Picture postcards! Splendid idea! What an idea! Picture postcards, picture postcards! [*He purchases a whole pile of cards from a salesgirl, sits at a table at some distance, and writes. He is now alone with* ZAUBERKÖNIG. *Dance music is heard from the bar.* MARIANNE, *in a bathrobe, enters slowly and stops in front of* ZAUBERKÖNIG. *He stares at her, looking her up and down—then turns his back on her. Pause.*]

MARIANNE: Why didn't you read my letters? I wrote you three of them. But you sent them back Unopened. [*Pause.*] I wrote you that he'd walked out on me—

ZAUBERKÖNIG [*turns slowly toward her and stares at her with hatred*]: I know that. [*He again turns his back on her.*]

[*Pause.*]

MARIANNE: Do you also know I have a child—?

ZAUBERKÖNIG: Naturally!

[*Pause.*]

MARIANNE: Things are going really badly for us, little Leopold and me—

ZAUBERKÖNIG: What? Leopold?! *I'm* Leopold! This is the limit! Naming your shame after me! On top of everything else! This is the end! You never listened, so now you just have to live with it! The end! [*He rises but has to sit down again.*]

MARIANNE: Papa, you're drunk—

ZAUBERKÖNIG: Don't be vulgar! And once and for all, I'm not your papa! And don't be vulgar, or I'll—[*He gestures as if to box her ear.*] Better you think of your mother! The dead hear everything!

MARIANNE: If my mother was still alive—

ZAUBERKÖNIG: You leave your mother out of this, you hear me? If she'd seen you like that, naked up on that stage—for everybody to look at—Have you no more shame? Jesus!

MARIANNE: No, I can't afford shame. [*Silence. The music in the bar has come to an end.*] I earn two schillings here a day. It isn't much, considering there's little Leopold.—But what else can I do? You never let me learn anything, not even eurythmics, you raised me only to get married—

ZAUBERKÖNIG: You miserable creature! So now you're blaming me!

MARIANNE: Listen to me, Papa—

ZAUBERKÖNIG [*interrupting her*]: I am not your papa!

MARIANNE [*pounds the table with her fist*]: Shut up! You *are* my papa! Who else would be? Listen to me now! If this goes on much longer, I won't be able to earn a thing—and I can't walk the streets, I can't, I've tried it, God knows, but I can't give myself to a man that I don't love with all my heart—as an uneducated woman it's all I have to offer—there's only the train left now.

ZAUBERKÖNIG: What train?

MARIANNE: The train. The train people travel on. I'll throw myself in front of it—

ZAUBERKÖNIG: I see. This too, now. You'll do this to me too, now—[*He bursts into tears.*] Filthy bitch, what are you doing to me in my old age? One disgrace after another—I'm a poor old man, how have I deserved this?!

MARIANNE [*sharply*]: All you ever think about is yourself!

ZAUBERKÖNIG [*stops crying, stares at her, and goes into a rage*]: All right then, throw yourself in front of the train! Go on! Do it! But take the brat with you!!—I'm not well—I'm not— I wish I could be sick—[*He bends over the table, then quickly straightens up.*] You'd do better to think about God, about our dear Lord God in Heaven—[*He staggers off.*]

MARIANNE [*watches him leave, then looks upward toward heaven; quietly*]: In heaven—

[*Dance music is heard again coming from the bar. The* AMERICAN *has now finished writing his postcards and notices* MARIANNE, *still looking up toward heaven.*]

AMERICAN: Ah, a chippy—[*He watches her, smiling.*] Say, um—you wouldn't have any stamps, would you?

MARIANNE: No.

AMERICAN [*slowly*]: What I need are ten twenty-groschen stamps that I'll pay fifty schillings for. [*Pause.*] Sixty schillings. [*Pause. Takes out his wallet.*] I've got schillings and dollars in here—

MARIANNE: Let me see. [*The* AMERICAN *hands her his wallet. Pause.*] Sixty?

AMERICAN: Sixty-five.

MARIANNE: That's a lot of money.

AMERICAN: It'll be earned.

[*Silence. The dance music has stopped again.*]

MARIANNE: No. Thank you.

AMERICAN: What's that supposed to mean?

MARIANNE: I can't. You've made a mistake, sir—

AMERICAN [*suddenly grabs her by the wrist and bellows*]: Stop! Stop, you stole my wallet, you bitch, you thief, you criminal, open your hand, open up!

MARIANNE: Ow!

AMERICAN: There! A hundred schillings! You thought I wouldn't notice, you stupid whore!? [*He slaps her on the ear.*] Police! Police!!

[*Everyone appears from the bar.*]

MASTER OF CEREMONIES: For Chrissake, what's the matter now?!

AMERICAN: This whore stole my wallet! A hundred schillings, a hundred schillings! Police!

MARIANNE [*tears herself away from the* AMERICAN]: Don't you hit me again! I won't be hit by you again!

[*The* BARONESS *appears.* MARIANNE *cries out in terror.*]

2

Out in the Wachau

[ALFRED *is sitting with his* GRANDMOTHER *in front of the cottage in the evening sun—baby carriage not far off.*]

GRANDMOTHER: I always knew you for a liar, but in my wildest dreams I never thought you were such a shit! You borrow three hundred schillings from me to go work for some forwarding business in France—and you come back three weeks later, confessing you never set foot in France, and you gambled it all away at the races! You'll end up the same place as that fine Marianne of yours! In jail!

ALFRED: In the first place, she's not in jail, she's in custody, and her trial comes up tomorrow—besides, it was only attempted theft, no one suffered any harm, and there were mitigating circumstances—she's sure to get a suspended sentence because of no previous convictions—

GRANDMOTHER: That's right, stick up for her, stick up for her.— You certainly made a fool out of me, I always knew you were a criminal.

ALFRED: You won't forgive me, then?

GRANDMOTHER: Go to hell!

[ALFRED *sticks his tongue out at her and bleats like a goat and* GRANDMOTHER *does the same at him. Silence.* ALFRED *rises.*]

ALFRED: You won't be seeing me around here anytime soon.

GRANDMOTHER: And the three hundred schillings? And the hundred and fifty from the year before?!

ALFRED: I don't care if you have a fit, but I still feel to a certain extent responsible for what's happened to Marianne—

[GRANDMOTHER *gasps for air.* ALFRED *raises his straw hat.*]
ALFRED: *Enchanté*, Granny! [*He goes off.*]

GRANDMOTHER [*beside herself with rage*]: I don't want to see you again! Dirty fucker! To talk to me like that! Go on! Get out of here! You shit! [*She sits down at the table on which her zither lies and tunes it.*]

MOTHER [*enters from the cottage*]: Has Alfred left already?

GRANDMOTHER: Thank God!

MOTHER: He didn't even say goodbye to me—

GRANDMOTHER: That's some fine son you've got there—cocky as he is lazy! Like father like son!

MOTHER: Let my husband be! Dead and gone ten years now, and still you won't let him be!

GRANDMOTHER: And what brought him to his grave so soon? Me? Ha? Or his precious alcohol?—He boozed away your entire dowry.

MOTHER: I won't hear anymore of this, I won't!

GRANDMOTHER: —Shut up! [*She plays* The Double Eagle March *on her zither.*]

MOTHER [*bends anxiously over the baby carriage and* GRAND-MOTHER *ends the march*]: I'm worried about little Leopold—first he was coughing so badly, and now his little cheeks are all red and he doesn't look like himself—that's how it started with poor little Ludwig—

GRANDMOTHER: The Lord giveth and the Lord taketh away.

MOTHER: Mama!

GRANDMOTHER: His mother's in jail and his father's a lazy bum. Better if he wasn't around any more—for a lot of people!

MOTHER: How would *you* like not to be around any more?

GRANDMOTHER [*shrieking*]: Don't you compare me with that *thing* there! [*Pointing at the baby carriage.*] My parents were a decent sort! [*Furious, she plays a minuet.*]

MOTHER: Will you *not play!*

GRANDMOTHER [*interrupting her playing*]: Why are you screaming like that?! Lost your mind?! [*They fix each other with a stare. Silence.*]

MOTHER [*frightened*]: Mama—I saw—

GRANDMOTHER: What?

MOTHER: What you did last night—

[*Silence.*]

GRANDMOTHER [*cautiously*]: And what did I do?

MOTHER: You opened both windows and pushed little Leopold's crib into the draft—

GRANDMOTHER [*shrieking*]: You dreamt it! You dreamt it!

MOTHER: No, I didn't dream it. You can deny it all you want!

3

And Back Once More in the Quiet Street of Vienna 8

[*The* CAPTAIN *is still reading the list of lottery results and* VALERIE *is standing in the doorway to her tobacco shop. In general everything appears the same as always, except that on the window of the dolls' hospital there is a sign that reads* CLEARANCE SALE.]

VALERIE [*maliciously*]: And so what have we won, then, Captain?

CAPTAIN [*hands the list back to her*]: It's Saturday, Frau Valerie. And tomorrow is Sunday.

VALERIE: Yes, well, that's life, Captain, it's the way it is.

CAPTAIN: Clearance sale! My conscience is clear, but even so. My reasons for being at Maxim's that day were entirely altruistic— It was a reconciliation I was after, a reconciliation and all that came of it was one tragedy after another. Poor Marianne, locked up and sentenced—

VALERIE [*interrupting him*]: A suspended sentence, Captain! A suspended sentence!

[*Silence.*]

CAPTAIN: Is he really still angry with me, Herr Zauberkönig?

VALERIE. About what?

CAPTAIN: Well, you know, the nasty situation I got him into at Maxim's.

VALERIE: Oh, now, Captain! After all that man's been through, the least thing he wants is to be angry with you—besides, he's become much more forgiving, he's a broken man. When he learned the other day that his beloved Marianne was a thief, he almost had a stroke!

CAPTAIN: A heart attack is nothing to joke about.

VALERIE: He heard the music of the spheres.

CAPTAIN: What do you mean, music of the spheres?

VALERIE: When a person's on the verge of dying, his poor soul begins to leave his body—only half the soul, of course—and it flies higher and higher, and there's a strange melody up there, and that's the music of the spheres—

[*Silence.*]

CAPTAIN: Possible. In and of itself—

[*The schoolgirl on the second floor begins playing a Johann Strauss waltz.*]

VALERIE: Can you keep a secret, Captain?

CAPTAIN: Of course!

VALERIE: Word of honor?

CAPTAIN: Imagine an old officer like me not keeping a secret! I mean, just consider all the military secrets I know!

[*Pause.*]

VALERIE: Captain. She came to see me.

CAPTAIN: Who.

VALERIE: Marianne. Yes, Marianne. She came to look me up. After four weeks in custody all she had left was her pride—and she still had that! Had it, that is, until I ripped it right out of her! Right out! You can count on me, Captain, I'll get her and her papa back together again, all right, we women understand these things a lot better than men. What you tried at Maxim's was far too direct—my God, what a fright it gave me!

CAPTAIN: All's well that ends well.

[ERICH *enters quickly from the right, on his way to the dolls' hospital, but catches sight of the* CAPTAIN *and fixes him with a stare. The schoolgirl breaks off the waltz in mid-phrase. The* CAPTAIN *looks at* ERICH *with utter disregard, then bows politely to* VALERIE *and goes off passing very close to* ERICH, *who stares after him with a lowering look, then looks at* VALERIE, *who starts into her tobacco shop.*]

ERICH: No, wait! Excuse me, dear lady. I merely wanted to bring to your attention that most likely we will not be seeing each other again—

VALERIE: I certainly hope not!

ERICH: I'll be leaving first thing in the morning—for good.

VALERIE: *Bon voyage!*

ERICH: Thank you. [*He bows formally and is about to go off into the dolls' hospital.*]

VALERIE [*suddenly*]: Halt!

ERICH: As you were!

[*Silence.*]

VALERIE: This is no way to say good-bye.—Come, let's shake hands—we'll part as good friends—

ERICH: Fine. [*He shakes hands with her, then takes a notebook from his pocket and leafs through it.*] I have it all here in black and white. Debit and credit—every cigarette.

VALERIE [*genially*]: I don't need your cigarettes—

ERICH: It's a point of honor!

VALERIE [*takes his hand holding the notebook and strokes it*]: You're just not a psychologist, Erich—[*She gives him a friendly nod of the head and goes slowly off into the tobacco shop.*]

[*The schoolgirl begins to play again.*]

ERICH [*looks after* VALERIE, *and is now alone*]: Fifty-year-old rotting piece of shit—[*He goes off into the dolls' hospital.*]

OSKAR [*enters with* ALFRED *from the butcher's shop*]: Well, in any case, thank you kindly for coming to see me—and for being so understanding in regard to Marianne.

ALFRED: All right, then, agreed. I give up all claims on her—for ever. [*He catches sight of the sign on the window of the dolls' hospital.*] What? Clearance sale?

OSKAR [*smiles*]: Yes, that, too, my friend.—Soon all the magic around here will have played itself out; which is to say, if he doesn't come to terms with our Marianne, there's no way the old man can keep the business going on his own—

ALFRED: How sad it all is. Believe me, I'm really not at fault in all that's happened—I think about it, and I just don't understand, I had it so good in the old days, no troubles, no worries—and then, without thinking, to fall headlong into an adventure like that—but I deserve whatever I got—God knows what got into me!

OSKAR: I'd say it was love, true love.

ALFRED: Oh, no. I don't have the talent for that.—I was too gentle-hearted. I just can't say no, and when that happens a relationship automatically goes from bad to worse. The fact is, at the time I really had no intention of breaking up your engagement—but for Marianne it was all or nothing. You understand?

OSKAR: Of course. It's only an illusion that men play the active role and women the passive—when you really consider the matter, that is—

ALFRED: The abyss is opening.

OSKAR: I mean, that's why I was never really angry with you personally—I never wished you anything bad—whereas Marianne [*he smiles*]. No question, she's had to pay a bitter price, poor thing—for the great passion of her life—

ALFRED: To bring so many people to misfortune! I really think we men ought to stick together more.

OSKAR: We're just too naïve.

ALFRED: No question about it. [*The schoolgirl's playing breaks off again.*] Herr Oskar. I really don't know how to thank you for offering to get me and Valerie back together again—

OSKAR [*interrupting him*]: Ssh!

[ZAUBERKÖNIG *enters with* ERICH *from the dolls' hospital—neither of them noticing either* ALFRED *or* OSKAR *who withdraw into the doorway of the butcher's shop.*]

ZAUBERKÖNIG: I'll say it again, have a good trip, Erich! Stay well and have a safe trip to Dessau!

ERICH: Kassel, Uncle!

ZAUBERKÖNIG: Kassel, Dessau—I'm always mixing them up. And don't forget our Vienna and your poor old uncle!

[ERICH *clicks his heels together once more, bows stiffly and goes off without looking back.* ZAUBERKÖNIG, *moved, watches him as he leaves—then catches sight of* VALERIE, *who, upon hearing* ERICH's *voice, appears once more in her doorway to listen.*]

ZAUBERKÖNIG: A real winner, that one! Mm?

[*The schoolgirl begins to play again.* VALERIE *nods slowly in agreement.* ZAUBERKÖNIG *takes a newspaper from the stand in front of the tobacco shop and leafs through it.*]

ZAUBERKÖNIG: Yes, yes, Europe's going to have to unite, because when the next war comes we'll all be wiped out—but how are we expected to put up with all this?! What do those Czechs think they're doing? Take my word for it: another war's on the way, and soon! No two ways about it! There'll always be wars.

VALERIE [*still elsewhere*]: True enough. But that would mean the end of our civilization.

ZAUBERKÖNIG: Civilization or no civilization—war is a law of nature. It's no different from competition in business. Personally, I haven't got any competition, because I'm in a specialty trade.

And still I'm going to rack and ruin. I just can't manage it any more alone, every customer that comes in makes me nervous.— In the old days, I still had my wife, and when she started getting sick, Marianne was old enough to—

VALERIE: How old?

ZAUBERKÖNIG: Old enough!

[*Pause.*]

VALERIE: If I were a grandfather—

ZAUBERKÖNIG [*interrupting her*]: I am *not* a grandfather, if you don't mind! [*He grabs at his heart and the waltz breaks off.*] Just don't get me excited! Ow, my heart—

[*Silence.*]

VALERIE: Does it hurt?

ZAUBERKÖNIG: Like a bastard—you know what the doctor said— I could have a heart attack just like that—

VALERIE: I remember that from my husband, rest his soul.—Stabbing pains, is it?

ZAUBERKÖNIG: Stabbing pains—yes—

[*Silence.*]

VALERIE: Leopold. God has given you a sign—a sign that you're still alive.—So just calm down. Don't excite yourself, don't excite yourself—or you'll have a heart attack, a heart attack, and then—then—well, you should learn to forgive, you old goat— learn to forgive, and you'll be getting back to business, and things'll get better and better and better!

[*Silence.*]

ZAUBERKÖNIG: Think so?

VALERIE: All right, now, look—Marianne's not a bad person, she's just stupid—a stupid, silly little woman—

ZAUBERKÖNIG: She's stupid, all right. Stupid as a pig in shit!

VALERIE: And she got the notion to change the world to suit herself—but the world works according to reason, right, Grandpa?

ZAUBERKÖNIG: Grandpa?

VALERIE: Yes.

[*Silence. The schoolgirl resumes playing.* ZAUBERKÖNIG *leaves* VALERIE *standing there and turns toward the dolls' hospital—stops in front of the show window and looks at the clearance sale sign. He then gives* VALERIE *a friendly nod, tears the sign from the window and disappears into his dolls' hospital.* VALERIE *grins with satisfaction and lights a cigarette.*]

OSKAR: Frau Valerie! I've got a surprise for you!
VALERIE: A surprise?
OSKAR: Someone wants to make up with you.
VALERIE: Who? Erich?
OSKAR: No.
VALERIE: Who, then?
OSKAR: Over there—

[VALERIE *approaches the butcher's shop and sees* ALFRED. ALFRED *bows. Pause.*]

VALERIE: Oh!

[*The music stops again.*]

ALFRED: You'll never know the inner struggle this has cost me—this trek to Canossa.—I'm not ashamed any more, because I know the wrongs I've done you.
VALERIE: Me?
ALFRED: Yes.
VALERIE: But when? [ALFRED *is perplexed.*] You've done me no wrong.
ALFRED [*even more perplexed, smiles in embarrassment*]: Well, I mean, I—I did leave you—
VALERIE: Leave me? You? I left *you!* Besides, there was nothing wrong in that, it was a good thing, very good in fact; remember that, you conceited monkey!
ALFRED: Still, we *did* part as good friends, understood?
VALERIE: We're two people who *parted*—understood?! I want nothing to do, now or ever, with a total bastard!

[*Silence.*]

ALFRED: Total bastard? You just said yourself that I did you no wrong!

VALERIE: Not me! Marianne! And your baby!

[*Silence.*]

ALFRED: Marianne always said I had the power to hypnotize— [*He shouts at her.*] How can I help it if I have such a powerful effect on women?!

VALERIE: Don't shout at me!

OSKAR: It seems to me, Herr Alfred was relatively good to Marianne—

VALERIE: You men are always coming to each others' rescue! Well, believe me, I have *my* share of women's solidarity, too! [*To AL-FRED.*] I'd like to see you cut down to size, just cut down to size!

[*Silence.*]

ALFRED: I'm a stricken man. You needn't tell me twice that I'm bad, I know that, because when it comes right down to it, I'm weak. I always need someone I can look after, it's a necessity, without it I'm a goner. But with Marianne, I just couldn't do it, look after her, I mean—it was just bad luck on my part.—Of course, if I'd still had some capital, I'd've bet on the races again, even if she disapproved—

VALERIE: Disapproved?

ALFRED: On moral grounds.

VALERIE: That certainly was stupid of her, it's the one thing you do well.

ALFRED: That's it! A different way of seeing things—it's why it broke up finally—our relationship. All by itself.

VALERIE: Don't lie to me.

[*Silence.*]

ALFRED: Valerie. I sold skin cream, I sold fountain pens and oriental carpets—it was a total catastrophe, and now I'm stuck in a really god-awful mess. In the past you were always so understanding of other people's bloody messes—

VALERIE [*interrupting him*]: How was France?

ALFRED: About the same as here.

VALERIE: And how are the French girls?

ALFRED: The same as all of them. Ungrateful.

VALERIE [*smiling*]: You bastard. What would you do if I loaned you fifty schillings?

[*Silence.*]

ALFRED: Fifty??
VALERIE: Yes.
ALFRED: I'd immediately send it off to Maisons-Laffitte, of course, and lay bets on both sides—
VALERIE [*interrupting him*]: And so? What then?
ALFRED: How's that?
VALERIE: The winnings?

[*Silence.*]

ALFRED [*with a cunning smile*]: My presumed winnings I'd deliver tomorrow personally to my little son—
VALERIE: We'll see—! We'll see!

[MARIANNE *enters quickly in a fright.*]

OSKAR: Marianne!
VALERIE: My, my! [MARIANNE *stares at one after the other of them and is about to rush off.*] Wait! Don't leave! It's time we got this mess cleared up—it's spring cleaning time! The time has come to forgive and forget, and *basta!*

[*Silence.*]

OSKAR: Marianne. I'm happy to forgive everything you've done to me—because loving brings greater happiness than being loved.—If you have so much as a spark of feeling in you, then you must know at this moment that, despite everything, I'd lead you to the altar, if you were still free, that is—what I mean is, the baby—

[*Silence.*]

MARIANNE: What are you saying?
OSKAR [*smiles*]: I'm sorry.
MARIANNE: About what?
OSKAR: The baby—

[*Silence.*]

MARIANNE: Let's leave the baby out of this.—What has the baby ever done to you? And don't look at me so stupid!
VALERIE: Marianne! This is a reconciliation.
MARIANNE [*pointing at* ALFRED]: But not with him!
VALERIE: Him, too. All or nothing. After all, he's only human.

ALFRED: Thank you.

MARIANNE: But yesterday you called him a common beast.

VALERIE: That was then, and this is now, and you'd do well to mind your own business.

ALFRED: He alone who loves change will be my friend.

OSKAR: [*to* MARIANNE]:

> *If in your heart ye have not love*
> *For death and resurrection,*
> *Ye will never look above*
> *The earth's dank putrefaction!*

MARIANNE [*grins*]: Goodness, how educated—

OSKAR: It's just a saying off a calendar.

VALERIE: Saying or no saying, he's only human, with all the failings and vices that go along with it.—You failed to give him the kind of inner support he needed.

MARIANNE: I did the best I could!

VALERIE: It's just that you're too young.

[*Silence.*]

ALFRED: What it comes down to is I was no angel myself.

VALERIE: What it comes down to is that, in a relationship like yours, no one's at fault. But what it really comes down to is, it's all in the stars, the way people are attracted to one each other and all that.

MARIANNE: But they threw me in jail. [*Silence.*] They humiliated me something awful.

OSKAR: You shouldn't expect the police to wear kid gloves.

VALERIE: Were they at least women officers?.

MARIANNE: Some.

VALERIE: Well, then! [*Silence.*] Dear, dear Marianne. Be good now and go on in there quietly—[*She points to the dolls' hospital.*]

MARIANNE: And?

VALERIE: Just go—

MARIANNE: Only if you take responsibility—

VALERIE: I take responsibility—

[*Silence.* MARIANNE *turns slowly toward the dolls' hospital, places her hand on the doorknob, and turns once again toward* VALERIE, ALFRED, *and* OSKAR.]

Marieluise Fleisser

Purgatory in Ingolstadt

Characters

BEROTTER

OLGA

CLEMENTINE } HIS CHILDREN

CHRISTIAN

ROELLE

ROELLE'S MOTHER

HERMIONE SEITZ

CRUSIUS

PEPS

GERVASIUS

PROTASIUS

1. ALTER BOY

2. ALTAR BOY

STUDENTS

SCENE 1

Living room of the BEROTTERS. BEROTTER, OLGA, CLEMENTINE. CLEMENTINE *calls in from backstage.*

CLEMENTINE: Where's that key to the linen closet? Everything always gets misplaced around here.

BEROTTER (*to* OLGA): Can't you tell her?

CLEMENTINE: I have to get these beds made.

BEROTTER (*to* OLGA): You want Hermione Seitz to lie in an unmade bed?

OLGA: On top of the bureau.

BEROTTER: Did you take something without asking again? How often do I have to tell you that's not permitted around here?

OLGA: Clementine never gets me things.

CLEMENTINE (*enters*): I always have to yell first. Olga, your blouse is dirty again.

OLGA: You never get me anything new.

CLEMENTINE: What's Hermione going to think?

OLGA: If it were up to me, she doesn't have to come at all.

BEROTTER: Mrs. Seitz is in the hospital. Where is she supposed to go?

OLGA: You don't know Hermione.

BEROTTER: In the convent she was your friend.

CLEMENTINE: She always ate your rice soup which you didn't like.

OLGA: Mother wouldn't have liked to see her coming to our house.

CLEMENTINE: Look who's talking about Mother!

BEROTTER: I can't do that to Mrs. Seitz.

OLGA: And you like seeing Mrs. Seitz.

BEROTTER: I am not going to argue with you. What a blessing you are to your father. (*to* CLEMENTINE, *about* OLGA) She knows Latin. She wants to impress me.

CLEMENTINE (*about* OLGA): She didn't even cry at the funeral.

BEROTTER: Wants to have a say around here.

CLEMENTINE: And she didn't go to church today either.

BEROTTER: You didn't go to church? You're setting a nice example. Some older sister!

OLGA: In church the evil enemy circles around the confessional.

CLEMENTINE: That's your bad conscience.

BEROTTER: I never know if I should make you go. I don't want to hear about your mortifications. You always exaggerate.

CLEMENTINE: If only we didn't have you!

OLGA: That's what you tell me every day.

BEROTTER: I'd like to know why you're coming home at all after school. (*to* CLEMENTINE, *about* OLGA) She never goes near the kitchen.

OLGA: And you never take me to a restaurant.

BEROTTER: You don't know how to talk.

OLGA: That has something to do with you. You wouldn't let me grow up like a human being.

BEROTTER: I never favored one child over another.

OLGA: You didn't like my face—a child notices that kind of thing. You always told me I hold my head all twisted.

BEROTTER: You didn't get your meanness from your mother.

CHRISTIAN (*enters*): Hello.

BEROTTER: You don't throw your school bag like that. Pick it up and put it down properly.

CHRISTIAN: Don't worry, the writing tablet's not in there.

BEROTTER: Are you getting fresh with me?

CLEMENTINE: He got that from Olga.

CHRISTIAN: Roelle really can annoy me.

OLGA: What about Roelle?

CHRISTIAN: Is there something between you and Roelle?

OLGA: That was a long time ago.

CHRISTIAN: I always say you can make that up about any girl. I know my Olga.

OLGA: He stinks. He is afraid of water.

CHRISTIAN: He says he knows something about you, and, if he wants to, he'll report you to the police.

OLGA: Boys always think they can force you.

CHRISTIAN: He wants to come here when he has the time.

OLGA: All talk!

CLEMENTINE: Olga interrupted me. Now your collar's not ready.

CHRISTIAN: Convent dummy!

CLEMENTINE: Listen to that. He would never insult his Olga.

CHRISTIAN: Your Roelle keeps telling everyone how Hermione Seitz lost her petticoat in the middle of Regent's Square.

CLEMENTINE: My Roelle doesn't say that.

BEROTTER: Olga, you shouldn't treat young Roelle like that.—You passed him as if he were air, although he said hello to you.

OLGA: He has a neck like a worm.

CLEMENTINE: Well, he wears such tight collars.

BEROTTER: Poor thing. His face was flaming red. Now if I know someone takes an interest in me. You'll suffer someday, you are harsh.

OLGA: When we were children, he wanted something dirty.

CLEMENTINE: He never wanted anything dirty from you. Olga always claims everybody for herself.

BEROTTER: He's human, after all. The nuns must have taught you to be so well mannered. You aren't that dainty otherwise.

CLEMENTINE: Our Olga is too good for us.

CHRISTIAN: You shouldn't scold her because of Roelle. Roelle is a coward. No one likes to be around him. He doesn't want to smoke with all the others so he won't get sick. He doesn't dare go in the water.

CLEMENTINE: Of course, you have to help your Olga. Now I want to say something: What about that dog?

CHRISTIAN: It wasn't her fault.

CLEMENTINE: Someone put pins in his eyes.

OLGA: Not me.

CLEMENTINE: He kept tripping from one side to the other. And you watched.

BEROTTER: What kind of person are you?

OLGA: They chased him in front of my window. That's no way to act. It made them feel so strong.

BEROTTER: Who did the chasing?

OLGA: Let me go.

CLEMENTINE: He might haunt you someday.

OLGA: It was the little brown one, with the soft ears. (*to* CLEMENTINE) You always tell lies. Whenever she's near you, she seems to be a different person.

CLEMENTINE: You think Olga loves you. Olga has no heart.

CHRISTIAN: She is not like you.

CLEMENTINE: So take your Olga.

BEROTTER: Don't get your neck all twisted again. Do they have to fight because of you? Don't annoy me with that look.

CLEMENTINE: She'll keep haunting us.

BEROTTER: What happened with the dog? Did you watch?

OLGA: You want to beat me?

BEROTTER: When was the last time I beat you?

OLGA: That was a long time ago. And I know what a relief it is for you.

BEROTTER: Don't make me sin against my blessed Anna.

OLGA: Go on, beat me, and you'll beat my mother in me.

BEROTTER: I can't do it. Listen to me when I talk to you, flesh of my Anna. (*He falls down.*) Look at me lie here: It is he who was so harsh with his Anna. The children must know.

CLEMENTINE: I can see she is getting away with it again.

BEROTTER: You're no angel either.

OLGA: Am I right?

BEROTTER: You are right. Everyone is always right. Only I am not right.

CHRISTIAN: Don't embarrass yourself in front of your children.

BEROTTER (*to all his children*): You shouldn't always leave your father out. I want to know why we don't have anything to say to each other.

OLGA: I can't always show it.

BEROTTER: Now that's my good girl. If only Anna were here.

CLEMENTINE: Do you like Olga better than me?

BEROTTER: You must have a lot of time to waste. Here you stand. What about Christian's collar? Does he have to ask for it again?

CLEMENTINE: That's all I am good for.

BEROTTER: You know what you have to do.

CLEMENTINE: Olga doesn't have to do anything.

BEROTTER: She doesn't feel well.

CLEMENTINE: What kind of illness could that be?

BEROTTER: You be quiet.

CLEMENTINE: I know you all hate me. Everybody hates me.

BEROTTER: Now she's starting too!

CLEMENTINE: They always want to gag my mouth. Mother looks down on me. She sees how you treat her child.

OLGA: You really believe that?

CLEMENTINE: She's my mother.

OLGA: I didn't want to do anything bad. She mustn't think that of me.

CLEMENTINE: You ran away from her when she was dead.

OLGA: Could you let her know that. . . .

CLEMENTINE: She won't help you. Mother looks straight into the heart.

OLGA: I didn't want to kill it. It's not human yet. That's what they told me. So it won't be hurt. The catechism teacher says they go to another place.

CLEMENTINE: You're scared.

OLGA: I didn't steal a soul from heaven. It had no soul. It was too small for one.

CLEMENTINE: You won't get to heaven. You'll have to burn in hell, and I'll be lying in Abraham's bosom.

OLGA: And you won't even know me.

CLEMENTINE: I won't hear you scream. The distance'll be too great.

OLGA: It's your child. That's how the pious are.

CLEMENTINE: What is it that you are?

OLGA: Keep hitting my head against it. That's what never ends.

CHRISTIAN: You want to be someone else?

OLGA: I wouldn't like that either. I can't ever know for sure.

CLEMENTINE: Roelle is here. He is coming up the stairs.

BEROTTER: Stop jumping around in front of my face. He didn't come for you.

CLEMENTINE (*to* OLGA): You want to take him away from me too?

OLGA: Did I say I want him?

ROELLE (*enters*): Greetings everybody.

CHRISTIAN: Politeness personified. Why don't you turn right around.

BEROTTER: Christian, please. Let him come in first. Why don't you keep an eye on our oldest, young man? She is so unpredictable. It must come from chlorosis. She felt sick today.

ROELLE: Yes, of course. I, for my part, am more than willing.

CLEMENTINE: Here I see a beautiful young man bright and early in the morning.

BEROTTER: You come along, Clementine. Young man, you behave yourself now. (*exits with* CLEMENTINE)

CHRISTIAN: Sissy! In front of an adult he shows a completely different side.

ROELLE: You'll never understand the subtleties of dealing with people.

CHRISTIAN: Olga doesn't want you.

ROELLE: Let her tell me herself. Get out of the way. (*He pushes him aside.*)

CHRISTIAN: Wimp!

ROELLE: There's my signature! (*He hits him.*) My father sells snuff. That's the kind of father I have.

OLGA: I never said that.

ROELLE: In front of the Lutheran church. You said I stink.

OLGA: I was a child then.

ROELLE: It's an import business.

CHRISTIAN: He never produces a bill. He just shows his yellow face.

ROELLE: We don't stink. I want you to say that.

OLGA: You'll have to wait a long time.

CHRISTIAN: You just dare to come over here. I'll show you my grip. Open your collar so nothing restrains you!

ROELLE: My dear lady, let me give you an overview of the situation. You look at me; you don't see a dog with his tail between his legs. You don't see a creature filled with fear. But what do I see when I turn to you? Before my inner eye you stand there like a bundle of misery.

OLGA: Something irritating must've gotten in your eyes.

ROELLE: I won't blush over someone like you. You are a real beauty. Good thing I know. It's time to spread the news.

OLGA: What can you do to me?

ROELLE: I know from Mrs. Schnepf. It's not bad for me. It's only bad for you.

OLGA: I don't know the woman. I was never in her house.

ROELLE: You were seen.

OLGA: I don't understand.

ROELLE: Maybe you thought Mrs. Schnepf would keep quiet for you. The woman doesn't have to be afraid of anything.

OLGA: I don't even know what you're talking about.

ROELLE: She doesn't do it anymore. That's what she told my mother. It's against the law. She's fed up with it. And then she went on about who had asked her to do something like that. A talk between women, straight and plain—you should take a closer look at the people you deal with.

OLGA: You—monster!

ROELLE: So, what are we going to do now? Can't you guess? Come here. Just one more tiny step. (OLGA *moves unconsciously toward him.*) Now tell me what you've learned.

OLGA: You are running an import business that doesn't stink.

CHRISTIAN: Olga! You let him do this to you?

ROELLE: Your sister doesn't want you.

OLGA: Christian, where's your courage?

CHRISTIAN: Congratulations—to that bloated neck! (*He exits.*)

ROELLE: May you be miserable through me. That's what I begged on bloody knees. Now you are paralyzed.

OLGA: You are wearing such tight collars. I want to look up to you again.

ROELLE: That's nice. I'm much obliged to you. Could it be you feel remorse? Are you beginning to see? Someone told me I stink, my flame, so to speak—perhaps it was you. I won't talk about my feelings. You went swimming, and the others came along. I saw you from afar, me, the fellow who stinks. But it was Horn who followed you, and he said, "Has she got legs." You didn't even bother to slip your stockings back on at night. And Horn wasn't any older than I. But I stood at the wall as if my skin was different from the others.

OLGA: You had bad thoughts in your head.

ROELLE: I had brought a matchbox, and I waited until you'd pass. I held it in my hand. My neck was bloated. I thought, in a minute I'll set her skirt on fire. You should have said, "Man, you're so pale." "Horn," you said, "don't go with him." And I was disgusted with myself.

OLGA: I had no idea.

ROELLE: Today no skirt'll be set on fire. The moon crosses the window. From my room I can see the light in yours. But it doesn't matter that I stink. It won't kill me—not from someone like you. There is vengeance. With your permission I'll light one now. It calms me down.

OLGA: Do you know how to smoke?

ROELLE: I always did. (*He smokes.*)

OLGA: I want to walk arm in arm with you, in front of the whole town.

ROELLE: I don't want to be seen with someone like you in a dump like this. I prefer my untouchable skin.

OLGA: What do I have to do for you to . . . be quiet.

ROELLE: I, too, can have power for once. . . . you don't get it, do you? I think she wants to be nice to me now because I might tell the whole town, everything—the way I want to. Did you change? You are the same. You'll treat me the same again.

OLGA: What do you know of me?

ROELLE: I ask you, as your father confessor: This child of your maculate conception—what is it to you, object of love or hate?

OLGA: It is no different from my enemy.

ROELLE: I ask you as your father confessor: Can you deny that you wanted to do away with it?

OLGA: If only my mother had done it with me!

ROELLE: So she goes and beats it to death, so to speak, with some kind of tool.

OLGA: You are so sure that you are right. But you don't say what's to become of the child. And of me.

ROELLE: That's something you and your neat friend Peps should have thought of before.

OLGA: You try and think! When everyone's always coming after me and one longs to be free—and freedom comes in a beautiful shape and it's crashing down all over you—

ROELLE (*approaches her*): You mean—like this? (*She shudders.*)

OLGA: There he comes and wants us to sin together.

ROELLE: I say bend your knee, and she shall bend her knee and shall be as a woman in bondage before me.

OLGA: What are you doing with your greasy head so close to me?

ROELLE: Neck and arms are mine. Something to hold on to.

OLGA: Your voice is cracking!

ROELLE: So what? I don't care.

OLGA: I don't want to. It's sickening with you.

ROELLE: He does it. He does it not. He does it.

OLGA: Get away!

ROELLE: Oh no. We'll end up in hell no matter what.

OLGA: How dare you! Just touch your head! Go ahead! Feel what's sitting on your shoulders!

ROELLE: I hear what you're telling me. When I show my face among people, it makes a sick dog howl with laughter.

OLGA: Splash your forehead and get back to reason.

ROELLE: No water.

OLGA: Can you stand up straight?

ROELLE: You always have to insult me. That's all you do.

OLGA: I guess I should've slapped my mouth.

ROELLE: If you've more to say, do it fast—I am leaving.

OLGA: You won't see me fall on my knees. I'll send Peps after you.

ROELLE: Why don't you ask him if he'll marry you?

OLGA: I did already.

ROELLE: He's worse than I. I'm warning you.

OLGA: He can't just do what he wants either. He says, I have to be the smart one of the two of us.

ROELLE: Easy for him to say. He's praying his rosary while he's doing it with Hermione. (*He exits.*)

OLGA: I knew it.

SCENE 2

Later the same day. OLGA, PEPS, *and* HERMIONE *still backstage. Dialogue backstage.*

ROELLE: I don't want it. I won't be forced.

PEPS: You have to. (PEPS *pulls in* ROELLE *forcefully.* HERMIONE *follows. To* OLGA) Did he ask your forgiveness?

ROELLE: I can't do that. It never comes out right with me.

OLGA: What's wrong now?

PEPS: Olga, you just don't know.

HERMIONE: He went to confession and they wouldn't let him off.

ROELLE: I don't think that's so bad.

HERMIONE: It certainly is.

ROELLE: I'll just go to another priest.

HERMIONE: You'll have to confess that, too, if the first one didn't absolve you.

ROELLE: I'll never go to confession again.

PEPS: Then what do you do if you have to come up to communion with your whole class?

ROELLE: That's my business.

HERMIONE: People who don't go to confession go straight to hell.

ROELLE: I can achieve perfect repentance.

PEPS: You can't. Only saints can do that.

HERMIONE: I wouldn't want to know what he's got to confess to have this happen to him.

OLGA: What do you want from him? Leave him alone with what he has to confess.

PEPS: Olga, you just don't know. He filled the confessional with talk about you. He mentioned your name and dragged you through the dirt.

ROELLE: That's a lie.

PEPS: I stood close by and pricked my ears, young man. I heard everything.

HERMIONE: You should always be aware of that.

ROELLE: You can't reveal this. It's under the seal of confession.

PEPS: I'm not a priest.

HERMIONE: He's not bound by the seal.

ROELLE: You found out sinfully.

PEPS: Do you know what you did? You ruined her reputation in front of the priest.

ROELLE: I had to tell. It is a sacrament.

OLGA: You could have left my name out.

PEPS: He didn't need a name.

ROELLE: I'll leave it out the next time.

HERMIONE: So, you'll be going to confession again?

PEPS: He'll learn how to do it.

HERMIONE: He can't even genuflect properly.

ROELLE: Who could compete with you!

HERMIONE: Boys never know what to do with the sacraments.

ROELLE: I went in there with the best intentions.

HERMIONE: Did you have cramps?

ROELLE: No.

HERMIONE: I wouldn't call that the proper remorse.

ROELLE: Cramps are more for girls.

HERMIONE: Did you hold the missal close to your face?

ROELLE: No.

HERMIONE: These are rules one has to follow. I'm very strict that way.

PEPS: Hermione and pious!

OLGA: She carries on with Peps long after the church bells stop ringing.

HERMIONE: Who says I have to avoid him like bad company or a sinful opportunity?

OLGA: It's not because of me.

PEPS: Be quiet. You always were the smart one.

OLGA: You have become a completely different person.

HERMIONE: He just doesn't want to anymore. He's probably found someone else.

OLGA: Then I'll send out our engagement announcements next Saturday—just so you know.

PEPS: Guess how much Hermione's dowry is worth.

OLGA: I have to stop right here. I have to wait for my beloved to recognize me.

HERMIONE: He really would be stuck with you.

PEPS: She'd have her man get up first in the morning and grind the coffee quietly.

OLGA: Mother, you told me so.

HERMIONE: That's what you get for being so smart.

PEPS: For once it didn't turn out the way she imagined it.

HERMIONE: She thought she could always get her way.

ROELLE: That's no way to treat Olga. She was a child.

OLGA: Roelle is the only one.

ROELLE (*to* HERMIONE): All of this is your viciousness.

HERMIONE (*standing next to* PEPS): Have you gawked long enough at the chemical reactions between the two of us?

ROELLE: To me, Olga has a face like John, the favorite disciple.

HERMIONE: I'll smash your stinking halo. What happened to that dog?

ROELLE: What do you know! It isn't easy to close a dog's eyes. When he howled, it felt like my own soul. Olga understood.

HERMIONE: He admitted it. You are my witnesses.

ROELLE: Bitch.

HERMIONE: I'll tell the teacher. These are bad seeds; they must be thrown out of school.

ROELLE: You have no say in that.

HERMIONE: I'm going to get him hanged today—right now. (*She exits;* ROELLE *follows her.*)

PEPS (*stares at* OLGA): Is it gone?

OLGA: No.

PEPS: Why not? I gave you the address of Mrs. Schnepf.

OLGA: She doesn't do it anymore.

PEPS: You lie. You haven't been there.

OLGA: Cross my heart—I was there. She refused.

PEPS: You must have acted silly.

OLGA: She said she had done time for it. They keep an eye on her. She said we couldn't pay her enough to do it.

PEPS: Then you'll have to find someone else. I don't need a child.

OLGA: You don't like me anymore.

PEPS: Do something about it, or you'll really get to know me.

SCENE 3

A deserted, tree-lined street. PROTASIUS, OLGA.

PROTASIUS: It's so strange. You, of all people, walking all alone through this deserted street.

OLGA: Hey, you are following me.

PROTASIUS: Relax, relax, Miss Olga.

OLGA: If you don't leave me alone, I'll scream.

PROTASIUS: Timidity is an urge. It rises irresistibly in certain people. Let me tell you something. If I were you, I wouldn't want to be alone with some tough, low-class fellow in this deserted street. It's different with me. You know, I am an unbloody person.

OLGA: Begging's allowed only on Fridays in this street.

PROTASIUS: Thank you very much. I am familiar with that kind of cruelty. But I am not the needy beggar you take me for. I am sent by my doctor, Mr. Haehnle, who is an important man. Handle me with care, like an egg.

OLGA: You are bothering me.

PROTASIUS: Roelle is quite attached to you. I know that. You have the most influence on him.

OLGA: If you want something from Roelle, it's Roelle you should see. Why do you bother with me?

PROTASIUS: I am forced only by necessity, Miss Olga. I shall explain patiently. Because his mother, this hardened woman, wouldn't let me near him anymore. Even though he promised.

OLGA: Why should I care?

PROTASIUS: You are a possible detour to my goal.

OLGA: I don't understand.

PROTASIUS: Detour or escape route. Because my doctor always sends me on the difficult missions, and my Doctor Haehnle is not a patient man. Now, you see, I would have told you all that nice and slow.

OLGA: Why are you after Roelle?

PROTASIUS: Because he no longer comes on his own. That's why I have to get the boy. Because he won't do it voluntarily, because he's asked so many questions, and people keep taking notes about his inner life.

OLGA: I wouldn't want a doctor looking into my life.

PROTASIUS: That's supposed to be good for the eventual healing process.

OLGA: Is something wrong with Roelle?

PROTASIUS: What have I been talking about? There is sufficient speculation, and, if it is correct, there's something not quite right with that boy.

OLGA: But he doesn't know it.

PROTASIUS: He mustn't get excited, says Dr. Haehnle. But I think that's such a general statement; it holds true for anybody.

OLGA: Then why don't you leave him alone?

PROTASIUS: Because he's let us down. He's let science down.

OLGA: I am sure Roelle has his reasons for not going.

PROTASIUS: He doesn't have the perspective for that. It's just that this is the way it works: Whenever something happens with the boy and we can observe that, he can be written about. Those are the rarest people, says Dr. Haehnle—the ones that can be written about. And, if this boy stays away out of some silly resistance, where can I get a similar substitute?

OLGA: What could he possibly have to offer to you?

PROTASIUS: You surprise me. Through your self-absorption, you can't see what's right in front of you. This boy is a dark heathen, and he's involved with magic.

OLGA: Now don't get insulting. I'm leaving.

PROTASIUS: You can't do that to us. We've barely touched the surface with that boy; that's not enough for us. We do our research on him.

OLGA: And what am I supposed to do?

PROTASIUS: Make it clear to him that he has to come, that he is doing it for science.

OLGA: That'll go to his head.

PROTASIUS: Well now, that would be an advantage.

OLGA: I don't even know what kind of a person you are and where he'd end up.

PROTASIUS: I am inseparable from my doctor. I am his headhunter and his spy. Don't think lowly of me because of that. I get him the people who are right for his immortal discoveries. Without me, he'd be lost, I tell you.

OLGA: I see you are exploiting the boy.

PROTASIUS: We exploit him, and we skewer him, but we guarantee him a kind of immortality.

OLGA: This is getting very eerie.

PROTASIUS: It's the eeriness that makes us so precise.

OLGA: I don't want to tell him, that's all. It has to be his choice.

PROTASIUS: The boy doesn't have a choice.

SCENE 4

Sideshow at a country fair. Behind a Gypsy cart. ROELLE, TWO ALTAR BOYS.

1. ALTAR BOY:

> *Ingolstadt's my kind of place*
> *They have a fine track for a race*
> *But one of the horses won't move*
> *The other one's got a cracked hoof*
> *The coachman looks like an ape*
> *And the wheels are all bent out of shape*
> *And when it gets started at last*
> *The cart cracks right down in the dust.*

ROELLE: Will you stop that stupid noise!

1. ALTAR BOY: Listen to him. We aren't supposed to breathe.

ROELLE: You know I have to prepare. I have to listen for the voice deep in here; I have to go way inside myself.

2. ALTAR BOY: Stop showing off. You need us to hawk your audience. Without us, no one would give a damn.

ROELLE: Well, then, it just won't happen. Because I never can tell what day or hour the spirit'll come over me.

2. ALTAR BOY: You stay right here. No running away now. You claim you are a real saint; now you have to prove it. That's all.

ROELLE: Angels come to me.

1. ALTAR BOY: And they shall carry you so your foot shall not hit a stone.

2. ALTAR BOY: If you have friends like that, you have to show them to poor folks like us.

ROELLE: But it doesn't always work. I never know in advance when it'll work. The angels are there, or they aren't. I can't call them down just like that. The angels have to take me by surprise.

2. ALTAR BOY: You just have to try a little harder. We've told the people, and now they want to see real angels for once.

ROELLE: You can't see angels. You can only hear them.

1. ALTAR BOY: Tell that to your audience.

ROELLE: Oh, you are blind and deaf.

2. ALTAR BOY: We don't understand you, we know.

1. ALTAR BOY: How could we understand him? We are not his disciples.

2. ALTAR BOY: We are sick and tired of piety. We have too much to do with that stuff already.

1. ALTAR BOY: Believe me, I polish off the sacred wine in one move. (*makes gesture of drinking*) Because an altar boy knows what tastes good.

2. ALTAR BOY: Dominus your biscuit.

1. ALTAR BOY: What would they do without us?

ROELLE: I'll pray for you to figure it out . . .

2. ALTAR BOY: Karl, we are being transfigured. Let us give up to him our own holy spirit, our alcoholic spirit.

ROELLE: Have you ever heard of the active power of love?

2. ALTAR BOY: I don't get to the movies. My father takes the money I make as an altar boy.

ROELLE: It changes you. Beyond recognition.

2. ALTAR BOY: Is that so?

ROELLE: Saulus becomes Paulus.

2. ALTAR BOY: That's not too visible in you. I'd say you got worse.

ROELLE: What do you think the old Roelle would have done?

1. ALTAR BOY: He'd have taken off and yelled from behind a street corner, "They are all too low for me."

ROELLE: And the new Roelle?

1. ALTAR BOY: What does he do?

ROELLE: He stands right in front of you, looks you up and down, and says yes; he says, you are the poor in spirit.

2. ALTAR BOY: It is exactly the same in my book. Because you are proud and we are too low for you.

OLGA (*coming around the cart*): I've been running all over the fair grounds.

1. ALTAR BOY: I almost whistled just now.

2. ALTAR BOY:

> *A candle's lit on the second floor*
> *She might slip in her slip and slip through the door.*

OLGA: Roelle, come on, let's go behind the cart.

2. ALTAR BOY: What if we come with you behind the cart?

ROELLE (*to* OLGA): No one'll hurt you.

1. ALTAR BOY: Isn't she the bashful one.

2. ALTAR BOY: She needs to be pushed into it; that's when she gets hot.

ROELLE: Go, hide; I see the glow in her face.

OLGA: In mine?

ROELLE: One can die from it. The light from heaven.

2. ALTAR BOY: You can't fool us, you crazy devil.

1. ALTAR BOY: Religious maniac!

2. ALTAR BOY: You can't sell her to us for an angel. She's known all over town.

ROELLE: She's come for me. Be reasonable. Leave us alone, will you.

1. ALTAR BOY: She's come for him. And what do poor altar boys get?

2. ALTAR BOY: Come on, Karl, let them flirt. It doesn't matter.

1. ALTAR BOY: Let's get out of here.

2. ALTAR BOY: But we won't go far. We'll keep you under observation, you understand. You know what's waiting for you.

ROELLE: Fine with me.

2. ALTAR BOY:

> *Ding dong klick klick*
> *the priest fell sick*
> *the sexton rings the bell*
> *the billy goat starts to yell*
> *meh meh meh*

(*The* ALTAR BOYS *exit.*)

OLGA: I've come.

ROELLE (*strokes* OLGA's *forehead and face*): You must be completely open to me. You must respond to the most subtle emotional signals coming from me.

OLGA: I thought there was more to the story.

ROELLE: Would you like to become a saint?

OLGA: Come on!

ROELLE: Do what I tell you.

OLGA: But I don't want to.

ROELLE: It's too much for you; I can see that.

OLGA: Most people don't want to be completely open to another person.

ROELLE: Still, we are together, aren't we?

OLGA: Just don't think there is more to it. (*She watches him.*)

ROELLE: Your unrelenting scrutiny is about to wreck my mood.

OLGA: I have eyes. Can't I look?

ROELLE: But you are putting me in a bad mood.

OLGA: I look at that twist in your face.

ROELLE: One can't choose one's face.

OLGA: I say there's something not quite right about you.

ROELLE: What's not quite right about me?

OLGA: That's how physiognomy works. The instincts show right up there, even though they're hidden.

ROELLE: I never noticed that.

OLGA: Why don't you move? You are like an animal that pretends to be dead.

ROELLE: I'm always clumsy before such sharp eyes.

OLGA: You have to move; your movements will show me what I don't yet know.

ROELLE: When you stare at me that way, I can't think my own thoughts.

OLGA: Then I don't know if I should sit down with you at all. I want to find out something.

ROELLE: Who or what am I to you?

OLGA: That shouldn't matter to you.

ROELLE: But it does matter to me.

OLGA: You were right about Peps. He doesn't like me anymore. He is getting so mean.

ROELLE: He is no great loss.

OLGA: But I'm having a child.

ROELLE: That's the way it is.

OLGA: My belly's getting fat.

ROELLE: You mustn't abort it. The child is already alive, even though it isn't conscious.

OLGA: Thou shalt not kill.

ROELLE: That's what I thought. The child was created in love. Perhaps it's a beautiful child.

OLGA: Most certainly.

ROELLE: It should be allowed to live, even if it isn't beautiful.

OLGA: But what am I supposed to do?

ROELLE: You won't let me help you. Even if you don't want to admit it, I am the important man in your life. Do as I tell you. You have to go to the country, before it shows. You have to give birth to the child where nobody will know you.

OLGA: That costs money.

ROELLE: I guarantee you, I'll come up with the money.

OLGA: You?

ROELLE: I'd love to have a beautiful child.

OLGA: You don't have to have it.

ROELLE: But I want to have it.

OLGA (*bitter*): And me with it.

ROELLE: It shouldn't turn out like its father.

OLGA: You are meddling in something—

ROELLE: By it becoming human, it makes humans of us.

OLGA: A person can't lean on anyone else. It won't do any good. (*She runs off.*)

ROELLE: That isn't true at all!

MOTHER (*enters with a soup container*): I finally caught up with you, spoiled brat. You just do what I tell you now.

ROELLE: You can't come after me with your stupid soups. You don't know what that does to me. Let me tell you slowly.

MOTHER: You eat now. I have to tell you that every Thursday! You don't just leave your oatmeal soup. You can sit here for an hour; I won't leave till it's gone.

ROELLE: Mama, I'm trying, but I really don't feel like it at all.

MOTHER: And that delicious egg in there. Do I have to force it into you?

ROELLE: The way you treat me today.

MOTHER: Just wait, I'll lock you up in the cellar and let you scream there.

ROELLE: That's a classic threat. Look, Mama, now can you see how I force myself? But that's for the pigs! It's cold.

MOTHER: I poured it in here the way you left it. Eat it now.

ROELLE: And that's supposed to make me strong?

MOTHER: Do I have to count? (*She takes the spoon and feeds him.*) There, this one is for Saint Joseph; this one is for your dead little sister. Now close your eyes. This one is for your guardian angel; you never know when you'll need him. This one is for all the poor souls in purgatory—

ROELLE: Man doesn't have to eat.

MOTHER: How are you going to grow up? You'll starve to death.

ROELLE: Maybe that's what I want.

MOTHER: You abuse yourself. I'd be scared, too.

ROELLE: It *is* pretty scary.

MOTHER: They should've never thrown you out of school. It's eating inside you.

ROELLE: I do what I must do.

MOTHER: You got that from your father. Jesus, Jesus! I'm just a simple woman.

ROELLE: The teachers decided together that I am no good.

MOTHER: As if others don't get into trouble when they are young! It's something to outgrow.

ROELLE: I'm the only one they are after; the others get away with it. I don't know why.

MOTHER: It is unfair, son.

ROELLE: They said I'm a pest.

MOTHER: Don't take it to heart so much.

ROELLE: I'm not a pest. They'll see.

MOTHER: We are not the dregs.

ROELLE: And they don't know it all. They'll be surprised.

MOTHER: There are schools in other towns. I'll just have to spend the money. I'll send you to a boarding school.

ROELLE: I don't want to go to a boarding school.

MOTHER: But you can't finish here. You need to finish.

ROELLE: I want to stay here. Olga hasn't left either.

MOTHER: You'll drive yourself completely crazy over that person. Do you want to cut off your life?

ROELLE: Nothing comes easy with me. The crown of thorns is for me. I know that.

MOTHER: So get pricked. Really work on it! See if you like it!

ROELLE: You can't follow me, woman. I'm telling you, something is calling me.

MOTHER: Son, just don't go too far.

ROELLE: They'll see. I'll pull myself up by my own hair from the bottom of the swamp.

MOTHER: There are no miracles. Everything advances step by step.

ROELLE: They don't know who I am. Maybe I've made up my mind to become a saint.

MOTHER: Keep dreaming!

ROELLE: That's right. One just has to think big. And then one has to do something about it. Others have done it, why shouldn't I?

MOTHER: You do that!

ROELLE: One just has to have willpower when it gets difficult. Not eating, for example.

MOTHER: Not eating, not eating! Until light can shine right through you? Until you get every possible illness? Who'll want you then?

ROELLE: You have to eat so little that supernatural visions will come in bright daylight.

MOTHER: I don't think that's healthy. I think it's dangerous.

ROELLE: It can be done. I've tried it, and it's possible. It pushes you beyond your limits.

MOTHER: Aren't you terrified of your own daring?

ROELLE: It is terrifying. That's why I stopped.

MOTHER: You see.

ROELLE: But now I'm starting again. I hadn't gone far enough. I wasn't a saint yet.

MOTHER: It's gone to his head. Jesus! Jesus!

ROELLE: You can't stop me, woman.

MOTHER: Son, I don't want you to be a saint.

GERVASIUS (*appears behind the cart*): This time we caught him. He is just a mama's boy.

ROELLE: You have no business here.

GERVASIUS: You should know. I am everywhere.

ROELLE: You're shortsighted. You didn't see everything.

GERVASIUS: I've been standing back there the whole time, and I enjoyed it. This one is for Saint Joseph—just keep working on your willpower.

ROELLE: I don't want to say what you are.

GERVASIUS: So what am I?

ROELLE: You are a misguided soul.

GERVASIUS: I kept thinking, Should I come out and embarrass the boy for all eternity? At first I felt sorry for you, but then I felt more like embarrassing you.

ROELLE: That shows your filthy character.

GERVASIUS: Because now I can tell it in the schoolyard, where you find the better boys. I have a notion those boys will show no mercy to a mama's boy. One more spoonful. That one's for your guardian angel; you never know when you'll need him.

ROELLE: Go ahead, run to your dirty schoolyard. They all know who you're after. I can also hint to the police what you're up to, and they'll be waiting for you.

GERVASIUS: You'll have to prove it first. (*He exits.*)

ROELLE: Gone—like a skunk.

MOTHER: Jesus, I got the shivers.

ROELLE: You see now how embarrassing you are?

MOTHER: Yes, and I stood there like eternal misery in pain and remorse.

ROELLE: Are you going to chase me with that soup again?

MOTHER: I'm cleaning it up, I am. I suppose this is the cross I have to bear. (*She exits.*)

ROELLE: Now let's get ready for sainthood. I get stuck all the time.

CLEMENTINE (*comes around the cart*): I would have talked to Mrs. Roelle, but she was all confused. She didn't even see me.

ROELLE: My mom is quite peculiar about whom she does and doesn't see.

CLEMENTINE: Not with me. She once said, Clementine, should there ever be something going on between you and my son, I would have nothing against it because you are such a hard-working girl, and that is like a capital investment. She is right. The entire household rests on my shoulders.

ROELLE: Well, I pay a lot of attention to my mother's judgment. I tell you, she lived and learned.

CLEMENTINE: She has lived her life, and that's what I want to do too. How did Olga's bow get here?

ROELLE: The wind blew it.

CLEMENTINE: It wasn't the wind. That's her wide one, and it's not ripped. I don't understand you. You're after her. How someone can be so wrong about a person!

ROELLE: I wasn't following her; she came on her own. And she also left on her own.

CLEMENTINE: I must say, Olga is something. And I feel sorry for anyone who is after her. From the side she looks like a man.

ROELLE: You see everything.

CLEMENTINE: You've known me since I was a child. Now that you're a man, you can't play stranger with me.

ROELLE: I'd never compare you to your sister.

CLEMENTINE: I have to get away from home. It's no place for me.

ROELLE: I'm not the dregs. I can show myself to a woman.

CLEMENTINE: You'll know yourself who is better for you. Olga can only lead to misery.

ROELLE: Just let me get through this day.

CLEMENTINE: You won't regret it.

1. ALTAR BOY: It's time: People are waiting for your appearance.

ROELLE: Out of the question.

2. ALTAR BOY: Some people were inclined to call it a hoax, but I got them inspired.

1. ALTAR BOY: Hermione Seitz complains the loudest.

CLEMENTINE: What's he gotten himself into now?

ROELLE: We won't tell.

2. ALTAR BOY: He didn't elaborate for the other one either.

1. ALTAR BOY: He just means that you're already the second one today.

2. ALTAR BOY: The face she made, she should get stuck with it. (CLEMENTINE *exits.* ROELLE *tries to leave.*) Don't let him get away. Roelle tries to avoid the crowds.

ROELLE: Now we're getting somewhere, I'm being assaulted.

1. ALTAR BOY: You must go there.

2. ALTAR BOY: You are the beginning of everything.

ROELLE: I'm not prepared.

2. ALTAR BOY: Think up something on your way over.

1. ALTAR BOY: Your followers want to welcome you; your enemies do too.

2. ALTAR BOY: You can't run away.

1. ALTAR BOY: Your Olga's waiting there, craning her neck.

2. ALTAR BOY: Your teachers are standing there, your classmates.

1. ALTAR BOY: And they all want to see what you have in store for them.

ROELLE: Have you drawn the chalk circle?

1. ALTAR BOY: We forgot.

ROELLE: First a chalk circle must be drawn because I have to step inside it.

2. ALTAR BOY: It will be done as soon as you get there.

ROELLE: And you expect it to work that way? Does everyone know that they can't talk to me?

2. ALTAR BOY: Let's go.

ROELLE: You can lift your hand like this. It can also be lifted like that.

1. ALTAR BOY: You want to show yourself like that? Good luck.

ROELLE: I call it an unusual posture.

(*A few students pass by.*)

1. STUDENT: We came the wrong way.

2. STUDENT: This way. You can go through this way.

3. STUDENT: Half the school's supposed to be there.

(*They exit. Some girls pass by.*)

1. GIRL: Here's one who believes it.

2. GIRL: They are not like other people. They don't live long, people say.

3. GIRL: Come on, I see him every day walking by the ravine.

2. GIRL: The organs, the inner organs can't take it.

(*The girls exit. A student comes around the cart.*)

STUDENT: They don't want to wait any longer. When is this odd savior supposed to come?

2. ALTAR BOY: We have to walk him around the square three times so he can concentrate.

1. ALTAR BOY: Three is the sacred number.

(*The student exits.* PROTASIUS *and* GERVASIUS *pass by.*)

PROTASIUS: What do you call it, whatever it is Roelle is doing?

GERVASIUS: Don't start with Roelle, or I'll get nasty. That rotten bastard with his spiritism!

PROTASIUS: What did you say? Say it for me one more time.

GERVASIUS: Spir-it-ism.

PROTASIUS: Aha!

GERVASIUS: It's got nothing to do with alcohol. That man'll think up any obscenity.

PROTASIUS: Half a year ago someone did that kind of nonsense in the beerhall, just to make something happen on the podium. I assume that's where he got it. It's something with ghosts. They materialize, you understand.

GERVASIUS: That's too esoteric for me.

PROTASIUS: They look out of the medium, they look out of his throat and tell you things you don't know yourself. And you have to believe them; otherwise, the ghosts will strangle you.

GERVASIUS: And that's what Roelle is trying to imitate?

PROTASIUS: You can get famous that way. All you need is someone from the university to get interested, and he'll make something out of you.

GERVASIUS: You're kidding.

PROTASIUS: And you're jealous of the boy. I can see it.

GERVASIUS: That fellow should be arrested. I'll arrest him right now.

PROTASIUS: I doubt you can get away with it.

GERVASIUS: Have you never read in the papers: The perpetrator, showing signs of mental disturbance, was taken into custody?

PROTASIUS: Do you have a stamped photograph?

GERVASIUS: I've never needed one.

PROTASIUS: If you don't have a stamped photograph, you can't arrest anybody.

GERVASIUS: Says who?

PROTASIUS: You have to show it every time you do something in the name of the law; otherwise, the police'll get you.

GERVASIUS: It's really a strange thing, your education.

PROTASIUS: And then you need handcuffs that lock automatically because he isn't going to come with you voluntarily.

GERVASIUS: Wouldn't you know! I'd have arrested him.

(They exit. Unrest and voices.)

1. VOICE: Where is our promised angel? Let's get that angel up here.

2. VOICE: We want to see that angel.

MANY VOICES: Get that angel! Get that angel!

2. ALTAR BOY: They're ready. Let's go. Throw yourself among them.

ROELLE: I can't. I can't.

2. ALTAR BOY: You have to.

1. ALTAR BOY: I'll die laughing. What a fiasco!

(The ALTAR BOYS *drag* ROELLE, *who is behind the cart trying to resist, up onto the platform.)*

2. ALTAR BOY (*offstage*): Ladies and gentlemen, in these times of unbelief, an ordinary young man managed to make contact with real angels. Let me introduce to you a man who is visited by his angel, just like that. Without charging you admission and only to shake up the skeptics, to shatter the nonbelievers, my man here will show you this creature from heaven. May I have your utmost attention? I ask you not to startle this man with shouts or cheers; they could cause a fatal crash. Contact with an angel is life-threatening.

VOICE: He's sweating already.

VOICES: Shhh.

2. ALTAR BOY: Quiet back there. Absolute quiet. Otherwise, he can't get hypnotized. It's difficult.

VOICE: Be quiet, he's becoming hypnotized.

VOICE: But we don't see anything.

VOICE: Quiet, it's coming.

VOICE: Stupid tricks.

VOICE: Just hands and feet.

VOICE: He stands there like an idiot.

VOICE: What a flop.
VOICE: Swindler. Cheat. Police.
VOICE: What he is doing is a sacrilege.
VOICE: It's the devil in him.
VOICE: Down with him.
VOICE: Stone him.
VOICE: Watch me stone him.

(*Rocks are thrown. Some roll under the cart.*)

VOICE: I hit him.
VOICE: He's dead.
VOICE: Everything's just hocus-pocus.

(*Some students pass by.* OLGA *tries to pull* ROELLE *away.*)

Intermission.

SCENE 5

BEROTTER'S *house. Balcony between two buildings.* ROELLE *wears a bandage.* OLGA, CLEMENTINE, CHRISTIAN, PEPS, HERMIONE. *They are drinking wine.*

PEPS: Maybe he finally learned his lesson.
HERMIONE: Not him. If anything, he'll get worse.
ROELLE: I am different. I stand out in a crowd.
PEPS: Just don't come to me when you've hit rock bottom.
ROELLE: It turned out I have a few followers.
PEPS: More enemies than followers.
ROELLE: That's nothing yet. There's one fellow, I just have to approach him with my slow tiger's gaze, and he turns white as a sheet.
CHRISTIAN: I'd like to know who he is.
ROELLE: Why don't you go and ask for him? His name is Crusius.
CHRISTIAN: Never.
ROELLE: Crusius fell on his knees and asked my forgiveness; he didn't recognize me.
CHRISTIAN: I don't believe it.
ROELLE: He said, Roelle, man, mercy, he said. You weren't there. That's your problem.

CHRISTIAN: Then why didn't you get your book back when he took it right from under your eyes!

ROELLE: That was when he had no idea who he was dealing with.

OLGA: You better take Roelle's word for it. You weren't there.

(CHRISTIAN *moves farther away from them and sits down again.*)

HERMIONE: Oh, how precious.

PEPS: And it's such a great night for getting drunk. Cheers.

ROELLE: Olga understood me. I let them smash a hole in my head.

CLEMENTINE: Was that necessary?

ROELLE: Can you believe it? Believe it, if you can.

OLGA: With Clementine, it's just envy.

CLEMENTINE: He didn't do it for you. It was for his own self-importance.

ROELLE: Angels do come to me, but they only come in solitude. They don't come to the market.

OLGA: They don't know, that's all.

HERMIONE: We don't believe it.

OLGA: You are the stubborn ones. You'll see how you end up.

HERMIONE: How will we end up?

PEPS: We are the ones you can't scare.

OLGA: I believe in angels.

PEPS: Now look what you've done, Roelle.

OLGA: I can't bend my little finger without being watched from heaven.

PEPS: That's what you would like, wouldn't you?

CLEMENTINE: And I have to wash the dishes all by myself.

HERMIONE: We didn't see you at mass.

OLGA: I don't need to be at a specific place.

CLEMENTINE: Won't Roelle soon be fed up with Olga aping everything he says?

OLGA: My Roelle can't be shaken.

CLEMENTINE: Don't always say he's your Roelle.

OLGA: I know what I know.

HERMIONE: Oh, how precious.

CLEMENTINE: I don't want to talk about how Roelle went on about you. He wouldn't say it to your face.

ROELLE: She wants to ruin my honor.

CLEMENTINE: Even if he won't admit it afterward.

ROELLE: When did I say anything negative? Tell me now.

CLEMENTINE: I can't do it when he's looking at me so closely.

ROELLE: You better think before you say something.

OLGA (*to* CLEMENTINE): Big mouth!

CLEMENTINE: Which one of us is right for you? I want to know right now.

OLGA: Clementine, you never run after anyone who doesn't pay attention to you.

CLEMENTINE: I know, because my hands are rough; I have to stick them in cold water. I'd like to see Olga do that.

CHRISTIAN: Look what he did to you.

CLEMENTINE: I've had enough. Always Olga. Mother, when she was still alive, always favored you.

CHRISTIAN: Hush now, not in front of strangers.

HERMIONE: I won't tell.

CLEMENTINE: They always go after me. Christian and Olga and the rest. Now I want to talk. High school, all of that, I wasn't allowed to go.

PEPS: That's all we needed.

CHRISTIAN: Get out of here. Scram!

CLEMENTINE: I just want to cry, and you can't stop me. I'm crying.

OLGA: Come now, Clementine. Let's wash your face. They don't have to see you like that.

CLEMENTINE: I don't care. I am my own person. I stay because I want to.

OLGA: You're coming with me.

CLEMENTINE: I can't even cry. (*She exits with* OLGA.)

PEPS: Did somebody stick a fork in your fat neck?

ROELLE: Someone like her can end up a traitor. She takes one step and gets stuck in evil.

PEPS: Who doesn't?

(CLEMENTINE *and* OLGA *return.*)

OLGA: They know that Roelle's with us. When we turned on the light in the living room, they yelled up his name from the street.

CHRISTIAN: How dare they!

ROELLE: They are my adversaries.

CLEMENTINE: I won't leave through the front door. They'll break our windows too.

PEPS: They'll get tired and go away.

OLGA: Do they know what they're doing?

HERMIONE: That's what you get with your Roelle.

ROELLE: Nothing will happen to you.

CLEMENTINE: Don't stand there as if you're at home here. It would be better for you to leave now.

ROELLE: You can't chase me away like a dog. I let them smash a hole in my head.

HERMIONE: Let's put three fingers in it. He's got a wound, that's his excuse.

PEPS: We don't want to know any of that. We have no use for someone like him.

ROELLE: That's even better. You'll pretend I don't exist.

OLGA: God, I've had enough. I can't put up with him forever.

PEPS: It's up to you.

ROELLE: It's not fair how she stares right past me at a distant point. I am sick.

PEPS: Didn't you get it? We don't want anyone sick in here.

CLEMENTINE: He's turning green.

CHRISTIAN: If you're sick, go home.

ROELLE: I won't find my way all by myself. I'm dizzy.

HERMIONE: Wouldn't you be happy now if someone would hold your head up for you?

ROELLE: I won't be able to make it.

OLGA: Lie down if you feel sick.

CLEMENTINE: No, take him away. Get him out of my sight.

OLGA: Not me.

HERMIONE: We don't want to touch him.

PEPS: He has lost a lot of blood. Maybe it's too much.

CLEMENTINE: Sit up, you! Sit up, will you?

ROELLE: I didn't come here for your pity.

CLEMENTINE: I can't stand the sight of this man!

ROELLE: I have my weaknesses, and I always have to defend myself because of them. Look, among other things, I am afraid of water. I can't go in. I get nauseated. I have to cover my mouth when the water rises up my body.

OLGA: I find that quite disgusting.

HERMIONE: I can't stop laughing.

ROELLE: If she won't look at me, I won't let her go to the country.

PEPS: You don't even have the money.

ROELLE: Who wants some? Who needs some? (*He shows them his money.*)

PEPS: You stole that from your mother's store.

ROELLE: It's not stolen. Besides, the store's in our house.

PEPS: That's called a double theft.

OLGA: And you come to me and make me accept stolen money.

CHRISTIAN: He pulled it off pretty well.

OLGA: I am going to take it back to your mother.

ROELLE: Then I'll tell her it was you who took it out of her cash register. She'll believe it on the spot.

OLGA: I'm cutting off our relationship. You are bad company. (*She starts to leave.*)

ROELLE: That's one of those classic lines. I know it well.

OLGA: Do you know who you're talking to? (*She stops.*)

ROELLE: I'll be seeing you again. You are no different than I.

OLGA: I'm much better.

ROELLE: How did you do it? Stand there right in front of me waiting for me to have a seizure.

OLGA: Because I collect people like that.

ROELLE: If it were up to you, I might as well have died.

OLGA: To me you aren't human. You haven't got the nerve for it.

ROELLE: I made up the thing with my nerves, so I can just as easily take it back again.

OLGA: Oh? So there is nothing wrong with you?

(PROTASIUS *and* GERVASIUS *enter.*)

PROTASIUS: Looks like another eating and drinking orgy.

PEPS: Who let you in?

PROTASIUS: I am supposed to act as a kind of carrier for the sick man.

GERVASIUS: I am the other one. I help him carry.

ROELLE: No one's sick here.

PROTASIUS: I am delighted that things took care of themselves.

GERVASIUS: How come your head is bleeding?

ROELLE: I am not the one you are looking for.

PROTASIUS: You are a damned provocation.

ROELLE: I have recanted. You must leave me alone.

PROTASIUS: You can't get away from us. We come flying. We come swimming, if need be. But let there be no need for force.

GERVASIUS: Let the insects live, even if they sting you.

PROTASIUS: You wouldn't want a corpse in the gulley.

ROELLE: I won't let myself be kidnapped. I'm not coming. I'm not walking into your trap.

PROTASIUS: You have to do it voluntarily.

ROELLE: I'll never come with you again.

PROTASIUS: We know too much. Did I ever tell you, brother, how you can alter the sex of your children?

GERVASIUS: I don't want any children, and you are not my brother. You are only my tormentor.

PROTASIUS: That's what you need. If you don't want to know, I'll tell this gentleman, who isn't as tough with me and who, I hear, plans to get married.

PEPS: I'm interested.

PROTASIUS: I'll make it short and intimate: If you're really hot for your lady, it'll be a girl. That's because you'll be with her too much. A boy comes only after a longer period of abstinence. Abstinence regulates the sexes.

PEPS: I am converted. Let's drink to that.

PROTASIUS: I call such voluntary conversions a sign of intellectual adaptability. And, I say, without this kind of adaptability man is lost altogether. Take me, for example, where would I be if I weren't so adaptable, intellectually? You'd be able to look right through me for reasons of nutrition. But that's not the case. Come along, brother.

GERVASIUS: I am not your brother. I'm fed up. This town has nothing left to offer me. I've done most of it.

PROTASIUS: You've lasted a long time, all things considered.

GERVASIUS: You can't make things up about me, you snoop.

PROTASIUS: It's your own fault. You're colorless. You bore me. You're getting old. You have no more new ideas. You're too ordinary. Nobody'll shed a tear for you.

GERVASIUS: You all sucked me dry like vampires. And then you dumped me.

PROTASIUS: You're like the dirt on the road. Invisible. You're too ordinary.

GERVASIUS: You took all the pleasure out of me. I feel empty.

PROTASIUS: You have to do the taking. That's what counts. But you don't take anymore.

GERVASIUS: I still take the boys.

PROTASIUS: They don't need what's left of you. You are finished, finished, finished. You better hang yourself. Come on, you half-corpse.

GERVASIUS: I'm not your corpse either.

(PROTASIUS *and* GERVASIUS *exit.*)

PEPS: I don't trust these men.

HERMIONE: I can't see straight anymore. Maybe they weren't even here.

ROELLE: You just can't get involved with them. I know that. It's best to stay away from them.

CLEMENTINE: Would you prefer someone shy?

ROELLE: I don't like such general questions.

CLEMENTINE: Do you know how to convert a person even if he's very difficult?

ROELLE: I wanted to, many times. But how could I succeed with another if it doesn't even work on me?

CLEMENTINE: What if the two of us stick together really tight?

ROELLE: It can't come from the outside. The real help must be inside oneself. And in my case it's just not there. They say it's the curse of this generation.

CLEMENTINE: You have to be able to wait. It takes a long time to develop.

ROELLE: Just try it with confession. You confess the same thing over and over again. I've stopped believing in a movement upward a long time ago. It might even be better to do something really bad. Stealing, for example. And feeling good because you've stolen and you attacked somebody. And not being afraid at all because of it.

CLEMENTINE: Did you really steal?

ROELLE: As soon as I begin to comprehend what a person really is, I'd rather exit from this horrifying life. I want to renounce it.

CLEMENTINE: You can't do that, renounce something. If you've done something, it'll stay with you always, and, I say, it stares right at you.

ROELLE: That's the greatest injustice.

PEPS: I come to you with my digestive problems.

HERMIONE (*about* ROELLE): And suddenly he looks all transfigured again.

CLEMENTINE: A lot of drinking here, I see.

HERMIONE: Just pour it down your throat.

ROELLE: Are you also always feeling hot?

CLEMENTINE: That's the American heat wave.

HERMIONE: Man has five toes and one head. Man has five toes and one head.

CLEMENTINE: But man has ten toes.

HERMIONE: Man has ten toes and one head.

OLGA: Clementine, time to get ready.

CHRISTIAN: I've had it. The way Hermione carries on.

HERMIONE: I'm not a crocodile. I'm not a crocodile.

PEPS: And everything keeps turning grayer and grayer.

ROELLE: I'll take Clementine to where it is completely dark.

CLEMENTINE: Will you let your daughter attend high school?

ROELLE: I won't let you preach to me. None of you is a saint.

CLEMENTINE: We don't need Olga. In the starlight.

ROELLE: And what about your presumed innocence? You can tell me.

CLEMENTINE: A person doesn't talk about that.

ROELLE: She just does it. She's probably just like Olga.

CLEMENTINE: You'll find out soon enough.

ROELLE: First they make you do it; then they plead innocent.

CLEMENTINE: Christian, he's not nice.

CHRISTIAN: You'd better apologize.

ROELLE: She's asking for it, that's what I think. I know what you want.

CLEMENTINE: He wants to slander me right here.

ROELLE: Don't try to deny it. It's obvious.

CLEMENTINE: Then why did you follow me, and why were you mad at Olga? You made me believe it was because of your love for me.

ROELLE: It's not my fault you're so dumb.

CLEMENTINE: Did he always have his eye on her and just pretended it was me? Now you're really going to get it. He thought I wouldn't mind. You don't know me: I'll come up with something for you.

CHRISTIAN: Let's use him to set an example. I've always wanted to do that.

CLEMENTINE: We'll dump him in cold water.

ROELLE: You can't do that to me.

PEPS: Let there be enmity between you and the water.

HERMIONE: Now we've got something. Now we can really get to him.

CLEMENTINE: Someone has to keep him here. (*She exits.*)

CHRISTIAN: He knows he can't get away from us. We'll block him.

ROELLE: I don't want to, I don't want to!

CHRISTIAN: Stupid ass!

CLEMENTINE: Here's the tub. Let's take off his shoes.

HERMIONE: Why not more?

(*They start to undress him.*)

ROELLE: I'll never talk to you again.

CHRISTIAN: Look at us cry.

ROELLE: I have my guardian angel, so this foot shall not hit a stone.

OLGA: You think Olga will help? Olga won't help.

ROELLE: I seek refuge with you.

OLGA: Grab him.

ROELLE: What kind of world is this?

OLGA: The kind where your neighbor must die in misery.

ROELLE: I want to confess. I want to confess something important.

CHRISTIAN: What?

ROELLE: I am a bad person.

HERMIONE: We know that.

CHRISTIAN: You won't die, man. It's only water.

ROELLE: Hold it. I want to do it myself.

CLEMENTINE (*pushes him in*): There. Let's see you sit in there.

ROELLE: Olga shouldn't look.

PEPS: She's still getting to him. (*General sobering up. They give* ROELLE *his clothes.* CLEMENTINE *drags the tub offstage.*) Clementine disgraced herself the most.

CLEMENTINE: It's all Olga's fault.

CHRISTIAN (*to* CLEMENTINE): Because of you we have to face ourselves like this.

OLGA: We don't want to keep you in this place any longer. You probably won't mind leaving.

ROELLE: I was naked, and you did not give me any clothes. You have poured your scorn over me, and now it stares you in the face.

OLGA: Oh, that we fall every day into a world of viciousness, just as we fell into our bodies, and now we're stuck with them.

BEROTTER (*enters*): Are you leaving, Mr. Roelle?

ROELLE: I had a sweater.

BEROTTER: Now *he* wants to leave too. Look at me, children, is there something wrong with my suit? I was at the Café Ludwig, but I left right away. People gave me such strange looks and moved away from me. Then one after the other paid and left. Did anything happen?

OLGA: Father, I have something to tell you. I am expecting a child.

BEROTTER: Christ in heaven! (*He collapses.*)

PEPS: That's such a sad thing to hear about a daughter.

HERMIONE: Someone help me hold him.

CLEMENTINE: Let's go inside, but without Olga.

OLGA: Now he's having a fit again.

PEPS: I begin to understand: This man doesn't have a chance today.

OLGA: You don't have to come after me. I'm going to the quarry. (*She exits.*)

SCENE 6

Meadow at the bank of the Danube. PROTASIUS, GERVASIUS.

PROTASIUS: Olga Berotter, much to her credit, went into the water. But Roelle, in an incomprehensible bout of whatever, pulled her out.

GERVASIUS: You don't say.

PROTASIUS: I stood at the bank. I even helped with the final pull. I showed myself to be human.

GERVASIUS: Makes me sick to my stomach just hearing about it.

PROTASIUS: Afterward she got mad at both of us.

GERVASIUS: The thanks you get.

PROTASIUS: She wanted to drown herself to get away from it all, but Roelle wouldn't let her. She won't forgive him for that.

GERVASIUS: No sense of reality. And it's guys like us who could easily pay the price for it.

PROTASIUS: We simply can't be good. It always backfires.

GERVASIUS: It doesn't suit us.

PROTASIUS: We aren't cut out for it.

GERVASIUS: It fails automatically.

PROTASIUS: A tiny lapse, so easily avoided.

GERVASIUS: We can make up for it pretty fast.

PROTASIUS: That's why I got my story in the paper. I do things in writing now.

GERVASIUS: You—that's all they need there.

PROTASIUS: Don't say that. I have a domed brain; that's a sure sign.

GERVASIUS: They'll chase you to hell soon enough.

PROTASIUS: So I went with an empty stomach to the local news desk. The fellow who sits there never knows where to get the news for his column. I say to him, you have no information about the nocturnal drama at the quarry, but I was there. And here's the story, signed: A lifesaver. That's me, I say, and another fellow.

GERVASIUS: Was he thankful?

PROTASIUS: Oh yes. But it still has to pay off.

GERVASIUS: Did you name names?

PROTASIUS: That's the nice thing about papers: You can intimate that it was someone, and that someone can do nothing about it. The news has already hit the stands.

GERVASIUS: That's sure awful for the Berotter girl.

PROTASIUS: I'll say. Reading that about oneself! Now I'll make myself at home with the local newsman and work as his informer as well.

GERVASIUS: But never again as a lifesaver.

PROTASIUS: I have to stay alive for my reports. Anyway, I am not one for big gestures. To me it's more of an inner thing.

(PROTASIUS *and* GERVASIUS *exit.* CRUSIUS, FIRST STUDENT, *and* ROELLE *enter from the other side.*)

CRUSIUS: You forget that to your former classmates you are an outcast.

ROELLE: I gave you money. Every time I saw you.

CRUSIUS: Don't tell me you wanted to buy me.

ROELLE: I don't want to offend you, but you have to do something for me.

CRUSIUS: I already do you a favor by taking it.

ROELLE: But I have to steal it out of my mother's cash register. That's a real problem for me.

CRUSIUS: We just don't like you. You are not like everyone else.

ROELLE: How am I supposed to be?

FIRST STUDENT: What kind of face did they stick on your skull? The way he dangles his paws gets me in a rage.

ROELLE: I am not aware of it. I don't know what I do with them. I would change it, really. I just don't notice.

FIRST STUDENT: Wouldn't do any good. You are who you are.

ROELLE: I don't like being an outcast. I'll do anything if you take me back again.

CRUSIUS: Anything? Really?

(ROELLE *nods*.)

FIRST STUDENT: Now hold it. Not so fast.

ROELLE: And you will take me back eventually?

CRUSIUS: I'm already doing the best I can.

FIRST STUDENT: But we aren't impressed. To us you are not a man.

ROELLE: I am the father.

CRUSIUS: I told them already. But they don't like it so much.

FIRST STUDENT: A woman's slave. That's what he turned into. That's something to brag about!

ROELLE: She eats out of my hand.

FIRST STUDENT: We'd need a demonstration.

ROELLE: Shall I bring you the girl, so you can try her out yourself? It's nothing to me: I wave; she comes.

CRUSIUS Would you spit at her in front of me to pay your way back in?

ROELLE: Will you sit down and break bread with me?

CRUSIUS You'll be just like one of us.

ROELLE: I have to buy my way in. It's the only way.

CRUSIUS: You are exactly who I think you are.

FIRST STUDENT: Unbelievable. So this Berotter girl puts up with everything from you.

ROELLE: And she knows why.

FIRST STUDENT: She always acted so smart. Now she's got a child from someone like you.

ROELLE: You said it. I am the father.

FIRST STUDENT: You're in real trouble if you're telling stories.

ROELLE: I don't lie.

CRUSIUS: Can it be true? He's starting to cry.

ROELLE: I hate myself. You drag me down.

CRUSIUS (*referring to money in* ROELLE's *pockets*): You got some more in there? Give it here. And don't say I robbed you.

(OLGA *is being chased in the distance. She has been hiding outside for a few days now. Sound of whistles and shouts; someone cries, "Hold her!" A few students enter.*)

FIRST STUDENT: The twelfth-graders have caught her.

CRUSIUS: You hear that? Everything's ready. You don't even have to bring her yourself.

(*More students come running in.*)

FIRST STUDENT: Now we'll cast her out. Let's stand right here.

(*Other students drive* OLGA *and encircle her. Whenever she tries to push through, they push her back.*)

FIRST STUDENT: You can't pass through here, noble virgin.

SECOND STUDENT: Now you can take a good look at her.

THIRD STUDENT: Have you dried off from your swim?

FIRST STUDENT: Olga Berotter was stung by a wasp.

OLGA: Make room. I have to get through.

THIRD STUDENT: You want to see your Daddy, after you ran away from him and became the talk of the town.

FIRST STUDENT: Honeyman, the Turk will marry anyone. He needs no ad in the papers.

OLGA: Why don't you go home where you belong?

THIRD STUDENT: Is that the way to treat us?

OLGA: How do you treat me!

FIRST STUDENT: She belongs to Roelle.

SECOND STUDENT: Nothing's too disgusting for her.

FIRST STUDENT: She'll be cast out, just like him. Then they'll see what they've got in each other.

SECOND STUDENT: Maybe she doesn't even like him that much.

THIRD STUDENT: She let him sting her, didn't she?

FIRST STUDENT: From now on you'll always be alone. There'll be no girlfriend to keep you company.

THIRD STUDENT: They'd be afraid to come with you.

OLGA: You have no right to do that.

FIRST STUDENT: We just made it our right.

CRUSIUS: You deserve to be spat at. Now let's have the two confront each other. (*He drags* ROELLE *in front of* OLGA.)

OLGA: What's he up to now?

CRUSIUS: Look up to your special lady, if she can stomach you.

OLGA: You dragged me down with you.

ROELLE: Then pull me up to you.

OLGA: Get your nails out of my feet.

ROELLE: These are the only feet that get me on the ground. I want to lie right here. You don't need to kneel. You are forgiven for everything.

OLGA: I don't belong to him; he won't let me go. You can see that. Get him off me. I don't want him.

FIRST STUDENT: I am beginning to have my doubts.

ROELLE: I am not the father. That's the truth.

CRUSIUS: So you made it all up? You just wait!

ROELLE: I'll never say it again.

CRUSIUS: What you went through so far was only a harmless beginning.

OLGA: He pulled me out of the water, as if I haven't been through enough, and now he's like this. He couldn't let me out of my misery, and he plotted it all to the last detail. You should have let me float, let the water flow through my teeth. I knew why I went in. Everything would be over now. You too.

FIRST STUDENT: She doesn't belong to him. So we have nothing to do with her either.

SECOND STUDENT: You can have your brat with anyone else, we don't care. But don't get involved with him, or you'll get it too.

(STUDENTS *and* CRUSIUS *exit.*)

OLGA: And so it came to pass: I've seen him among his own. Yes, indeed.

ROELLE: Don't leave. I'll scream.

OLGA: Go ahead, scream.

ROELLE: I'm going to hold on right there. And here—here's a knife. (ROELLE *hands her the knife.*) Stab me until my eyeballs turn upward for good.

OLGA: Annihilation.

ROELLE: Salvation.

(OLGA *hesitates, then she throws away the knife.*)

OLGA: On a heap of revulsion we have mounted two faces so that they shall stare at each other for all eternity.

ROELLE: Can't you ever give me relief?

OLGA: Take your evil wishes off my branded face.

ROELLE: Kneel down.

OLGA: No.

ROELLE: Wait, I'll get you by the throat. I'll make you scream.

OLGA: No.

ROELLE: One nice word, just once. Nice Roelle, good Roelle, say it. Nod. You can't even nod. Nothing. Roelle! What do you expect?

OLGA: The only excuse I have for you is that I am right with you on the same level of purgatory.

ROELLE: I'm not the man who praises the Lord just for the privilege to breathe next to you. I can do without your feelings for me. (*He takes back the knife.*) Whatever I would do for you, you wouldn't care. For you I am scum. But I'll get you. I'll get you. If the priest's hands are too hairy, take communion with your eyes closed. From now on I'll come over you in an evil shape. You might as well know it: Angels stopped liking me a while ago; they haven't come to me in a long time. Now I am visited by another. You'll find out soon enough who lives inside me. I am the devil. (*He points the knife at her.*)

OLGA: Animal! (*She hits him.*)

MOTHER (*enters*): Let me see her touch you in front of me.

ROELLE: Mother, can't you see you're in the way?

MOTHER: Look what you've done to him. My son is out of his mind. I saw it coming. I knew it, I, his mother. Yes.

ROELLE: This isn't meant for you. This is between us.

MOTHER: I know your "between us." And I don't like it, your "between us." I'll prevent it.

ROELLE: Mother, it's time for you to go home now.

MOTHER: Not without you, son.

ROELLE: You really are a cross to bear.

MOTHER: Look how frightened he is, and pale.

ROELLE: You're a big help! Building me up in public as this idol with a monkey face.

MOTHER: You are talking to your mother, son. Be happy you still have me.

ROELLE: I am punished enough.

MOTHER: You seduced him. It's you who dragged him into everything.

OLGA: They haven't cut his head off.

MOTHER: Who are the ones who torture my son? You're coming with me to the school right now. You'll report yourself and all the others by name.

OLGA: If you want to get names, stick to your son.

ROELLE: You won't get any names out of me.

MOTHER: Jesus, son, did they ever give you anything but bruises? But I am going to the teachers, and I'll tell them it was Boettcher and Wimmer, who will deny it, and then it'll all have to come out. I can pull that off. I'm still here to reckon with. I demand severe punishment.

CRUSIUS (*enters*): There are no informers among us. We stick together. Out of necessity.

MOTHER: You are one of them. What did you do to my boy?

ROELLE: Not he. He isn't one of them. That's Crusius. He wasn't there.

MOTHER: You are lying. What is he doing here, then?

CRUSIUS: Just passing by. That's the best way to see a lot. From a distance I thought I recognized the young lady.

MOTHER: Maybe when I'm in heaven they'll tell me what's so special about her.

CRUSIUS: Excuse me, aren't you the young lady who kept looking at me during mass?

OLGA: Don't give me your dumb talk.

ROELLE: You can see that she doesn't know him.

MOTHER: Boy crazy!—You want to get under her skirt too?

CRUSIUS: My apologies, I mistook her for someone else. It happens.

MOTHER: You didn't. She keeps her men warm, one right on top of the other.

OLGA: I don't have to listen to that.

CRUSIUS: I am quite embarrassed. I cast the wrong suspicion on the young lady.

ROELLE: So get the fastest way out. Now.

CRUSIUS: But now I do have to stay. Young lady, don't do this to me. Don't avoid my eyes. You might miss something.

OLGA: Control yourself.

CRUSIUS There are young ladies who think every man's out to get them. What am I going to do to you, in bright gray daylight?

ROELLE: She is mine. Just so you know.

OLGA: You aren't like Roelle.

CRUSIUS: I am not like that one there. Things are different with me.

MOTHER: He just walked in, and she's throwing herself at him.

CRUSIUS: What are we doing afterward?

OLGA: I'm looking for someone who'll emigrate to America with me.

CRUSIUS: I don't quite understand—you?—To America?—That's far.

OLGA: I want to go to America because no one knows me there.

MOTHER: She should be my daughter.

(ROELLE *wants to protest.*)

CRUSIUS: If you want to be pigheaded, it won't work with me. Let me tell you right off, I believe in the spiritual strength of women.

ROELLE: What an egomaniac. If she goes with him, he'll drag her down completely.

CRUSIUS: That's no reason to shed a life-sized tear. America's no good. You weren't really serious.

ROELLE: I'd like to know how you know.

CRUSIUS: I just do. Why do you look so dazed? Cat's got your tongue?

OLGA: I should be home.

CRUSIUS: That's a revelation. So why are you standing there?

OLGA: I'm going.

MOTHER: I won't put in a good word with your father to make him let you stay.

OLGA: I can do that myself. I let him beat me. (OLGA *exits.*)

CRUSIUS: She's got airs.

MOTHER: I like how she stalks out of here and doesn't know what's in store for her at home.

CRUSIUS: She knows.

MOTHER: She might arrive just in time for a house search.

CRUSIUS: Why?

MOTHER: You may tell that to everyone. I had my suspicions about this person for a long time now. I always said, you can get in from the back. All she had to do was climb over the balcony.

ROELLE: Into our house?

MOTHER: But this time I tricked her. It was always bills. This time I wrote down the numbers, and I let the police know in advance. And I reported her too. And, sure enough, something's missing from the cash register again.

ROELLE: Mother, that was me, always. I took your money.

CRUSIUS: That's what they say.

MOTHER: God Almighty, it can't be true. My boy, what made you do it?

ROELLE: Because they're always after me. I have to give it to them.

MOTHER: I must go back right away and tell them I misplaced the money and found it. I have to make a retreat, that's all.

ROELLE: It won't do any good if Crusius tells.

MOTHER: What can he say?

ROELLE: He has the money. He took it out of my pocket.

CRUSIUS: You gave me that money.

ROELLE: You took the money. There were people who saw it.

CRUSIUS: We don't want a lying thief like you among us.

ROELLE: Then what happened to my book, which you took from my desk? I'll tell that too.

CRUSIUS: Why did you let me get away with it? Anyway, that was an experiment. (CRUSIUS *exits.*)

MOTHER: Jesus, boy, listen to me—

ROELLE: She is gone. That's my punishment. She never wants to see me again. Everybody took her away from me. You too.

MOTHER: Let her be gone.

ROELLE: I don't like you anymore. It's over between us. To me you are dead.

MOTHER: That's a sin, son.

ROELLE: To me you are dead. Let go of me.

MOTHER: He's possessed by the devil, that's what it is.

ROELLE: Yes! Make three crosses over me. Splash me with holy water from the cemetery. The devil is everywhere. Stay away! Why don't you stay away? Let go of me!

MOTHER: I don't recognize you.

ROELLE: When I die, I'll go to hell, and I'll be damned. I'll be with the devil and all the damned souls. And that will never end, never. How could there be anything more cruel than that.

MOTHER: Son, you mustn't even think such thoughts!

ROELLE: You want to know something? My God is the devil.

MOTHER: Let go of him, unclean spirit. Enter a swine, enter your swines.

ROELLE: Your prayers can't exorcise him. To hell with your prayers, whatever you're mumbling. You can't help me.

MOTHER: A priest. He must be saved. (*She exits.*)

ROELLE: I am in the state of mortal sin. I must confess. I've learned how, but I don't remember. I forgot how to do it. (*He takes out a piece of paper and reads from it.*) "I, poor sinner, accuse myself in front of God Almighty and you, reverend fathers, that since my last confession how many months ago I have committed the following sins: against the fourth commandment, how many times? Against the sixth commandment, how many times?" I am afraid. "Against the seventh commandment, how many times? Against the eighth commandment, how many times?" These are my notes to myself. I could eat them. "Against the seven deadly sins, I ask for healing penance and your priestly absolution." I'll try that. (*He eats the piece of paper.*)

Translated by Gitta Honegger

Acknowledgments

Every reasonable effort has been made to locate the owners of rights to previously published translations printed here. We gratefully acknowledge permission to reprint the following material:

Random House, UK, for permission to reprint *Spring Awakening* by Frank Wedekind, translated by Edward Bond. Copyright © 1980 by Edward Bond. First edition published by Eyre Methuen Ltd.

Carl R. Mueller for permission to print his translations of *The Marquis of Keith* by Frank Wedekind and *Tales from the Vienna Woods* by Ödön von Horváth.

Thomas Sessler Verlag for permission to reprint *Geschichten aus dem Wienerwald* by Ödön von Horváth.

Suhrkamp Verlag for permission to reprint *Fegefeuer in Ingolstadt* by Marieluise Fleisser. © 1977 by Suhrkamp Verlag. All rights reserved.

Gitta Honegger for permission to reprint her translation *Purgatory in Ingolstadt* by Marieluise Fleisser.

ROELLE: I don't like you anymore. It's over between us. To me you are dead.

MOTHER: That's a sin, son.

ROELLE: To me you are dead. Let go of me.

MOTHER: He's possessed by the devil, that's what it is.

ROELLE: Yes! Make three crosses over me. Splash me with holy water from the cemetery. The devil is everywhere. Stay away! Why don't you stay away? Let go of me!

MOTHER: I don't recognize you.

ROELLE: When I die, I'll go to hell, and I'll be damned. I'll be with the devil and all the damned souls. And that will never end, never. How could there be anything more cruel than that.

MOTHER: Son, you mustn't even think such thoughts!

ROELLE: You want to know something? My God is the devil.

MOTHER: Let go of him, unclean spirit. Enter a swine, enter your swines.

ROELLE: Your prayers can't exorcise him. To hell with your prayers, whatever you're mumbling. You can't help me.

MOTHER: A priest. He must be saved. (*She exits.*)

ROELLE: I am in the state of mortal sin. I must confess. I've learned how, but I don't remember. I forgot how to do it. (*He takes out a piece of paper and reads from it.*) "I, poor sinner, accuse myself in front of God Almighty and you, reverend fathers, that since my last confession how many months ago I have committed the following sins: against the fourth commandment, how many times? Against the sixth commandment, how many times?" I am afraid. "Against the seventh commandment, how many times? Against the eighth commandment, how many times?" These are my notes to myself. I could eat them. "Against the seven deadly sins, I ask for healing penance and your priestly absolution." I'll try that. (*He eats the piece of paper.*)

Translated by Gitta Honegger

Acknowledgme

Every reasonable effort has been made to
rights to previously published translations pr
fully acknowledge permission to reprint the

Random House, UK, for permission to reprint
Frank Wedekind, translated by Edward Bon
by Edward Bond. First edition published by

Carl R. Mueller for permission to print hi
Marquis of Keith by Frank Wedekind and
Woods by Ödön von Horváth.

Thomas Sessler Verlag for permission to re
dem Wienerwald by Ödön von Horváth.

Suhrkamp Verlag for permission to reprint
by Marieluise Fleisser. © 1977 by Suhrka
reserved.

Gitta Honegger for permission to reprint he
in Ingolstadt by Marieluise Fleisser.

Titles Available in The German Library

All titles available in hardcover as well as the paperback editions listed below from The Continuum Publishing Company, 370 Lexington Avenue, New York, NY 10017

22. HYPERION AND
SELECTED POEMS (Hölderlin)
320 pp 0-8264-0334-4 pbk

23. PHILOSOPHY OF GERMAN
IDEALISM
290 pp 0-8264-0307-7 pbk

24. ENCYCLOPEDIA OF THE
PHILOSOPHICAL SCIENCES IN
OUTLINE AND CRITICAL
WRITINGS (Hegel)
320 pp 0-8264-0340-9 pbk

25. PLAYS (Kleist)
352 pp 0-8264-0263-1 pbk

26. TALES (Hoffmann)
320 pp 0-8264-0264-X pbk

27. PHILOSOPHICAL
WRITINGS (Schopenhauer)
324 pp 0-8264-0729-3 pbk

28. COMPLETE WORKS AND
LETTERS (Büchner)
314 pp 0-8264-0301-8 pbk

29. GERMAN FAIRY TALES
288 pp 0-8264-0289-5 pbk

30. GERMAN LITERARY FAIRY
TALES
312 pp 0-8264-0277-1 pbk

31. NINETEENTH-CENTURY
GERMAN PLAYS
304 pp 0-8264-0332-8 pbk

32. POETRY AND PROSE
(Heine)
300 pp 0-8264-0265-8 pbk

33. THE ROMANTIC SCHOOL
AND OTHER ESSAYS (Heine)
308 pp 0-8264-0291-7 pbk

34. ROMANTIC NOVELLAS
320 pp 0-8264-0295-X pbk

35. GERMAN ROMANTIC
STORIES
272 pp 0-8264-0313-1 pbk

36. ESSAYS ON SCIENCE IN
THE NINETEENTH CENTURY
320 pp 0-8264-0745-5 pbk

37. GERMAN NOVELLAS OF
REALISM I
318 pp 0-8264-0317-4 pbk

38. GERMAN NOVELLAS OF
REALISM II
332 pp 0-8264-0320-4 pbk

39. GERMAN POETRY FROM
1750 TO 1900
280 pp 0-8264-0283-6 pbk

40. GERMAN SOCIALIST
PHILOSOPHY
320 pp 0-8264-0749-8 pbk

41. GERMAN ESSAYS ON
SOCIALISM IN THE
NINETEENTH CENTURY
320 pp 0-8264-0324-7 pbk

42. GERMAN LIEDER
360 pp 0-8264-0328-X pbk

43. GERMAN ESSAYS ON
MUSIC
324 pp 0-8264-0721-8 pbk

44. STORIES (Keller)
372 pp 0-8264-0266-6 pbk

45. NOVELS (Raabe)
318 pp 0-8264-0281-X pbk

46. SHORT NOVELS AND
OTHER WRITINGS (Fontane)
338 pp 0-8264-0260-7 pbk

47. DELUSIONS, CONFUSIONS
AND THE POGGENPUHL
FAMILY (Fontane)
292 pp 0-8264-0326-3 pbk

48. PHILOSOPHICAL
WRITINGS (Nietzsche)
324 pp 0-8264-0279-8 pbk

49. GERMAN ESSAYS ON
HISTORY
324 pp 0-8264-0344-1 pbk

50. GERMAN SATIRICAL
WRITINGS
322 pp 0-8264-0285-2 pbk

51. WRITINGS OF GERMAN COMPOSERS
304 pp 0-8264-0293-3 pbk

52. GERMAN OPERA LIBRETTI
324 pp 0-8264-0739-0 pbk

53. GERMAN SONGS
324 pp 0-8264-0731-5 pbk

54. GERMAN ESSAYS ON RELIGION
324 pp 0-8264-0735-8 pbk

55. PLAYS AND STORIES
(Schnitzler)
284 pp 0-8264-0271-2 pbk

57. PLAYS (Hauptmann)
324 pp 0-8264-0727-7 pbk

58. EARLY 20TH-CENTURY GERMAN PLAYS
292 pp 0-8264-0961-X pbk

59. PSYCHOLOGICAL WRITINGS AND LETTERS
(Freud)
324 pp 0-8264-0723-4 pbk

60. SOCIOLOGICAL WRITINGS
(Weber)
312 pp 0-8264-0719-6 pbk

61. GERMAN SOCIOLOGY
324 pp 0-8264-0959-8 pbk

64. THE LOYAL SUBJECT
348 pp 0-8264-0955-5 pbk

66. GERMAN EXPRESSIONIST PLAYS
320 pp 0-8264-0950-4 pbk

70. PROSE AND POETRY
(Rilke)
264 pp 0-8264-0287-9 pbk

71. SIDDHARTHA, DEMIAN, AND OTHER WRITINGS
(Hesse)
264 pp 0-8264-0715-3 pbk

72. SELECTED WRITINGS
(Musil)
346 pp 0-8264-0305-0 pbk

73. PROSE ESSAYS POEMS
(Benn)
298 pp 0-8264-0311-5 pbk

79. GERMAN ESSAYS ON ART HISTORY
284 pp 0-8264-0309-3 pbk

82. ESSAYS ON SCIENCE IN THE TWENTIETH CENTURY
320 pp 0-8264-0747-1 pbk

83. ESSAYS ON GERMAN THEATER
354 pp 0-8264-0297-6 pbk

86. GERMAN RADIO PLAYS
324 pp 0-8264-0342-5 pbk

88. NEW SUFFERINGS OF YOUNG W. AND OTHER GDR STORIES
372 pp 0-8264-0952-0 pbk

89. PLAYS AND ESSAYS
(Dürrenmatt)
314 pp 0-8264-0267-4 pbk

90. NOVELS PLAYS ESSAYS
(Frisch)
354 pp 0-8264-0322-0 pbk

92. MARAT/SADE, et al.
(P. Weiss)
336 pp 0-8264-0963-6 pbk

93. CAT AND MOUSE AND OTHER WRITINGS (Grass)
312 pp 0-8264-0733-1 pbk

94. SELECTED PROSE AND DRAMA (Bachmann/Wolf)
324 pp 0-8264-0957-1 pbk

98. CRITICAL ESSAYS
(Enzensberger)
254 pp 0-8264-0268-2 pbk

99. CONTEMPORARY GERMAN FICTION
324 pp 0-8264-0741-2 pbk

Complete Author Listing
in The German Library,
by Volume Number